## DATE DUE

|  |  |  |  |
|--|--|--|--|
|  |  |  |  |
|  |  |  |  |
|  |  |  |  |
|  |  |  |  |
|  |  |  |  |
|  |  |  |  |
|  |  |  |  |
|  |  |  |  |
|  |  |  |  |
|  |  |  |  |
|  |  |  |  |
|  |  |  |  |
|  |  |  |  |
|  |  |  |  |
|  |  |  |  |

The Picnic from *Selected Pen Drawings*

# Norman Lindsay
## THE EMBATTLED OLYMPIAN

*Homage to Balzac,* from the Collection, University of Melbourne

# Norman Lindsay

THE EMBATTLED OLYMPIAN

John Hetherington

MELBOURNE

OXFORD UNIVERSITY PRESS

LONDON   WELLINGTON   NEW YORK

*Oxford University Press, Ely House, London, W.1*

GLASGOW   NEW YORK   TORONTO   MELBOURNE   WELLINGTON
CAPE TOWN   IBADAN   NAIROBI   DAR ES SALAAM   LUSAKA   ADDIS ABABA
DELHI   BOMBAY   CALCUTTA   MADRAS   KARACHI   LAHORE   DACCA
KUALA LUMPUR   SINGAPORE   HONG KONG   TOKYO

*Oxford University Press, 7 Bowen Crescent, Melbourne*

*First published 1973*

ISBN 0 19 550388 0

*Published with the assistance of the Literature Board of the Australian Council for the Arts*

*Registered in Australia for transmission by post as a book*
PRINTED IN AUSTRALIA BY BROWN PRIOR ANDERSON PTY LTD

*To* JEAN
*for all the things you are*

# Contents

# List of Plates

## LINE DRAWINGS IN THE TEXT

# *Preface*

Norman Lindsay invited me to write his biography 'when the under-taker has disposed of my carcase'. He affirmed the proposal in a formal handwritten note dated from Springwood on 10 April 1957, and inserted a clause to that effect in his Will. To help me explore his character, personality, actions and thoughts he sent me a series of intimate papers on specific aspects of his life, and many long and outspoken letters; he also talked freely on several visits I paid to Springwood. More than once he bade me, 'Write anything you like as long as it's the truth', (which, he told me, was the novelist Norman Douglas's injunction to an intending biographer). I have tried to do that, but I do not pretend that Norman would endorse everything I have said of him in this book; for the legal maxim that no man is a good judge of his own cause applied to him no less than to any other mortal. I had a deep affection for him and still have—death does not cancel or abate one man's liking for another—but his conclusions were not always acceptable. I often found his version of a given event to be accurate when I studied the objective evidence; but nearly as often I found him, especially on issues which had heavily engaged his emotions and brought him into conflict with other people, to be wrong.

Norman was an agonizingly difficult biographical subject. The problem he posed to anybody writing about him has been succinctly stated by his nephew, Peter Lindsay, who says, 'He was a dozen different men'. While simple in his personal wants and needs, he was the most psychologically complex human being I have ever known well. Most men are inconsistent and do not know it; he was maddeningly so and well aware of it, and unrepentant. Once established, his views on any major proposition, such as the integrity of the artist, mankind's debt to Greece and Rome, and the immortality of the human spirit, were fixed and immovable, but his opinions on secondary questions were as changeful as a wild bird's flight. That he had said thus and thus yesterday was no assurance that he would not say this and this tomorrow; or even today. This book inevitably reflects his inconsistency—it would miss an essential element of him if it did not—but anyone tempted to condemn him on that score might temper the finding by remembering that he had so much more to be in-consistent about than all but perhaps one in five million men. The range of his swift, agile and restless mind saw to that.

All through this book I have found it best to identify him by his given name; sometimes I call him 'Norman Lindsay' but usually just 'Norman'.

Although we were close friends for many years I dislike this touch of familiarity. The ungarnished surname seems to me to be more appropriate for a biography but it did not work here. I discarded it on realizing that its use led to ambiguity because so many other Lindsay men—brothers, sons, nephews, and so on—were constantly moving in and out of the story. For this reason I ask readers to be lenient with me for what might appear to be an example of undue mateyness. I hope for understanding on another aspect also: this is a biography, not an attempt to analyse Norman's artistic, literary and other professional techniques and achievements, a learned discussion of which would fill another full-scale book. My purpose has been to bring the man himself to life, and I have said only as much of his work as seemed necessary to that end.

I take this opportunity of mentioning two practical matters. First, Norman's home in the Blue Mountains was known only as 'Springwood'; to all his friends, and to many people unacquainted with him except by reputation, 'Springwood' meant 'Norman Lindsay', and 'Norman Lindsay' meant 'Springwood'. For me to identify it in any other way would be inexpedient and clumsy, not to say pedantic and silly, but the Springwood label could cause confusion (and the more so since readjustments imposed by municipal developments mean that the house and grounds are no longer situated in Springwood but in the neighbouring postal district of Faulconbridge!) I have accordingly made every effort to differentiate between Norman's Springwood and the town of Springwood wherever the context seems to require it. I hope I have succeeded. Second, in dealing with money I have made no effort to translate £ s d into dollars; the answers produced would be meaningless. A rough idea of values mentioned in the narrative may be had if one remembers that a shilling in the years from 1900 to the outbreak of the 1914-18 war, or two shillings between the wars, would buy about as much as a dollar today. An economist or statistician would reject with horror this free-and-easy basis of calculation, but it will serve for practical purposes.

One Australian idiom figures fairly often in the text: *Wowser*. It was among Norman's pet words, just as the genus Wowser was among his pet hates. Although the word is less fashionable than it once was, most Australians probably understand its meaning, but it might mystify overseas readers. The Wowser has been described, among other things, as 'a puritan of advanced prejudices' and 'a killjoy', but nobody else has succeeded so well as C. J. Dennis, the Australian larrikin poet, in capturing its true essence. In the glossary to his first book, *Backblock Ballads and Other Verses* (Melbourne, E. W. Cole, 1913), Dennis described a Wowser as 'an ineffably pious person who mistakes the world for a penitentiary and himself for a warder'. Norman disliked Dennis's verses but that definition enraptured him.

# Acknowledgements

This book was written with the help of a Commonwealth Literary Fund fellowship. I wish to thank the C.L.F., and the sponsors of my application, Professor Zelman Cowen and Mr Frank Eyre.

Anybody who has tried to write a book of this kind will vouch for the quality of Australia's public reference libraries and the devotion of their staffs. I owe a deep debt to the State Library of Victoria (particularly to Miss Patricia Reynolds, La Trobe Librarian, and her staff, notably Miss Clarice Kemp and Miss Joan Maslen; and to Miss Joyce McGrath, Art Librarian); to the Library of New South Wales and the Mitchell Library (particularly to Mr G. D. Richardson, Principal Librarian and Mitchell Librarian, and Miss Suzanne Mourot, Associate Mitchell Librarian); and to Mr R. K. Olding, State Librarian of South Australia. I am no less indebted to Professor D. P. Derham, Vice-Chancellor of the University of Melbourne, and Professor Joseph Burke, Professor of Fine Arts, for having let me study a collection of letters and other papers, then in the possession of the Department of Fine Arts but now in the custody of the La Trobe Library.

It is impracticable for me to thank by name the hundreds of men and women who helped me in my search for enlightenment. Three stand out: Dr Jack Lindsay, of Castle Hedingham, Essex, England, surely one of the busiest of living authors, repeatedly interrupted his own work to answer, in detail and with unfailing good temper, my letters asking for guidance; Mr Peter Lindsay, of Sydney, supplied me with a wealth of material and time after time went to considerable personal trouble to unravel knotty points; and Miss Elizabeth Douglas, of Melbourne, on a working visit to England, scoured public libraries, newspaper morgues, and other repositories and brought up an astonishing collection of valuable information about Norman's two visits to Europe and his English exhibitions. I must also mention the generous help of Mr David Adams, Mrs Anne von Bertouch, Mr Godfrey Blunden, Mrs Colin Burke, Mr Horace Chisholm (Chief Librarian of the Melbourne *Age*), Miss Sonia Dean, Mr G. A. Ferguson, Mr John Frith, Mr Leon Gellert, the Reverend Harold J. Gorrell, Professor R. G. Howarth, Mr Peter Laverty, Miss Margaret MacKean, Mr Harry McPhee, Mr Justice A. R. Moffitt, Councillor E. J. Semmens, Mrs Henry Shaw, Mr Keith Sinclair, Mr Kenneth Slessor, Mr Douglas Stewart, Mr Walter Stone, Mr G. Kingsley Sutton, Mr John Tierney and Mr Eric Westbrook.

The frontispiece, *Homage to Balzac*, is reproduced with permission from the University of Melbourne; the half-tone plates are reproduced with the permission of Curtis Brown (Aust.) Pty Ltd on behalf of Mrs Jane Glad, with the exception of Plates 7, 14, 25 and 29 which are reproduced by courtesy of Mr Peter Lindsay, Plate 33 by courtesy of the *Age*, Melbourne, and Plate 34 and Figure 7 by courtesy of John Fairfax & Sons Limited.

I am grateful to Australian Consolidated Press for allowing me to reproduce cartoons and other drawings by Norman Lindsay from the Sydney *Bulletin*; and to Mr Vane Lindesay, of Melbourne, for his expert advice on the selection of illustrations.

I have left it to the last to record the special debt I owe to my wife on three counts: for having read my early drafts with a critical eye and made a multitude of suggestions for improving the narrative; for having typed and otherwise prepared the book for publication; and—perhaps above all—for having given me aid and comfort in periods when I was gripped by that mysterious but very real affliction, Writer's Melancholia.

J.H.

*Discretion is not the better part of biography.*
*—Lytton Strachey*

*There is something more to our interest in the*
*private lives of great men than the mere desire*
*to pry into other people's personal affairs.*
*—Edmund Wilson*

# I

## Creswick in the Morning
## 1879-96

He was like a small and delicately boned bird. The brilliant blue eyes seemed enormous in the still babyish face as he sat at the nursery table drawing, forever drawing. For most of the time he was lost to all else, aware only of his hand and the movement of his pencil and the outlines of the sketch taking shape on the paper, as he worked away with a cushion under him to lift him high enough to reach the table. Being sickly and condemned to live indoors, he admired men of action. His pictures were nearly all battle pieces, in which plumed knights clashed in deadly combat, Assyrian charioteers hurled themselves against the Babylonian hosts, kilted clansmen massed before the Sassenach oppressors on gloomy cloud-girt Scottish moors. Sometimes—not often—he paused and let his eyes stray to the window to watch his brothers and their mates climbing the willows and pines in the yard of 'Lisnacrieve' or whooping and galloping about in the paddock behind the Creswick Wesleyan Church next door. Then, knowing he must stay quiet, he went back to his knights and charioteers and clansmen and once more immersed himself in the world of his own making.

The Lindsay children born before him—easy-going and imperturbable Percy, fastidious but tough-fibred Bert, Lionel wearing his good looks and self-assurance with royal grace, even the little girl Mary who was two years older than Norman—were as hardy and healthy a family of young Australians as you could find. Only Norman, thin and inconspicuous alongside his brothers. was a weakling. There was no accounting for it. His father, a capable medical man, stroking his short pointed beard, shook his head and confessed himself baffled. He could find no physiological reason why Norman should suffer these attacks which caused small, white, acutely itching blisters to spring up all over his body immediately the mildest exercise heated his blood a little. Doctor Lindsay harumphed and examined and reflected. He prescribed ointments and lotions and oils and medicated baths, but none of these seemed to help. He told Norman's mother to keep the boy inside and let him do what he pleased so long as he did not rush about like the others.

So Norman filled in the early years, from the time his fingers were first able to grasp a pencil, by teaching himself to draw. He loved soldiers, all soldiers, any soldiers. He created his own on paper and did not care whether they were British, Roman, Trojan or any other kind so long as they were fighting men, and he drew them with meticulous care for the detail of uniforms and weapons. His were never the infant scratchings of an untutored hand; from the first they were the experiments of a child born with a special talent. To be sure, much that he drew was inaccurate or out of balance. This was not because his eye was faulty but because his small hand was not always equal to the tasks he gave it. And whenever a drawing was wrong he knew it. He would frown, make a tight ball of the sheet and throw it away. Then he would do the same drawing again, working to make the awkward hand or clumsy fingers obey him. The long struggle to master the means of expressing himself was to go on all his life, and nearly ninety years after he sat over his paper behind the sheltering walls of 'Lisnacrieve' he would die, still reaching outward and upward toward the unattainable.

His parents were comforted to know that the boy seemed happy enough, fiddling away with pencil and paper. He never rebelled when old Ellen Scott admonished him, 'Now, Master Norman, no jumping about and getting excited! You know it upsets you', but went back and lost himself in the dust, smoke and thunder of his battles. The world outside was barred against him except for sedate walks with Mary, under the eye of Ellen or one of the other servants. Doctor Lindsay was a busy man with a practice which often meant a buggy journey of many miles; he could give only a little time each day even to an ailing child of his own. Norman's mother was no less busy. There was always a cook as well as one or two housemaids at 'Lisnacrieve', and usually a nursemaid too; but cleaning, cooking, jam-making, sewing and the rest of the work never seemed to be done, and Mrs Lindsay had to oversee it all.

The older children were growing up fast, each becoming a personality in his own right, and every few years another child was born. Pearl came four years after Norman, then Ruby, then Reginald, then Daryl; then, after a lapse of four years, the delicate Isabel. Janie Lindsay had her hands full, but as she bustled about, seeing that the bed linen was aired, the furniture, Venetian glass and porcelain kept speckless, the Sunday roast done to a turn, supervising the patching of small boys' pants and little girls' skirts, and taking a thousand other duties in her stride, she seemed tireless and unflappable. She even managed to keep the peace between her children most of the time, not least between Bert and Lionel, whose bickerings could turn to blows in an instant. The two who gave her no trouble in that way were Mary and Norman. They were always content to be together—when Norman started speaking he called his sister Mame, which was easier for his infant tongue, and Mame she always remained—and they never wrangled or quarrelled. Nor, for that matter, did Lionel and Norman, who were remarkably good friends considering the difference in their ages. Lionel, who could read long before he went to school and read omnivorously then and all his life, did more than anyone else to open Norman's young eyes to the world of books. He spent hours reading aloud to the housebound child, and taught him to read for himself. Norman was five when he got through his first book unaided. It was R. M. Ballantyne's *The Coral Island.* He went on to Lewis Carroll, Talbot Baines Reed's school tales, Captain Marryatt's sea stories, *Tales from Homer, The Three Musketeers,* and Scott's livelier romances. Within a few years he was gulping down Dickens, Samuel Pepys and Boswell's *Johnson.*

And all the time he went on drawing. He found inspiration in the magnificent plates in the great family Bible; the two-volume Shakespeare illustrated with reproductions of steel engravings by famous artists was another rich source, and so were the bound volumes of the *Cornhill, Chambers' Journal,* the *Illustrated London News, Punch,* and the London *Graphic* in his father's waiting-room. He never lost his devotion to soldiers, but gradually his scope widened. He discovered subjects in Boswell's *Johnson,* in Dickens and Thackeray, and in some of the more swaggering poets. White drawing paper always seemed to be scarce, but somehow he got enough. Day after day, month after month, he worked at his drawings, teaching himself by trial and error, never forgetting anything once learned.

Although Doctor Lindsay had gone to Creswick because of the greatly increased population drawn there by the rush to the Ballarat goldfields, the raffish golden springtime was over when Norman Lindsay was born on 22 February 1879.* Millions of pounds worth of gold was yet to be won from the earth of Creswick and the near-by countryside by deep-level mining, but the riches lying on the surface and a few feet below were exhausted. Gold-getting had become a settled industry under the control of organized companies which could afford to buy expensive machinery, go down hundreds of feet and bore through great layers of

---

* Since practically all reference books, including those carrying entries checked by Norman himself, give his birth date as 23 February, it is worth emphasizing that 22 February is correct. This is confirmed both by the records of the Victorian Government Statist and the Creswick Register of Births.

solid basalt, and meet heavy wages bills. Most of the happy-go-lucky diggers of the rush period, when the population had briefly reached 25,000 to 30,000, had moved away to other 'rushes'. A few stayed behind, living in shanties scattered about the old diggings, panning a few pennyweights of gold from the ravished soil and mumbling on about their memories. And there were the Chinese, hundreds of them, who had come when gold was found. They formed a close-knit and homogeneous community. They kept to their own little Chinatown, worshipping behind the walls of their joss-houses and living by keeping shops and laundries. Some earned a few pence extra by making and selling such delicacies as fy-shang toffee to the Creswick young. They were quiet people, and law-abiding except when they gambled at fan-tan and pak-a-pu or when the old men floated off into exquisite opium dreams.

Doctor Lindsay remembered Creswick when thousands of diggers were still living along the creek in tents, wattle-and-daub shanties and bark humpies. An Irishman, he had landed at Melbourne in June 1864, after a passage of three months from London in the ship *Red Rose*, 1,445 tons. A few days later he took the coach for Creswick, some eighty miles north-west of Melbourne and twelve miles beyond Ballarat, on a southern flank of the Great Dividing Range. He was in his middle twenties, and inexperienced, but, having studied under able men at Belfast and Edinburgh and taken a good degree, confident of his skill.

When he climbed down from the coach at Creswick he took in his surroundings with mixed feelings. Everybody seemed to be flush of money but the place was only just beginning to acquire a permanent air. Nevertheless he stayed, and as he settled in and came to know Creswick better his sensibilities were shocked by the wild drinking sprees in the grog shops and by the number of professional ladies who prospered in a settlement where men heavily outnumbered women. Although no prude he had a simple religious faith and shrank from moral indiscipline, but had to make the best of it. Word that he knew his job quickly spread. He was not the only doctor in Creswick but there was more than enough work for them all.

He was warm and friendly, and nearly everybody liked him. While only of medium height, he was always a striking figure as he marched along, bearded, genial and immaculately dressed, stick in hand, square-crowned hard hat or summer panama on his head, a flower in his button-hole. He had a natural dignity, but gave himself no airs. To a pompous fellow citizen who complained that the townspeople did not like him, Doctor Lindsay grunted, 'They think you're a damned snob and so you are'. He could neither understand nor abide snobbery. He was not a man to go long unwed—he needed a wife beside him and a family around him. In May 1869 he and Jane Elizabeth Williams were married.

Janie was nineteen and fresh from boarding school in Melbourne. She was uncommonly pretty, and had all the accomplishments of a gently bred young lady of the day; these included a talent for fine needlework, proficiency on the piano and as a drawing-room singer, some modest skill at painting in water-colours, and a good seat on a horse. Her religious faith was strong, and even in girlhood her features reflected a firm and positive character, but neither then nor later was she the domestic tyrant depicted in a persistent legend nurtured by Norman and Mary. They—and, to some extent, Bert in later life—were the only ones who ever contrived to see her as a despotic wife and mother. Norman's memory of her was distorted when he looked back and recalled the restraints he had suffered in his frail childhood but forgot the reason for them; Mary's by the resentment of an unmarried daughter who felt trapped and defeated. The rest of Janie Lindsay's children endorsed the view succinctly expressed by her youngest son, Daryl, when he wrote that 'throughout her long life I never heard her laying down the law as regards her religion or anything else: except perhaps the making of strawberry jam'. She was exceptionally good at strawberry or any other kind of jam.

Her father was the Reverend Thomas Williams, who had been the Wesleyan minister at Creswick for some years. Thomas Williams had seven other children but Janie was the outstanding one; she was also her father's favourite. He saw much of himself in her, and turned to her whenever life seemed arid and cheerless. He was no ordinary cleric and no ordinary man. Full-bearded, stern, uncompromising and steady-eyed, he had something of the gaunt and craggy splendour of an Old Testament prophet—no great stretching of the imagination was required to see him leading the Children of Israel out of the land of Egypt. He was already well into his fifties when he was posted to Creswick, but although he had been pouring out his Christian fervour for many years, the power of his faith and his evangelistic ardour were still strong. He was no mere pulpit thunderer—his mind was too fine and flexible for that—but he had a gift of eloquence which took hold of his congregation.

An Englishman, born in Horncastle, Lincolnshire, he was educated for an architect's career but took holy orders and, having married, offered himself as a missionary. The Methodist Church sent him to Fiji in 1840 and he stayed for fourteen years, preaching Christianity to his cannibal flock. He also managed to find material for a book which is a standard work on the subject.* Thomas Williams was neither a bigot nor a crank but his faith was like a flame. He wanted to make all men see that the earth is the Lord's. His young wife worked beside him, tireless

* Thomas Williams, *Fiji and the Fijians*, vol. 1, 'The Islands and their Inhabitants' (London, 1858).

and uncomplaining. She bore him child after child, and Janie was said to be the first white child born in the Fiji Islands.

Robert and Janie Lindsay started married life in a timber cottage near the post office. Although Creswick's population was shrinking fast as the surface gold ran out, the town had a core of hard-working people and a solid and stable community was taking shape. Farms were springing up all over the surrounding countryside. Creswick had its own flour mill, a blacksmith employing six or seven ironworkers, a coach and buggy builder, a brick works, and a saddler who could hardly keep abreast of the demands on him.

There were three other doctors—Tremearne, Bell and Lyons—as well as Robert Lindsay. They had to work long hours and often make exhausting journeys, but they lived in good style. Doctor Lindsay was able to indulge his Irish fondness for high-stepping horses. He always kept a groom who was required to see that the horses, the buggy and the trap shone at all times. The doctor was easy-going but he would not tolerate slackness in the stables; any groom who neglected the horses got short shrift.

The cottage served the Lindsays well enough for seven or eight years. Then, after Lionel was born, Robert and Janie needed a bigger place. They bought a piece of land in Victoria Street, next to the Wesleyan Church, and built a large and rambling one-storey wooden house. They filled it with heavy furniture, assorted bric-a-brac, Robert's books, Janie's upright piano, and much more besides. Then, having called it 'Lisnacrieve' after the Lindsay home in County Tyrone, Ireland, they moved in. It was an ideal house for children. It had ample room for young minds to grow as well as young bodies, with the one reservation that the Lindsay children seem to have been fed rather more Christianity than they could digest. Perhaps this is the reason why most of them grew up to be either sceptics or out-and-out unbelievers. Lionel, who had the most scholarly and penetrating mind in the family, was a convinced pagan from his childhood until his death. Norman also was a fervent anti-Christian, but intuitively rather than by any process of reasoning; he held that Christianity was 'the one immortal folly of mankind'.

With the sole exception of Percy, who began making his own rules of conduct while he was in short pants and never observed any others, the Lindsay children were marched off every Sunday to the church next door, a building of depressing ugliness, and shepherded into a family pew to join in worshipping the Wesleyan God. Norman seized the opportunity afforded by the inordinately long sermons to decorate any white space in the hymn books with drawings representing Biblical figures. He made one notable study of Moses sporting a pork-pie hat and an umbrella, but this early example of his skill has been lost.

The Reverend Thomas Williams and his wife were regular visitors to 'Lisnacrieve'. They often came for midday dinner on Sunday. The Lindsay children liked Grandma Williams who, soft, frilly and a little vague, moved in an aroma of lavender water and gentleness, but it was Grandpa Williams whom they remembered. He dominated the talk at table. This was not because he would give no one else a hearing but because he had the faculty of riveting everybody's attention. He expressed himself in sonorous phrases and what he said usually went right to the heart of the matter. Doctor Lindsay was out of his depth and contributed little beyond a 'H'm!', a 'Ha!', or a 'Quite so!' He stood in deep and abiding awe of Grandpa Williams, and all his children knew it.

Thomas Williams had retired as an active minister of religion and moved from Creswick to Ballarat when Norman first became aware of him. He and his wife lived with an unmarried daughter in a small and pleasant house 'Horncastle', on Soldiers' Hill; their windows looked out on a section of the old gold diggings. Ballarat being only half an hour from Creswick by rail, one or another of the Lindsays was often there. Life at 'Horncastle' was stricter than at 'Lisnacrieve', with a long session of pre-breakfast prayers, but there were compensations. For all the old man's austerity and his somewhat terrifying presence, he understood children and never talked down to them. They liked and respected him for it.

The Ballarat Art Gallery was one of his favourite haunts from the time it opened in 1887. To him, that square and solid building was an oasis in a cultural desert. Before his death in 1891 he introduced all the older Lindsay children to the Gallery one by one, and did more than anyone else to wake the artistic curiosity of Lionel and Norman in particular. The Ballarat Gallery's collection of pictures was mediocre at the start; they were mostly English academic paintings of the Victorian era, safe, sound and unexciting. There was, however, one work, *Ajax and Cassandra*, by Solomon J. Solomon, which did something to relieve the dull respectability of most of the others. It was one of the first successful paintings done by Solomon, a young English artist who was to make a sound reputation in the next twenty years and be elected to the Royal Academy in 1906.

An oil eleven feet high and six feet wide, *Ajax and Cassandra* depicts the preliminaries to the rape of Cassandra in the temple of Athena during the sack of Troy. The two figures are painted with only a swirl of floating draperies to hide their nakedness. The picture was daring by Victorian standards but it did not shock Thomas Williams. He found inexhaustible delight in it and never wearied of extolling its virtues. Whenever Norman stayed at 'Horncastle' Grandpa Williams took him to the Gallery and led him on a conducted tour which inevitably ended with *Ajax and Cassandra*. The picture enchanted the little boy as it did the old man. Cassandra was the first painted nude he ever saw. The shapeliness of the body, the flesh tints, the grace of the splendid legs fired his imagination. *Ajax and Cassandra* must have played a part in creating the central pillar of his mature artistic philosophy that 'the nude body is the most beautiful thing on this earth', and to the end of his life Norman upheld it as an excellent work, both in conception and execution. Norman later said that he knew every brush stroke by the time he was six, after standing before it many times and listening while Grandpa Williams held forth on its merits and also on what he considered a conceivable defect—whether or not the portrayal of Ajax's right foot was anatomically acceptable.

Grandpa Williams was the only adult in Norman's young life with a strong and assured pictorial instinct; his mother's taste was pedestrian and his father's worse. Doctor Lindsay was an eager buyer of a type of oil-painting reproduction called an oleograph, much in vogue when the Lindsay children were growing up. He never returned from any visit to Melbourne without one or two. He loved studies of cherubic children lisping prayers at their mother's knee or sleeping with a guardian angel watching over them, of St Bernard dogs succouring lost travellers and other works on the same philosophical plane. To his perplexity such pictures never lasted long at 'Lisnacrieve'; he would look at the wall and exclaim 'Extraordinary, extraordinary! I'd have sworn I hung it there. Well, well!'

So the young Norman looked for aesthetic enlightenment and stimulus to Grandpa Williams, who never visited 'Lisnacrieve' without asking to see his grandson's latest drawings and delivering a critical appraisement of them. Thomas Williams was a frustrated artist. In the Fiji Islands he nearly always had a sketchbook handy, and many of his drawings, having lain forgotten, were reproduced eighty or ninety years later as illustrations to *The Journal of Thomas Williams*.\* These are careful factual studies but never amateurish. An artist can admire them no less than an anthropologist.

His pictorial talent skipped a generation, then reappeared in four of Janie's sons and one of her daughters, so that Creswick people said, 'The moment they're born the Lindsays grab a pencil and start to draw'. Each of the five became a successful professional artist, and in Norman the faculty manifested itself in a variety of forms which some of his admirers called genius. And he alone inherited another of his grandfather's qualities. This was the old man's evangelistic zeal. It took a different turn in Norman but his consuming need to make other men believe what he believed came straight from Thomas Williams.

---

\* Edited by G. C. Henderson (Sydney, 1931).

Doctor Lindsay was right. Time cured the disorder which caused Norman's skin to erupt in itching blisters and when he was seven or eight he could run and jump and climb trees to his heart's content without suffering for it. Nobody sent him to sit down and be quiet. It was good to be alive.

Making up for lost time, he ran everywhere. He was a thin wisp of a child, light on his feet, quick in his movements, and he liked to feel the wind streaming past his face and rushing through his hair. His blue eyes were brighter than ever and his nose, which had been pudgy and rather formless, strengthened and sharpened into a beak. His brothers teased him about it. Norman did not mind. Life was easier if you took the chaffing of older brothers in good part; or, better still, ignored it altogether.

And older brothers had their uses. He started at the Creswick State School when he was six. Bigger boys saw him as a good subject for bullying and introduced him to arm-twisting, nose-grinding, the 'dry shave' and other approved torments. Lionel, four years older than Norman and muscular, while pretending outside 'Lisnacrieve' to be oblivious of his younger brother's existence, yet kept an eye on him at school. Word went round that it wasn't healthy to bully young Norman Lindsay—if you did you'd have his big brother on your neck and end up with a thick ear! So Norman was left in peace.

That made school more tolerable, but he did not like it. Most of those in authority over him and his fellows at Creswick State, particularly Snorky Simmons, Nosey Norton and Black Sammy, revered the cane as a teaching instrument and laid it on hard. Norman's hands were delicate and supersensitive throughout his life, and he could never recall those school canings without wincing. Most of the stuff they tried to teach bored him. Even the drawing lessons were fatuous. What satisfaction could he find in sketching a wooden cone, a milk jug, a slouch hat or a hurricane lamp when he might be letting himself go in an illustration to *The Three Musketeers* or *Don Quixote* or *Gil Blas?*

His passion for drawing what interested him was as strong as ever but, with his itching trouble cured and animal energy flowing through him, he discovered that life held a multitude of other, if lesser, joys. He explored the old diggings with his brothers and mates until he was familiar with every shaft and drive. One afternoon he nearly drowned while Lionel was teaching him to swim in an old waterhole. The others pulled him out and pumped water out of him, and he tottered home.

The tales told by the horsy chaps who succeeded one another in the post of groom at 'Lisnacrieve' were an unfailing delight. Dennis Denny was a prime favourite. He specialized in the Kelly Gang of bushrangers, claiming inside knowledge.

'Me brother Tom owns Dan Kelly's saddle to this day', he told the gaping Norman. 'I'll tell y'all about that some time.' According to the Denny version, Ned and his gang became an Australian equivalent of Robin Hood and his merry men, robbing the rich and giving to the poor. Norman never wearied of hearing about the Kellys' vengeance on a lustful policeman who had tampered with their sister Kate.

'Any fella who messes around with a bloke's sister is asking for trouble', Denny always remarked, fixing a severe eye on his young listener. 'You wanta remember that!'

Norman promised that he would.

And there were friendships; or what pass for friendships with the young. His drawing skill ensured that he had plenty of pals. He was in demand to make sketches in their pocket notebooks; knights in armour, ruffled swordsmen and other men of action predominated at the start but by the time he was eleven or twelve he was producing a popular line in nudes. These were based largely on imagination and pictorial hearsay. For although Norman, by his own account, did some bold experimenting with girls in his pre-adolescent years, other evidence suggests that he was less of a juvenile libertine than memory led him to suppose. The truth is that, in sexual matters, he was, throughout his life, much more the inquisitive theorist than the active researcher.

And, in boyhood, no matter what other diversions took his fancy, nothing else equalled his craving to draw. It possessed and obsessed him; he never ceased working at it for more than a few hours at a time. His eldest brother, Percy, had decided that he'd like an artist's life. Percy studied for a while under a Melbourne painter, Walter Withers, who came to Creswick and ran a class, and also under a Ballarat teacher named Sheldon, then went to work. At nineteen or twenty he was turning out landscapes which were always competent, and at their best delicate and lucent. Norman, who was nine years younger, liked Percy's pictures but was not tempted to try his hand at colour; that could wait. First, he wanted to draw with pencil and pen, and since no teacher was available he had to slog away and teach himself.

Copying drawings in books and magazines was useful but it was not enough. It was no good being a monkey, an imitator—he'd have to go deeper. Where to start was the question. Well, there were horses. He decided to work right over the horse and familiarize himself with every detail of its anatomy. He went out to the 'Lisnacrieve' stables and examined a hoof from the front, then went inside and drew it. Then he went back and examined the hoof from one side, and went in and drew that. He studied the hoof from every angle, even lifting it to examine the underpart, and each time he went inside and drew from memory what he had seen. He could have drawn direct from the horse but that would not have done. The only effective way, for him at any rate, was to take a mental photograph of each detail, then go inside and put it on paper. Once having mastered the hoof, he went on to the fetlock, the knee, the shoulder, the neck, the head, studying each item in sections, then going away to draw it.

It took weeks but time did not matter. He had a whole life before him. He persevered until he could draw any and every detail of a horse's anatomy from memory without faltering. He did each drawing on a small piece of paper and pasted this in a book. Now when he wanted to draw a horse he could do it swiftly and unerringly, rarely pausing to wonder if he was right or wrong about this detail or that—each image was stamped on his memory like a head on a coin; and as a check he had his scrapbook notes for instant reference. The Lindsays kept a cow and he memorized her by the same method. Then he worked through hens, ducks, cats, dogs. He never forgot any form which he memorized in this way. And the exercise taught him something of lasting value: it made him see that all forms were based on certain geometrical principles and that the artist who ignored these must go wrong.

Creswick had a public library. Norman discovered it when he was nine or ten. He spent hours there, brooding on illustrations in English and American magazines. One day, in an issue of *Harper's*, he came on an article about Albrecht Dürer, the fifteenth-century German artist. A number of Dürer's black-and-white works were reproduced and, as the small beak-nosed boy pored over them, he was at one and the same time transported by seeing what an inspired hand could do and harrowed by a conviction that he would never be able to match it. This thought depressed him for only a day or two; then he went back to his drawing book and flung himself into the struggle again.

Norman's mind was haunted by the men, the women and the scenes that Dürer had created; they gave him no rest. He had been taught to respect other people's books but he had to have that article about Dürer. The librarian, an old man who liked books and did the job for a tiny stipend, knew Norman well. The boy came and went as he pleased, saw what he liked, sat over books and magazines for hours on end. One afternoon he went along, gathered five or six magazines together and took them to a corner table. He spent an hour or two with them, then closed them up, put them back in their places, and went home. A sharp eye might have noticed a bulge under his jacket but the librarian was not suspicious. Doctor Lindsay's boy filching from the library? Unthinkable.

In his own room at 'Lisnacrieve', Norman slipped the copy of *Harper's* from under his jacket, opened it up at the article on Dürer, and gloated. He got scissors and snipped out each of the Dürer reproductions. then pasted them into the book which held his anatomical studies of horses, cows, hens and other assorted livestock. That was the birth of his lifelong habit of collecting and filing any published item which seemed likely to be useful for reference. Thus he built an honest and worthy practice on dishonest and unworthy foundations. In later life he was never sure whether to blush for his wrongdoing or to exult on the ground that the end justified the means. Somehow he could never pretend to repent.

From the first he had a feeling of kinship with Dürer. This gained strength some years later when the Creswick library acquired a book about the great painter and engraver's life and work. Norman was among the first to borrow it. One of the illustrations was a reproduction of a black-and-white self-portrait which Dürer had done when he was thirteen—the very age Norman happened to be at that time. To Norman's eyes, the face was his own. With the aid of the mirror he drew a study of his face in the same position as the young Dürer's. Line for line, the faces were almost identical—even Dürer's long hair and the odd-shaped hat he wore did not weaken the uncanny likeness. That cemented Norman's sense of what he liked to think of as a blood tie. Looking at the two self-portraits side by side, he was filled with surging excitement.

He plunged into the book's descriptive account of Dürer's life. It was competent, but suddenly a phrase pulled him up. The writer called his subject 'the simple Dürer'. Simple? Norman felt the adjective was disparaging, belittling, contemptuous. He snapped the book shut and hurled it from him. It struck the wall with a thud, then slithered to the floor and lay there with a burst cover. Dismay quenched his anger. There might be trouble about this; he might even be barred from the library. He took the book to his table, and worked over it with scissors, cardboard and strong glue. The repair job came out well. When he returned the book the old librarian noticed nothing wrong. Norman breathed again.

The library was an unequalled source of pictorial inspiration but one other public institution in Creswick also offered something. This was, improbably, the bar-room of Sandy McPhail's Phoenix Hotel. Passing by one night, Norman happened to glance through the open door. Hanging on the wall at the back of the bar he saw a lithograph depicting the death of Nelson. The study of the dying Nelson lying in the cockpit of HMS *Victory* with his officers about him was skilfully composed and expertly drawn. Norman stood gaping at it over the heads of the evening drinkers breasting up to the bar inside. The Phoenix was near 'Lisnacrieve', and after that he often found an excuse to escape for a few minutes at night and stand in the darkness outside the bar-room peering in. It had to be night, when the bar-room was brightly lit—the daytime twilight blurred the detail of the picture for a watcher outside the door, where Norman's tender years condemned him to stay.

For him, the picture outranked even *Ajax and Cassandra* and he doubted if any other ever made a like impact on his eye and mind. He knew that thousands of pictures which he saw later were incomparably better works of art but he did not care. The Phoenix Hotel's *Death of Nelson* stayed first, even though his memory of it was always and unalterably entangled with the odour of beer.

A moralist would have been troubled had he been privy to certain actions of the young Norman Lindsay. There was not only the filching of the Dürer article from the library, and later and equally successful filchings of other magazine illustrations. There was also a matter of forgery.

It was not difficult. He had been working to acquire a command over the pen and pencil for years and could produce a creditable replica of pretty well any item capable of being copied. So early in 1894 he composed a note in an imitation of his mother's firm, clear and pointed handwriting and, having stowed it away in his pocket, went whistling off to school. The note, addressed to the head teacher, explained that the writer had decided to transfer Norman to Creswick Grammar School. It worked. Norman, who was about to turn fifteen, left school, wagged it for six months, and was never unmasked. He continued to leave 'Lisnacrieve' after breakfast each morning and head for the State School. Then, having hidden his books, he spent the rest of the day doing what he wanted instead of what stuffy adults believed he ought to do. He nearly always made for the old diggings which straggled away for miles along the creek. Nobody likely to betray a truant schoolboy ever went into that region of mullock heaps and abandoned shafts; the only other living things were an occasional fossicker and a few starveling goats. Norman did not just idle his time away. He made hundreds of drawings while roaming the diggings; and when he was not drawing he was scribbling in an exercise book, trying to write one or another of the romantic tales which haunted his mind. None of these ever got far; inspiration always ran out after a few pages and every story ended in the air.

Norman always insisted that his truant period was an invaluable experience. For one thing, it satisfied him 'that solitude has a charm that no other system of existence can give', which was to become one of the guiding principles of his life. He knew he could not go on wagging it indefinitely, and the time came when he had to find a way out; painless, if possible. Percy, Bert and Lionel had each been finished off, in the accepted phrase, at Creswick Grammar School, so Norman went to his parents and urged them to send him there too. The State School, he said, could teach him nothing more, which was true enough, if not for the ostensible reasons. His parents consented and in the middle

of 1894 Norman's name was added to the Grammar School roll. He was
fitted out with a cap bearing the black and gold colours and, after being
initiated by having his head plunged into the slimy chaff-flecked waters
of the horse-trough outside the Phoenix Hotel, became a member of the
student body in good standing.

The school was fighting a losing battle. It took girls as well as boys
but even so the number of pupils was diminishing every year; it was only
about forty when Norman enrolled. Creswick's shrinking population was
to blame, not the quality of the schooling. The Principal, Samuel Fiddian,
M.A., a distinguished Cambridge scholar, had come to Australia as the
first headmaster of Prince Alfred College, Adelaide. Mr Fiddian, a delicate
and sensitive man, had bought Creswick Grammar School in 1872, three
years after it was founded, and was to see it close in 1903. Many of the
boys he sent out into the world won positions of some eminence but it
is unlikely that he numbered Norman Lindsay among those who would
go to the top. Norman's talents were not of the kind which impress
schoolmasters, and he chiefly distinguished himself by showing a liking
and talent for journalism. This was mildly ironic, seeing the derision
in which he later held the daily newspaper branch of that calling. Nobody who once heard him spit out the word 'newsrags' could ever forget
the contempt he put into it, even though, paradoxically, in manhood he
found common ground with many working journalists and made some
intimate friends among them.

Norman was the editor and general mainstay of the school's unofficial
magazine, a four-page sheet called the *Boomerang*. Percy and Lionel
had each in his own time edited the *Boomerang* but it had been dormant
for a period when Norman revived it. He and his helpers printed it by a
facsimile process from a handwritten and hand-drawn master copy. The
ink was mauve. This gave it a vaguely decadent look but the contents
would have passed the most puritanical censor. The *Boomerang* published school football news, original verses, correspondence, and an occasional story. A particularly memorable tale which began in one issue
and ended in the next, bore the almost unbearably alliterative title of
*The Mystic Midnight Murder* or *The Manor Master's Revenge*. Few of
the drawings rose much above schoolboy level, but sometimes Norman
took a fancy to do something ambitious. In one issue he published a
full-page study headed 'The Prisoner of Chillon', over a telescoped version
of the Byron lines:

> My hair is grey, but not with years . . .
> My limbs are bow'd, though not with toil,
>     But rusted with a vile repose,
> For they have been a dungeon's spoil.

For all the crudity of the reproduction, the study of the shrunken man chained to a dungeon pillar with hopelessness stamped on his face was a striking piece of work for an untrained sixteen-year-old. It was also a tribute to a poet whom Norman Lindsay admired to the end of his life— one he ranked nearly, if not quite, beside Browning.

The *Boomerang* was important in his life for more than one reason. As well as letting him test his muscles as an illustrator and as the knock-about journalistic artist he was to become a few years later while striving to find his feet, it also founded a friendship between him and a boy of his own age, Ruff Tremearne, one of the *Boomerang*'s regular contributors. The nickname, short for 'Ruffian', was inspired by the boisterous way that young Tremearne, who had been christened John, hurled himself into any and every activity. A dark, handsome, warmly demonstrative boy, he was a son of Doctor Tremearne. Norman and he formed a close friendship which was never shadowed. It was the only friendship of Norman's life which began when he was young and lasted. They never exchanged an angry word, and Tremearne's serene and invulnerable amiability was the keystone of their unbroken compatibility. Norman made friends effortlessly and lost them nearly as easily. Ruff Tremearne had the same talent for making friends and a no less conspicuous talent for keeping them.

Norman's marks were just good enough to keep him clear of trouble, and he was doing largely what he wanted to do, which was to improve his technical skill as an artist. He knew even then that his battle to gain complete mastery over the pen and pencil would never be quite won, but his skill was increasing. After sixty-odd years, his sister Mary looked back on him at that time and recalled the usual night scene when the evening meal was cleared away and the big dining room 'belonged to the older members of the family'.

> . . . for the most part I see him sitting at the far side of the long dining-room table, the only completely quiet human in that hive of restless humanity, concentrating on his allotted task—to draw. Norman always sat with his back to the piano, apparently oblivious to any noise or movement in that room, intent on making pictures, and all the time experimenting with just one pen and a small bottle of Indian ink . . .
>
> The word art was seldom used in our household—certainly never in regard to the artistic performances, early or late, in the careers of the brothers, but each kept an eye on the other and knew that little Norman had something in him tremendously interesting and ahead of all the others. I remember Lionel sometimes saying to me behind Norman's back 'Did you see that drawing he did last night?', as one might say 'Have you seen Orpen's latest?'
>
> Sometimes passing, I'd glance over his shoulder and point at a new experimental bit of technique. 'Yes,' he'd say, looking up for half a second. 'I think you get the shine on the armour better with that stroke.' Then he'd go on drawing, absorbed in his work, only now and again lifting his eyes for a moment to gaze into space, seeing something in his mind's eye that only he could see.

Sometimes I'd go to the piano, right behind Norman's chair, and strum impartially a bit of one of Beethoven's slow movements, or perhaps something catchy from the latest musical comedy. There was a cheap popular tune in vogue called *The Parade March*, which he loved. It had a good thumping bass. When, without looking up, he'd say 'Play that thing, Mame', I knew what he wanted and thumped away at *The Parade March*. Many years later, when he came home on a visit, I went to the piano and played a few chords of *The Parade March* and said, 'Why did you like that old tune so much?' 'Oh,' he said, 'it always made me see a cavalcade of soldiers on horses, or troops of soldiers on the march.'. .

*Men of Harlech* was another favourite. He often asked Mary to play it and went on drawing to the beat of its swinging rhythm.

Norman grew restless as 1895 drew on. Creswick was lifeless, stuffy, dismal—like a prison with invisible walls. To make matters worse, Ruff Tremearne had been sent to round off his schooling at Ballarat College. Norman and he saw less of each other but their devotion was as strong as ever and their meetings were all the more precious. Whatever came or went they never missed Saturday night. That was the only time Creswick woke for a few hours. Then the windows of the shops in the main street were brightly lit, and farmers and their wives and families, who drove in from miles around, added to the crowds on the pavements. Hobbledehoys and girls paraded, elaborately unconscious of one another's existence. The Salvation Army provided the sole entertainment; grouped around the big drum in the light of a naptha flare, they proclaimed their faith in heavenly bliss with unflagging zeal. Norman Lindsay and Ruff Tremearne picked their way up and down the sidewalk together, pledging lifelong devotion to the arts and to their pact of friendship, and pausing to ask themselves now and then how much longer they would be stuck in this dreary hole.

Norman's older brothers came and went as they pleased. Why shouldn't he also be free? It was true that Percy, having taken himself to Melbourne for a year or so, had wandered back to Creswick and settled down at home again. That proved nothing except that Percy liked an untroubled life and was not driven by an inner compulsion to rush out and challenge the world. He would go back to the city again when the spirit moved him; meanwhile, in Creswick, life was easy, girls were friendly, and landscape subjects limitless, and at 'Lisnacrieve' board cost nothing, meals were regular and beds soft. A man could do worse.

Norman liked Percy—who didn't?—but had no wish to imitate him. Lionel's policy of galloping out to meet life head-on was more to Norman's taste. Lionel had gone off to Melbourne some years before to work at the Government Observatory and become an astronomer, but when that plan collapsed he had come home and gone back to school. Creswick

1   Grandpa Williams          2   Doctor and Mrs Lindsay

3   'Lisnacrieve' in about 1900

4 A Lindsay family group in 1888. *Back row:* Lionel, Percy, Bert
*Front row:* Mrs Lindsay with Reg in her lap, Ruby, Doctor Lindsay
with Pearl on his shoulder, Mary *On the ground:* Norman

seemed as stifling to him as it did to Norman but he stood it for a while. Then he escaped. Although he had none of Norman's passion for making pictures or Percy's feeling for colour, he had inherited some of Grandpa Williams's skill as a draughtsman and now and then played about with drawing. Through a friend he was offered the job of cartoonist for a shady little Melbourne weekly, the *Hawk*, which was a blend of sports tabloid and scandal sheet. He grabbed it. The work bordered on the disreputable but the pay, thirty-five shillings for a page of sketches illustrating the salient events of each week in Melbourne's sporting circles and underworld, was not bad. Victoria was still in the aftermath of the economic depression which had followed the bursting of the land boom in 1891 and a bachelor could live well on thirty-five shillings a week.

Norman's discontent quickened whenever Lionel came home to spend two or three days in Creswick. Lionel talked largely of the emancipated and gamesome life he lived. His accounts of studio parties, of his adventures with obliging girls, of his intimacy with heroes of the boxing ring and the cycling track, and his familiarity with dark and violent backwaters of the city, lost nothing in the telling. Norman listened with wide eyes and yearning heart. Bohemia lay just eighty miles away at the end of a railway track, and here he was stuck in Creswick where nothing ever happened. He began pressing his mother to let him go and join Lionel in Melbourne. She told him he was too young to be exposed to the trials and temptations of the city. And how did he propose to support himself? Ridiculous! He must put the idea out of his mind and settle down like any normal boy. He appealed to his father, knowing that he was wasting his breath. 'What's that, old man?' Doctor Lindsay huffed. 'Melbourne, you say! And your mother won't hear of it! Then that's the end of it, old man. No use badgering me about it.' And Doctor Lindsay scuttled off into his surgery and closed the door.

Grumbling and disconsolate, Norman put the 1895 Christmas *Boomerang* to bed a day or two before the school broke up in December. He had made up his mind about one thing: wild horses wouldn't drag him back to school after the holidays. Yet nothing about the *Boomerang* betrayed the editor's jaundiced mood. It breathed out a spirit of seasonable merriment and good will.

Christmas came and went, and then New Year's Day. To Norman the year ahead loomed drab and interminable, but within a few weeks everything changed for the better. Lionel wrote home with news that he was taking a step up in the black-and-white art world: he was joining the staff of a weekly, the *Free Lance*, which was about to be launched in Melbourne; his job would be to draw topical sketches and caricatures for a salary of two pounds a week. The *Free Lance* would resemble the Sydney *Bulletin* without being a slavish copy. It would thus aim higher

c

than the *Hawk*—it could hardly aim lower. The trouble was that Lionel could not cram into a single week the task of drawing topicalities for two different sheets. He needed an understudy, but one who would stay in the shadows, for he did not contemplate telling the editor of the *Hawk* that he was working for the *Free Lance*; nor did he intend handing over to a deputy any more of the *Hawk* salary than he must. Letters flitted back and forth between Lionel and 'Lisnacrieve' and a proposal took shape: Norman should go to Melbourne and, for ten shillings a week, 'ghost' the *Hawk*'s weekly page, which would still appear under Lionel's name. Thus Lionel would have two pounds a week from the *Free Lance* and twenty-five shillings a week from the *Hawk* while Norman . . . well, Norman would have ten shillings a week and would gain priceless experience.

Mrs Lindsay was against the idea, but she knew the day was lost when her husband mumbled 'Can't keep the boy tied to your apron strings for ever, what!' and darted out of the house, supposedly to go and see a patient. She still did not give in but she was wilting. Lionel vowed that Norman would come to no harm, either physical or moral—he would see to that. Norman sulked about the house and seized every chance to nag his mother and break down her resistance. Poor Mrs Lindsay realized that Norman had left boyhood behind him and turned into a young man. Even his voice had lately deepened and acquired a strong masculine timbre which was surprising in one of such slight physique. After all, Norman pointed out, he would be seventeen in a few weeks, and he was going to be an artist, come what may. And what, he asked her, could an artist do in Creswick? Or, for that matter, in Ballarat? In Melbourne it would be different. There he could keep himself by drawing Lionel's page for the *Hawk* and spend his free time studying at the National Gallery school, under the best teachers.

Mrs Lindsay suddenly surrendered and Norman went bounding off to pack his bag. He did not have much, only a couple of extra shirts, three or four pairs of socks, and a few other articles of clothing; and, of course, most important of all, his pens, pencils and paper, and the precious scrapbook. He was sorry to abandon one of his possessions. This was a model of a three-masted square-rigged ship which perched on a shelf above his bed. Old Bill Ayres, a ship's carpenter turned landsman, whose daughter Jane was a housemaid at 'Lisnacrieve', had made it for him when he was four or five. Slim, spare and graceful, it stood on the shelf all through his childhood and adolescence. That was the beginning of his conscious love of ships. He would miss his miniature square-rigger in Melbourne but it was too awkward to pack, so he had to leave it.

Mary helped him to stow his stuff away in a battered old portmanteau of his father's. She kept up a stream of laughing chat all the time because she did not want him to guess how heavy her heart was. She was not blind to Norman's faults—among them, his unthinking selfishness, his capacity for self-deception, his incipient but growing dislike of criticism—but of all her brothers he was closest to her and his going would leave a huge gap.

He ate a quick breakfast in the kitchen next morning. Then, still half-fearful of being stopped, he said a hurried goodbye to 'Lisnacrieve' and, snatching up his bag, set off to walk to the railway station and catch the eight-forty to Melbourne. He trudged up the dusty road, and when he topped the low rise and saw the station he had to suppress the temptation to halt and do a little victory dance.

His head was too full of what lay ahead to have room for so much as a thought for the girl he was leaving behind him; or, rather, the young woman, for she was twenty-four, with warm thighs and eager breasts. One of her brothers had introduced Norman to the family farm, and in his disgruntled period, between leaving school and persuading his mother to let him go to Melbourne, he had several times stayed there. He had previously done a little novice fumbling with girls of his own age but the farmer's daughter had initiated him into the mysteries of adult sex. Their affair, intense on his side and half-derisive on hers, was carried on under the very noses of her family. They made him free of the house and, with one exception, treated him as a light-hearted and innocent youngster who was fun to have around. The exception was a beefy older brother who seemed, Norman sensed, to doubt whether the young visitor was quite so harmless as the others fancied. One Sunday afternoon the lovers were in the sitting room when the suspicious brother came padding along the hallway in stockinged feet. He would have surprised them in the midst of an illicit embrace if a creaking floor board had not given the alarm. Norman was just in time to flop into an armchair and snatch up a novel lying at hand. He never forgot that book; it was F. Anstey's *Vice-Versa*.

But all that was behind him as he went to the ticket window at the Creswick station, pushed over 10s 3d, and asked for a second-class single to Melbourne. On the platform he stood waiting for the train, glad to be getting away without any tearful family leave-takings. He glanced up and saw a slim young man strolling toward him. It was his brother Bert—exquisite, finicky, a shade effeminate, who was pained by his brothers' rowdyism and their choice of uncouth friends. Bert was a clerk in the National Bank at Creswick and, detesting the figures, the ledgers and the stodgy routine, he found an outlet by exercising a talent as a designer and maker of costumes. This was invaluable whenever amateur stage shows and tableaux were being organized in Creswick, but the other Lindsay boys jeered at his interest in silks, satins and brocades and his skill with scissors, thimble and needle. Yet here he had come to say farewell and Norman was touched. He had never dreamed that Bert, behind the modish bow ties, well-cut jackets and other foppish niceties, harboured a brotherly affection for him.

The engine lumbered into the platform, drawing a string of passenger coaches and freight trucks—it was a mixed train as far as Ballarat. Norman found a corner seat in a dog-box compartment and heaved his bag up on to the rack. Then Bert and he talked through the open window until the guard called 'All aboard!' and blew his whistle. The brothers exchanged a quick handshake and the train went clanging on its way.

# 2

# *City Lights*
# *1896-1901*

Norman and his cronies lived from hand to mouth and loved it. Yesterday had never been, and tomorrow would never come; only today mattered. They slept, woke, walked and breathed in an aura of divine irresponsibility, wrangling, affirming, denying, proclaiming, denouncing, extolling, and sometimes working. Whenever two or three of them gathered together theories about life and art rioted and spun like fallen leaves in an autumn wind. They could smell a debt-collector three blocks away and a bailiff even farther off. When they had sixpence or if their credit was good they ate in cheap hash-houses—'dog-shops' to the art students and their circle; at other times they tightened their belts and filled their bellies with dreams.

It did not matter that Melbourne was still in straitened circumstances; to Norman it was a magic city, with its network of cable tramways, its fashionable women in picture hats and bustles, its night streets brilliant with light, its theatres staging melodrama and vaudeville. Bars were open until the small hours of the morning, and the wheels of hansoms and four-wheeler cabs and private carriages rumbled until dawn. The population was still below half a million but it was the largest city in Australia, and Norman was proud and glad to be a member of its artists' colony.

At first he lived with Lionel in St James Building, near the Law Courts. They slept on stretcher beds in a dingy cell above a work-room grandly styled the studio. As often as not one or two others belonging to the brotherhood of artists, journalists, aspiring writers and undefined refugees from middle-class respectability also slept there. The door of the studio was always open and the laws of hospitality required that you invite a friend to make himself comfortable on the floor when the talk had run on and the hour was late.

Lionel paid the rent out of his £3 5s a week, so all Norman had to worry about was finding money for food, tobacco, drink, clothing and other creature comforts; and, of course, for pens and ink and drawing paper. Ten shillings a week allowed for no frills. At the time Norman never paused for long to brood on Lionel's affluence and his own poverty —he was too grateful to his brother for having rescued him from Creswick and transplanted him to 'Baghdad-on-the-Yarra'. The joys of *la vie de Bohème* far outweighed the material shortcomings. He would gladly have toiled as Lionel's 'ghost' for no pay at all.

The work was not hard. It called for speed and versatility rather than artistic elegance. Every Sunday morning Lionel told him what to draw for the weekly page in the *Hawklet* (as the *Hawk* had been renamed to circumvent a legal complication which had threatened to put the rakish sheet out of business). The eight items usually crammed into the page were chosen with an eye for, on the one hand, the sporting tastes, prejudices and loyalties of the *Hawklet*'s readers, and, on the other, their appetite for the salacious, the violent and the seamy. To keep the editor in the dark about the arrangement with Norman, Lionel still had to do a little leg-work, perhaps plodding down to the morgue to sketch the body of a murdered girl fished out of the Yarra or dodging into Mick Nathan's Victoria Hall in Bourke Street to jot down a rough likeness of a crowd-pleasing pugilist. But the real labour of turning the ideas and the raw material into a coherent page fell to Norman, so he spent much of each Sunday drawing hard for the *Hawklet* in one corner of the studio while Lionel drew hard for the *Free Lance* in another.

Norman quickly learned how to stretch his ten shillings. He found a sixpenny restaurant which sold for five shillings a book of twelve meal-tickets, valid for a week. Having eaten two meals a day—soup, meat and vegetables, and a slab of leaden suet pudding—for six days, he could scramble through the seventh day on tea and toast. If emergencies upset his budget, he ate less. At such times he sagged with hunger; now and then he blacked out and came round to find himself lying on the floor. 'Malnutrition', he remembered later, 'was what might be called an occupational infirmity in those days'. A quarter-pound plug of tobacco costing a shilling could, with care, be made to last a week. Tobacco was a necessity; a pipe when he woke in the morning allayed hunger and made it easier to skip breakfast. He spent a further shilling to have his shirts washed and ironed at a Chinese laundry; while untroubled by many crudities of living which would have horrified his parents he was never happy in a grubby shirt. Another shilling went to pay his way into the weekly Life Class at the National Gallery school, so that he could practise drawing from a live model. The rest of his earnings bought drawing materials, and there was sometimes enough left over for a couple of beers or a glass of wine while he roamed the city in the company of a kindred spirit, eyeing the girls, damning the *bourgeoisie*, and arguing the eternal artistic verities.

Somehow he managed to buy a book once in a while. A shilling volume of Rabelais went everywhere in his pocket like a priest's prayer book. To Norman and the brotherhood, Rabelais was the fountainhead of wisdom, the supreme authority on life and how it should be lived. A well-thumbed copy of Rabelais had been among Grandpa Williams's books at 'Horncastle'. Being in French, it had defied Norman's efforts to read it, but he had seen Grandpa Williams chuckling over it. Now that Norman had made the acquaintance of Gargantua, Pantagruel, Panurge and the others, it baffled him to understand how a man could have read and enjoyed Rabelais and yet still remained a devout Christian. He would have liked to debate the matter with Grandpa Williams but it was too late. The old man had died five years before.

Norman's income did not leave him much money to buy books but the public library was full of them. And as well as books to read there were fine reproductions of the work of Millais, Whistler, Frederick Sandys and other famous artists in old files of English periodicals; he spent hours with them. He liked Cole's Book Arcade, in Bourke Street, even better. The atmosphere was so cheerful. Every afternoon a small string band made music which was punctuated by the screeching of parrots and other ornamental birds and the chattering of a small cageful of monkeys. Anybody was welcome to spend all day and every day if he chose, dipping into and reading any of the million-odd books on the shelves. Cole's opened Norman's eyes to Balzac, Gautier, Theocritus and Petronius. There he read Browning again, worked through Byron's letters, and discovered the poetry of Rossetti and Swinburne.

The National Gallery was another of his haunts. He found something new whenever he wandered through the gloomy old place. It was a rich moment when he came on Dürer there. The Gallery had prints of three Dürer etchings: *Melancholia, The Knight, Death and the Devil*, and *St Jerome In His Cell*. Norman went back and back to them and the more he studied them the more they revealed. After two or three hours with them he would walk away with his mind reeling as if he had drunk too much wine.

He had never before worried about colour, had hardly thought about it. The struggle for mastery in black and white was to obsess him for many years, but in exploring the National Gallery he at least began to glimpse the possibilities of colour. Wanting to find out more than he could learn from the Melbourne collection, he had to satisfy his curiosity by reading about the lives and methods of the great colourists and poring over reproductions in books. It was a poor substitute for seeing the original paintings, but when he went to Europe nearly fifteen years later and visited the great galleries he saw nothing to make him amend the honour roll of colourists which he had drawn up in Melbourne. The names on it were Rubens, Titian, Rembrandt, Goya, Turner, Corot and Delacroix. For Norman, Rubens always remained supreme, the equivalent in painting of Shakespeare in poetry and Beethoven in music. 'This Giant, in his sense of inexhaustive vitality has the effect of a torrent that drowns all feeble efforts', Norman was to write many years later. 'Those who scramble out stand on the banks, uttering cries of exasperation at the size, force and volume of this creative stream.'*

Wild parties were rare but now and then an unexpected fee for a drawing made one possible. On such a night Norman had his first sight of a square-rigged ship, more or less the twin many times magnified of the model he had left in Creswick. It was a Saturday, and with two cronies he had been roaming from bar to bar. They ended at a sailor's pub, Antonio's, at the western end of Flinders Street. Turned out at closing-time, about midnight, they found their way, muzzy with beer, to the near-by Yarra wharves and, after some witless skylarking, stretched out on the bare planks. The other two were soon snoring, but Norman was wakeful. A late moon rose and shed pale bright light over the river, and then he saw the square-rigger, lying at a wharf lower down. His eyes dwelt on the tapered masts, the slight dip from poop to waist, the long sweep up to the bows, the thrust of the bowsprit, the lift of the cutwater to the figurehead—a woman with one arm upraised. Propped up on an elbow in the silver night, he was entranced by this vision of beauty. He believed he would never see any man-made thing to surpass it.

An apocalyptic experience of the kind was rare but no day or night was drab or humdrum or quite without its touch of wonder. He told himself that this was life. He could go on living it for ever. Parnassus was not around the next corner. It was here.

One day Lionel told Norman he'd have to find somewhere else to live. Lionel said that two of his friends, Ernest Moffitt and Jack Castieau, were coming to join him in St James Building. Moffit, a fine musician and a talented painter as well as an orchestral administrator, and Castieau, a public servant who dabbled in journalism, were both in their late twenties, and Lionel explained that he would be failing in his duty if he exposed his seventeen-year-old brother to the influence of these mature men by letting him live under the same roof.

Norman grunted, 'Boiled down, all this gab means that you want to get rid of me'.

* *Creative Effort*, p. 82.

'If that's the way you talk to me after all I've done for you', Lionel retorted, 'you can go to hell'.

It was their first falling-out and they soon forgot it. They had not yet learned to harbour grievances. Besides, Norman still needed Lionel's ten shillings, and Lionel still needed Norman as a 'ghost'.

Norman went to live in a Collingwood slum with two friends, Hugh Conant and Herbert de Burier. Conant, who had once been a bank clerk in Creswick, fancied himself as a poet; de Burier, an English bishop's son, was an amiable remittance man who worked at any job on offer which did not intrude on his pleasures. For six shillings a week they rented a narrow-gutted terrace house in Little Fitzroy Street. Since Norman's stipend from Lionel was still ten shillings he had to learn to eat less. He took comfort in reflecting that the experience more than compensated for the hunger pains. Their neighbour on one side was a scrawny man with a hoarse voice who kept his wife and children by hawking rabbits through the suburbs in a handcart; on the other side was a brothel. The rabbit-oh and the harlots were citizens of a world different from any Norman had known. He watched and he listened, noting down idiosyncrasies of action and speech, and storing these away for future reference.

The move to Little Fitzroy Street was only the first of twenty-seven which he made in his Melbourne years. He stayed in some places for a few months, in others for a few weeks. The only one he really regretted leaving was a gardener's cottage in the grounds of 'Charterisville' on the banks of the Yarra at Heidelberg. 'Charterisville' had been an artists' retreat for some years and when Lionel and Ernest Moffitt, having dissolved partnership with Castieau, decided to quit St James Building and try Heidelberg, they asked Norman to join them.

The Lindsay brothers came together again with no rancour. They were soon calling one another 'Joe', in the old comradely way. This was a form of address which they and Percy had evolved among themselves because none of them liked his given name. One or two others including Ruff Tremearne, although not Lindsays, had the status of Joes, and Daryl was admitted to the fraternity later. For the benefit of the uninitiated they sometimes identified any Joe under discussion by speaking of him as 'Joe Norman', 'Joe Lionel' or the like, but among themselves this was never necessary—distinctions were made by some esoteric system of inflection.

A few other cottages and outbuildings were scattered around the grounds of 'Charterisville'. Most of these were rented by artists, musicians, journalists and theatre people, and the little colony numbered twelve or fourteen in all. Norman was younger than most of the others but they accepted him; he was a quiet youth, readier to listen than talk, and when argument ran high he sat back, taking it all in but keeping his thoughts to himself. Any seventeen-year-old could do little but hold his tongue in that company of garrulous egotists.

Norman liked Ernest Moffitt best. Although Moffitt was living a free and full Bohemian life, dining, drinking and womanizing, he was not so immersed in his own affairs as to be unaware that Norman was troubled. Norman had reason to be. He felt he was getting nowhere. He gave most of every Sunday to the *Hawklet* page. He also did an occasional commercial job for a printer or an advertiser; these tasks were wretchedly paid but they brought in a few shillings, and every little helped. For the rest he spent his days lying about the cottage and reading Lionel's books, swimming in the Yarra when the weather was warm, trying—vainly, it is said—to seduce the pretty daughter of a neighbouring dairy farmer, and making sketches of any stretch of the river, stand of trees or other spot which took his eye.

It was all rather aimless, and Norman knew it. He still went to the Life Class but it had lost much of its enchantment. He was out of step with his contemporaries and out of patience with himself. He had shown his pen drawings to George Coates, Hughie McLean and other of his fellow students, only to meet derision. He was on the wrong train, they told him—he'd never get anywhere with that stuff. French Impressionism had lately come to Australia, and they all said it was the only thing. You had to paint like a French Impressionist or you exposed yourself as a footling amateur. Although Norman had nothing against the French Impressionists he felt this judgement was extravagant, but he was still too unsure of himself to argue. Then when George Coates won the National Gallery Travelling Scholarship in 1896 it seemed to establish his artistic authority beyond all challenge. And since he was saying what all the others were saying, there was really no room for dissent.

One day Norman had a long talk with Moffitt. Encouraged by the older man, he opened his heart and expanded on his intellectual predicament. Moffitt watched the play of emotion over the thin, intense face in which the blue eyes burnt like flames, and listened to the gabble of words tumbling from the sensitive mouth. It was a little incoherent, but he understood and dropped in a word here and there to keep the flow going. Presently Norman got out a series of his pen drawings. Moffitt studied them in silence, taking his time about it. Then he spoke.

'Never take any notice of what people tell you you ought to do', he said. 'Do the thing you want to do. Nothing else matters.'

The words jolted Norman. He suddenly realized that he had gone close to letting himself be jockeyed into doing what everybody else was doing— he had all but capitulated and joined the mob. Moffitt's advice became one of the cornerstones of his philosophy. 'Charterisville' would have been worth while if it had given him nothing else.

The *Free Lance* died while they were at Heidelberg. That was a blow. Lionel no longer needed a 'ghost' for the *Hawklet* page, so Norman lost his ten shillings. He chased about for more commercial jobs and found enough to keep his head above water, but it was a struggle.

Lionel was also short of money. He had grown used to living well, dining at good restaurants, and entertaining any lady of his fancy with a flourish. Now he had to skimp. A dashing and spectacular man, his compelling personality, his overwhelming powers as a talker, and his repertoire of gay and bawdy ditties which he sang in a pleasant tenor voice while strumming an accompaniment on a guitar, made him the centre of any gathering. He decided they must leave Heidelberg and find cheaper lodgings. Moffitt concurred; he wanted to get away on affairs of his own anyway. Norman, as the very junior partner, was not consulted; he was simply told to pack his stuff. He and Lionel loaded their mattresses and other possessions on to a borrowed handcart, trundled the load eight miles to the city, and moved into a room whose window looked out over an expanse of grey rooftops. Heidelberg seemed a thousand miles away.

They lived like nomadic Arabs and acquired an intimate knowledge of the city's topography. They did not move their quarters every night or even every week, but the problem of finding money for rent and the reluctance of landlords to let them live free kept them from ever settling in one place for long. Although Lionel's *Hawklet* pay came in regularly he was always out to earn more, but there was little money for the kind of work that he and Norman did, the only kind that either was qualified to do. They illustrated jokes for the weeklies, designed posters, made sketches for labels on bottles and cans, even decorated religious texts for Sunday schools. They did everything that came along at the meagre ruling prices and liked it. Or tried to like it. Occasionally something novel came up. The management of the Melbourne Aquarium wanted a bold sign to flaunt above the entrance. They summoned the Lindsays, gave them a strip of calico twenty-four feet long and told them to adorn it with likenesses of the seals, fish, penguins and other marine creatures to be seen within. Lionel and Norman toiled over it, off and on, for two weeks. The fee was a starveling £2 10s, but Norman at least was satisfied. He had never seen a penguin before and was enchanted by what he called 'the little gentleman in the flogger coat'. He spent hours chuckling at the antics of the Aquarium's penguins as they popped in and out of their pool and strutted around the edge like miniature aldermen. His observations were probably the genesis of Sam Sawnoff the Penguin, one of the principal characters in *The Magic Pudding*, the tale for children which he wrote nearly twenty years later.

Another commission, which Norman took alone, was to design a poster advertising a contraceptive called 'Solvit'. Puritanism was riding high and the problem was to tell the public about the wonders of 'Solvit' without bringing the manufacturer to grips with the law. Norman did his best to be at once lucid and discreet, but the poster was hardly up on the hoardings when the police struck. They arrested the manufacturer and seized his stock. He was sentenced to six months in gaol. Worse, Norman was never paid for his work.

Then, suddenly, his fortunes improved. Lionel went off to Western Australia to work for the *Clarion*, a flamboyant newspaper launched by Randolph Bedford, a brilliant but erratic journalist, writer, mining promoter and adventurer. Norman took over the *Hawklet* page. With thirty-five shillings a week all to himself he felt like a plutocrat. He had to submit his page of sporting curiosities, scandals and criminalities to the editor and owner of the *Hawklet*, Billy Williams, every Monday morning. And nearly every Monday morning there was a gigantic row. Billy Williams, a lanky slouching man with large ears and a drooping moustache, rarely let the meeting pass without damning the quality of Norman's work and loudly appealing to the gods to bring Lionel back.

'Y' call that drawing!' he would hoot. 'What's it supposed to be? A sheila, a bloke, or a horse with the strangles? That's no bloody good for our paper! 'Ere, come an' look at this an' y'll see how it oughta be done!' He would hustle Norman across to a file of the *Hawklet*, throw it open and slam the flat of his hand down on a page of drawings bearing Lionel's initials—as often as not a page that Norman had ghosted. 'That's drawing, that is! That's what our paper's got t' have. That's what I'm paying y' for, an' paying y' a damn' sight too well.'

The Monday explosions never led to any lasting ill feeling. At other times Norman and Billy Williams got along well enough, although there was sometimes tension when Norman went to the office on Saturday morning to collect his money and the boss told him he'd have to wait because 'those bastards haven't paid up'. Norman never found out who the bastards were. Anyway he wasn't interested in the *Hawklet*'s financial troubles but only in his own. Knowing that Billy Williams was a welsher on principle, he never let himself be put off. More than once Billy was missing, and then Norman tracked him down, usually to a brothel, and made him disgorge, always bitterly protesting, 'Suck a man's blood, would y'! All right, here y'are, take the bloody money an' I hope it chokes y'!'

Billy Williams had many interests. The *Hawklet* was only one. He also promoted fights in partnership with Mick Nathan, took a hand in organizing other professional sports events, and managed a number of music hall performers. The *Hawklet* office was always crowded on Saturday morning, for Saturday was pay-day not only for the *Hawklet* staff but for all Billy Williams's vassals. One Saturday morning Norman was in the outer office with the others when a brisk little man who earned a living by running a snake-charming act bustled in. He was carrying a canvas sack and as he planked it down it writhed gently.

'I'm off outa town for a coupla days, Billy', he said. 'Can I leave me snakes here?'

'Yeah', said Billy Williams, 'Shove 'em under that couch'. He jerked his head at a couch against the wall. 'An' don't forget to come back for 'em.'

'Don't fret', said the snake man, 'I'll be back', and, sliding the sackful of educated snakes under the couch, he left.

A few minutes later another music-hall performer strolled in. He was a tall Negro song-and-dance man, flashily elegant in a tailcoat and white waistcoat and a three-inch collar. He sat down and his eyes fell on the canvas sack under the couch.

'What you got there, Billy?' he asked, prodding the sack with his silver-mounted stick.

'Sausages', said Billy Williams.

'Yeah, I believe you!' the Negro grunted.

He lugged the sack out and slipped off the string holding it closed. A snake pushed its head out and stared at him with bright beady eyes. He howled, dropped the sack, and fled, with everybody else on his heels. The open sack lay on the floor with snakes slithering out of it and writhing all over the room, a mass of sinuous bodies and darting fangs. They held undisputed possession until their owner showed up two or three days later. He pounced on the snakes and, snatching up one after the other, bundled them back into the sack, tied the mouth, and went off about his affairs.

It was some weeks before Norman again saw the Negro whose curiosity had caused the trouble. Once more it was at the Saturday morning pay parade. Billy Williams was going rabbiting in the country that afternoon and came to the office bearing a box of ferrets which he put down on the couch. A few minutes later the Negro stood in the doorway, looking about him.

'You got any snakes here today, Billy?' he asked.

'No', said Billy Williams. 'Y' can come in.'

The Negro lowered himself on to the couch. Staring into space, he idly worked a finger into one of the airholes in the ferret box and twiddled it. Nothing happened for a moment. Then the Negro let out a high-pitched wailing scream.

'A doctor, a doctor', he yelled. 'I'm bit by a snake.'

Clutching his hand, he raced for the door. The others in the room gave chase, but he was too terrified to heed them and went galloping off to find a doctor.

It was the kind of thing that happened when you worked for Billy Williams. Norman always said the *Hawklet*, although a cheap and rancid little rag, taught him more things—and stranger things—than ever he learnt at Creswick Grammar School.

Life was a tumbling, churning whirl. On the surface the art students and hopeful scribblers were a feckless lot, who laughed at misfortune, drank too much, and never harboured a serious thought, but only a few were like that under their skins. Nearly everyone had a driving spirit inside him, and in none was it stronger than in Norman Lindsay. After steeping himself in Greek mythology, he took to calling it his Daemon. That was as good a term as any for an intangible element which, unless illness put him to bed, never let him rest at any time in his life.

For his first three years or so in Melbourne he had no clear idea of where he was going. He was merely fumbling with serious art, but in working for the *Hawklet* he quickly developed into a highly competent journalistic artist. He knew that he would not be content to spend the rest of his life doing such shoddy and ephemeral stuff but at that time he was eager for any chance to practise his drawing, so when Lionel's friend, Jack Castieau, invited him to draw for a new Melbourne weekly, the *Tocsin*, he seized the chance. Castieau, a black-haired and olive-skinned man with a small, upturned moustache which gave him the air of a second-rate boulevardier, was one of a group of doctrinaire socialists who founded the *Tocsin*, in October 1897, to preach the liberation of the proletariat from the capitalist oppressor. Although Norman had no marked sympathy with the *Tocsin*'s political doctrines, he was not at that time an unbending enemy of socialism. It was only later that, while continuing to cherish many radical views on art and life, he acquired an attitude to the social order as conservative as any squatter's; he expressed this by reviling Utopianism, deploring the levelling of the classes, and refusing to believe that all men are born equal or that any political miracle will ever make them so. 'That the levellers themselves are destined to be dragged into the abyss of mediocrity of their own making is the only satisfaction one may get out of the miserable business', he once said. Yet in his Melbourne days, before his personal ideas had hardened, he took some pleasure in his *Tocsin* work. This was just as well, because there was no material reward—the *Tocsin* could not afford to pay him anything. The ideas he worked on were not his own; they came from Castieau and his socialist comrades, and Norman merely put them into pictorial form. He liked that arrangement; being a wholly tongue-in-cheek operation. it left him free to concentrate on his drawing technique. The experience certainly enlarged his journeyman skill and flexibility. He learned to skip from a *Tocsin* cartoon to a Sunday school text or a sauce label and then on to a page of topical vulgarities for the *Hawklet* without faltering.

Lionel came back from Western Australia with only a few shillings in his pocket and kept himself going in Melbourne with freelance work. He and Norman were closer than ever, and Castieau, who had a wife in a cottage at St Kilda but somehow managed to live the life of an emancipated Bohemian-about-town, was much in their company. They liked him, but when Lionel, who had also let himself be talked into contributing cartoons to the *Tocsin*, found that he was working for nothing, the cordiality lessened. Lionel not only disliked socialism but was an abler business man than Norman and saw no reason why he should starve in a garret to help the *Tocsin* flourish.

Perhaps it was in protest against Castieau and his fellows that the two Lindsays turned to pirates. Lionel started it. A voracious reader since early childhood, he began delving into the history of the pirates of the Spanish Main. Norman also soon became absorbed in the immense literature of pirates and piracy. Then Lionel conceived the idea: Why not, he asked, join forces in writing a pirate novel? Norman thought it a brilliant notion and they flung themselves into it. They invited a journalist friend, Ray Parkinson, to help them. He too had been captivated by the pirate cult and accepted with delight.

Lionel said that this act of creation could not be carried forward in a dismal city bedroom—they must have the right atmosphere. In a lane running off the eastern end of Little Bourke Street they found a one-roomed brick shanty and rented it for 2s 6d a week. They made a rough table and three chairs out of a packing case, hung a drawing of a Skull and Crossbones over the fireplace, and rolled in two or three old barrels to heighten the pirate atmosphere. They even managed an armoury. While painting the sign for the Aquarium Norman and Lionel had discovered a collection of antique pistols, swords and daggers gathering dust in a lumber room; these pieces had apparently been used in some pageant, then stored and forgotten. The Lindsays carried them off under the noses of the Aquarium people, walking out each evening when they finished work with an item or two hidden in their trouser legs. Now they decorated the walls with these vintage weapons, and stood back to admire. The place looked every inch a pirates' lair.

They drew up a kind of deed. In this they solemnly swore to navigate the *Royal Fortune* 'through all adverse winds, through fair weather and foul, through doldrums and tornado', and each of the three signed his

name in blood over a drawing of crossed cutlasses above a rum-cask.*
Thus committed, they began to work on the novel. To stimulate their
imagination, they clapped three-cornered hats on their heads around
which they knotted red-and-white cotton bandanas, slung swords and
pistols about their bodies, and now and then interrupted their labours
to take an inspirational swig from a bottle of Jamaica rum on the
table. Like Cinderella, Ray Parkinson had to shed his finery at midnight
and trudge off home to East Melbourne. The Lindsays sometimes went
back to sleep in their rented room but more often kept right on being
pirates. In hammocks swung from the ceiling they would fall asleep to
dream of plunder on the high seas, dead men hanging from the yard-arm,
and pieces of eight.

There was only one thing wrong with the lane. It was a night haunt
of assorted larrikins and bums, who gathered outside the shanty and sat
on the doorstep, arguing, squabbling, cursing, and sometimes singing.
These noises off did not help the three collaborators; they were finding
the going hard enough, and whenever one of them had a flash of revelation it was doused by a burst of discord from the lane.

'We'll put a stop to this!' Lionel shouted one night and wrenched the
door open, waving an archaic pistol and with a cutlass swinging from his
belt. Norman and Ray were at his heels and all three levelled pistols at
the men clustered outside. The pistols, although unloaded and probably
incapable of firing anyway, looked deadly enough.

'Get to hell out of it and stop making this row outside our door',
Lionel yelled.

The disturbers of the peace gaped for a moment at this trio of pistol-
waving madmen, then fled up the lane. One had been leaning against the
door when it opened and had fallen into the room; now he crouched on
hands and knees, goggling at the menacing pistols.

'Hop it', Norman told him, in unpiratical but unmistakable words.

He scrambled to his feet and bolted.

The three would-be authors were not disturbed after that, but invention still flagged. In the end they gave up. They had to admit it: the
idea wouldn't work. They drank the last of the rum and collected the
pistols, swords and daggers. Then, banging the door shut, they left the
shanty with the Skull and Crossbones over the fireplace to the ghosts of
Captain Kidd, Henry Morgan and Long John Silver.

Now and then Norman or Lionel went back to Creswick for a day
or two; sometimes they went together. They would have liked to go more
frequently, but couldn't often afford it.

* The deed is in the Australian manuscript collection of the La Trobe Library,
Melbourne. The blood has rusted and faded but the signatures are still legible.

5 *Ajax and Cassandra*, the painting by Solomon J. Solomon in the Ballarat Art Gallery which the young Norman Lindsay so much admired

6   Dressing up at 'Lisnacrieve'

7   Lionel noting down Norman's poetry   8   Lionel and Norman in pugilistic mood

A tremor of excitement rustled through Creswick whenever the Lindsay boys came home. They always looked under-fed (they were) and as if they bought their clothes off secondhand-shop pegs (they did), but they pranced along the main street with the air of young men who owned the earth.

They often took friends with them, never doubting that they would be bedded down and fed. And they always were. Their mother and Mary were unfailingly resourceful even when six or seven young men came storming into 'Lisnacrieve' without warning. Doctor Lindsay never minded his waiting-room being taken over as a bedroom for two or three youths he had never seen before and whose names he never managed to catch. Inexhaustibly affable, he could chat with them as readily as with men of his own age. To stay-at-home Percy these visitations brought a bracing whiff of the city; Percy liked Creswick and did not hanker after Melbourne for the time being, but he enjoyed hearing his brothers' brave and bawdy tales. And to the younger Lindsays, Ruby, Reg and Daryl, who were still at school, Lionel and Norman were as miraculous as men from Mars.

About this time Norman discovered a passion for photography and scraped together enough money to buy a cheap camera. On his visits home he was for ever digging into old chests and wardrobes and dragging out fading evening dresses, an old opera cloak, a moulting top hat, a superannuated bedspread and other like trifles to be used as costumes in the tableaux which he delighted in posing and photographing. Under his direction his helpers even improvised passable wigs for medieval characters out of rags and teased rope. The field was limitless—Lord Suckfist pleading before Pantagruel, a scene from a stage melodrama of the gaslight era, an episode from Petronius, or anything else that touched his fancy. He and Lionel revelled in stage-managing and appearing in these nonsensical performances. Each had a highly developed talent for mimicry and they often entertained their friends with comic duologues which would have gone well in a professional music hall. The kitchen garden of 'Lisnacrieve' was a perfect setting for their tableaux. Small boys dragged themselves up and watched over the high board fence, then went away round-eyed to spread the word, 'Hot stuff going on over at the Lindsays'.

Melbourne was not kind to Lionel after he came back from Western Australia, so one day he packed his bag—it didn't take long—and took ship for Sydney in a steerage berth which cost his last three pounds. Norman missed Lionel and his tearing enthusiasms, but life was too full for moping. Sometimes he wished he could bar his door against the young men who burst in on him at any hour of the day or night that suited them, but since none of the rooms he could afford ever boasted

D

a lock or bolt he was always accessible. He had a special liking for two or three friends, including Ray Parkinson. Although young Parkinson's mind was conventional and unadventurous, talk always flowed easily when they were together. The reason they got along so well seems to have been that Parkinson was always ready to embrace and affirm Norman's ideas. Even at nineteen Norman was beginning to value disciples who never challenged his opinions—anybody who agreed with him was obviously a man of clear vision, deep sensibility and balanced intellect.

The *Rambler* came into being out of his friendship with Ray Parkinson. Although it lived for only a few months and made no mark on the history of Australian journalism, the astonishing thing is that it was born at all. An English penny comic weekly, *Pick-Me-Up*, was popular then, and Norman and Ray decided that Australia needed something like it. Or perhaps Norman decided it and Ray merely assented. Norman brimmed over with optimism, but since their combined resources never amounted to more than a few shillings the whole thing was pure fantasy. Then a young doctor named Jack Elkington made it possible. Elkington, who was married to Ray Parkinson's eldest sister, Mary, was just starting out on his career. He had little money to spare but, liking the spirit in which Norman and Ray had conceived the idea, he offered to stake them up to a limit of a hundred pounds or so to see if they could make the *Rambler* go.

The first issue, twelve pages of theatre gossip, light verse, and illustrated and unillustrated jokes, appeared on 2 January 1899; it cost a penny a copy. Other than the name, any resemblance to Doctor Johnson's London *Rambler* was imperceptible. An editorial note proclaimed the 'exceptional advantages' of the *Rambler* as an advertising medium. A few people bought a little space but most potential advertisers were unimpressed. So were potential subscribers. Each issue sold a few hundred copies but every week Doctor Elkington had to find money to keep the *Rambler* going.

It brought Lionel back to Melbourne, however. After a spell in Sydney he had gone on to Queensland and managed to pay his way there, but when he heard about the *Rambler* he caught the first ship south. Norman and Ray were glad to see him. They needed help to get the *Rambler* out. Ray could crib only a few hours each day from his salaried job, while Norman still had to spend half his working week at pot-boiling tasks. Lionel's presence made all the difference.

They had an office at 175 William Street. It was a dingy room always littered with paper and decked with scattered pens and pencils, ink-bottles, a pair of scissors, a paste-pot or two, and other journalistic paraphernalia. As each weekly deadline approached it became a hive of frenzied industry, with the three editors racing against the clock, tense, short-tempered, grunting anything they had to say through set teeth. They kept the office boy on the run. A solemn, round-faced fourteen-year-old wearing a turned-down Eton collar and short pants, he was constantly darting here, running there, or hurrying somewhere else. He was a good office boy, quiet, willing, observant, intelligent. Like the Lindsays he had been born in Creswick, when his father was a police constable there. His three bosses liked him but they would have doubted it if somebody had told them that he was to become Prime Minister of Australia some forty years later. His name was Jack Curtin.

Advertisers were so few that even the least of them had to be treated with respect, if not reverence. Norman's defiance of this rule all but brought him to blows with Lionel and Ray one day. A brandy merchant gave the *Rambler* an illustrated advertisement with an order to repeat it in several issues. Norman saved the cost of having a block etched for the advertisement by making a small woodcut and using that. The brandy man came storming into the office as soon as he saw the *Rambler*, bellowing that he wasn't going to have his bloody grog advertised by a crude bloody picture like that. Norman bellowed back. Young Curtin stood by wide-eyed as the tumult rose.

'To hell with you!' Norman shouted. 'I admit it's a lousy woodcut but it's not as lousy as your brandy.'

Spluttering curses the brandy man stamped out of the office and sent back a hand-delivered note cancelling his advertisement. Lionel and Ray were furious. Norman had antagonized one of the *Rambler*'s few paying customers and what the devil game did he think he was playing! Lionel hastened to the brandy man, apologized for Norman's uncouth manners, and promised that nothing like that would ever happen again. Few people could withstand the torrent of Lionel's eloquence. The brandy man was mollified. He agreed to restore his advertisement and, after presenting Lionel with a bottle of brandy, shook hands and ushered him out remarking that he couldn't understand why such a charming fellow came to have such a bastard of a brother!

But it was all in vain. The end came a few weeks later. Doctor Elkington's money ran out, they put the last issue to bed and closed down.

Nothing stood still for long. Friends went off to other States and were seen no more in the old haunts; occasionally one raised the fare to Europe and was swallowed up in Paris or London, dreams and all. But a few old familiar spirits stayed, and the number of Bohemians never changed much, because new ones were constantly appearing. One of these was Hugh McCrae, a tall, broad-shouldered young man who had left his job as apprentice to an architect to cultivate a talent for writing lyric poetry and drawing gay and whimsical trifles. McCrae had a gift of laughter and could make a conquest of any pretty girl without crooking a finger—they came to him unbidden.

He literally strolled into the Lindsays' lives one day when they were sharing a room in the Premier Building, in Collins Street. McCrae, still with the architect at that time, was working in a room opposite and one morning he saw Norman, wearing shirt, trousers and, of all things, a scarlet fez, lope across the roof and, perching on the parapet, make a sketch of a scene in the street six or seven storeys below. It was McCrae's first sight of a young man 'whose radiant personality was destined to influence the rest of my life'. He lost no time in calling on his over-the-street neighbour and introducing himself. Thus two of the unique figures of Australian art and letters began a friendship which lasted, albeit with some bumpy patches and in later years a little cooling, until McCrae died in 1958.

McCrae noted that the Lindsays' room, strewn with the tools and materials of the artist's trade and a scatter of accumulated rubbish, was not over-furnished. There was a bed for Norman on one side and a bed for Lionel on the other and not much else, but screwed to one wall was a shelf holding books. McCrae ran his eyes over these with approval: Boswell, Shakespeare, Cervantes, Rabelais, Flaubert, de Maupassant, Gautier, Burns, Byron, de Quincey, Dickens. He knew he'd be on common ground with fellows who read this stuff. He was mildly surprised to see a set of boxing gloves hanging on a nail behind the door. These were one of Norman's cherished possessions; other items might be sold or pawned from time to time when money was short and the landlord—or Norman's belly—grew clamorous, but he clung to his boxing gloves through every trial. The slender Norman looked totally unpugilistic; his darkish hair fell down over his forehead in a soft fringe and, although five feet seven inches tall, he would have been hard-pressed to weigh in much above one hundred pounds. Yet boxing was one of his chief delights. As the *Hawklet* artist he was an honoured ringsider at Mick Nathan's squalid Victoria Hall, and even the dull-witted bruisers whom he sketched excited his admiration. Their brains were shambling and their tongues slow but he envied the muscular co-ordination which enabled them to throw a left hook or a right cross while he was thinking about it.

For him, there was a kind of poetry about any buccaneering man who swaggered through life with the aid of brawn as well as brains. Lionel's friend, Randolph Bedford, was a flawless example. Bedford, who had a lively intelligence, ready fists, husky shoulders, an aggressive jaw, few scruples, and total indifference to anybody else's sensibilities, was living in Melbourne on a small fortune which he had made in Western Australia. A man of prodigious personality, he became the centre of a gay and irreverent group which included the Lindsays and their Creswick friend Ruff Tremearne, as well as Ray Parkinson and Jack Elkington. Among others it embraced also three talented brothers, Ted, Ambrose and Will Dyson. Ted had already begun to make a mark as a writer, and each of his brothers had shown glimpses of the artistic talent which was to win Ambrose a reputation as a sound cartoonist and Will a name as one of the world's great cartoonists, caricaturists and draughtsmen.

Norman Lindsay and Will Dyson became close friends. It was a curious friendship, based on differences rather than similarities of taste and outlook. Will (who was Bill Dyson to all his Australian intimates but always Will Dyson to the British, American and Australian public from the time he made his name) was a devout socialist while Norman was not. They agreed, however, on at least two matters; these were the odiousness of popular morality and the intellectual power of the German philosopher, Friedrich Nietzsche, whose works had only lately become available in Australia in cheap translations. Nietzsche opened new horizons to both young men. For Norman, he affirmed also the advice which Ernest Moffitt had proffered at 'Charterisville'. Nietzsche's words, 'This—is my way,—where is yours? . . . For *the* way existeth not!'* were identical in essence with Moffitt's 'Do the things you want to do. Nothing else matters'.

Will was eighteen months younger than Norman but his supple mind was already mature. When one of Norman's enthusiasms sent him rocketing off into the clouds, Will delighted to shoot him down with a mocking phrase and a flash of sardonic brown eyes. Their furious arguments did not impair their friendship; the more savagely they disputed the better they seemed to like one another. Whenever a chance offered they put the gloves on and belted away for a few rounds. Will, who could have held his own with most professional lightweights, was physically stronger and a heavier puncher but Norman, although outmatched, always made a willing go of it. More often than not he ended one of these bouts with the bridge of his prominent nose skinned.

Norman was just then making his first major experiments in pen drawing. He and Lionel and an art student friend, Hughie McLean, had each set out one night to illustrate an episode from a story in Boccaccio's *Decameron*, as an exercise in composition. The other two soon pushed their half-finished sketches aside but Norman, elated and excited, went on working all through the night until dawn. It was the start of one of the major artistic adventures of his life. This was the production of homogeneous groups of drawings based on famous literary works but expressing his own creative instinct; these had to be called illustrations for

* *Thus Spake Zarathustra*, translated by Alexander Tile. (London, T. Fisher Unwin, 1899).

want of a better word but they went far beyond any meaning usually borne by that term. Petronius, Casanova, Rabelais, Villon and other imperishable writers were to command his mind and hand later but it was Boccaccio who first put the spell on him.

The *Decameron* characters swarmed through his mind, more real than the living men and women about him. Night after night he sat at his table working in the light of an oil lamp, with a blanket tucked around his legs. Often a drawing would not come right and he would rip it up and try again, fighting the artist's age-old battle to set down on paper or canvas the vision his inner eye can see in rich and intricate detail. The drawings grew in number. Scenes born in Giovanni Boccaccio's brain in fourteenth-century Florence were thus being given pictorial form in a scruffy room with damp-stained walls tenanted by an unknown Australian artist in nineteenth-century Melbourne.

One day Will Dyson pushed open the door and drifted in, grunting a salutation. He wore a narrow black silk scarf wound five or six times about his throat and the hard muscles of his slim body rippled under his tight-fitting clothes. He stopped at Norman's work-table and stood looking down at one of the *Decameron* drawings.　. .

'I'd give ten years of my life to do a drawing like that', he said.

That was all, but it was enough. Will rarely praised a drawing; he was more likely to damn its technical and aesthetic deficiencies, so his remark had the ring of a hosannah. Norman felt that the *Decameron* drawings marked a long step forward in his work but he was not sure until Will Dyson spoke. The laconic words sent him back to Boccaccio with renewed zest.

Then something else happened to stimulate his imagination and give his spirit wings. He fell in love. Or perhaps he only fancied himself in love. At twenty the difference is of little account. Whether real or imaginary the enchantment is compelling while it lasts.


The girl was Katie, a sister of Ray Parkinson. She was a few months older than Norman. She had black hair, black-lashed blue eyes, a generous mouth and a strong vibrant body. She was the kind of girl any young man would turn his head to look at in the street.

Norman met her for the first time one evening when Ray took him and Lionel home to the Parkinsons' in East Melbourne. Katie fetched coffee and sandwiches to Ray's den and, having seen her, Norman resolved that he must arrange to be invited again, and soon. A week or so later Ray asked him to dinner. That night Norman seized a chance to whisper an invitation to Katie to meet him next afternoon in the Fitzroy Gardens, only a few hundred yards from the Parkinsons' home. He waited on tenterhooks until he saw her, feminine and desirable, walking toward him. He gabbled a welcome and led her off along a tree-bordered path. An hour or so later, hidden by a screen of bushes from the eyes of strollers, perambulating nursemaids and gardeners, they became lovers.

Norman had no qualms about seducing a friend's sister. Not that it could be counted a seduction—Katie had met him half-way. Anyway he took the view that, pretty girls who would kiss and go on from there being hard to find, no man could afford to harbour far-fetched scruples when one came along. The romance moved fast. They made love in the Fitzroy Gardens, in hotel rooms hired for the afternoon, in whatever happened to be Norman's lodging of the moment with a chair wedged against the door to keep out callers.

None of the Parkinsons seemed to realize that Norman's actions and intentions were strictly dishonourable. Mrs Parkinson, the widow of an Englishman who had been a well-paid Civil Servant in India, was an abstracted old lady who maundered through life with little idea of what her three daughters and two sons were doing or thinking. Her eldest child, Mary Elkington, was the only Parkinson with any force of charac-ter. She had taken hold of the family when her father died suddenly some years earlier and left them penniless, and none of them ever ques-tioned her leadership. Even Mary, a handsome and resolute young woman, who managed the lives of those about her with an iron hand, seemed to have no suspicion about Norman and Katie. Jack Elkington's good opinion of Norman probably lulled Mary's doubts. Jack liked Norman and believed he had a big future as an artist.

The South African War had broken out in October 1899, and Victoria, like the rest of the Australian colonies, was well in it. There were loyal speeches, patriotic songs, military bands, marching soldiers. Young men were flocking to the Colours but Norman was not among them; the delights he found in Katie Parkinson's arms far outran any hypothetical glory to be had chasing Boers across the veldt. The thought of Katie made him want to dance and sing. His hack work for the *Hawklet* was a pleasure now instead of a groaning sweat. Even his unpaid cartooning for the *Tocsin*, done under Jack Castieau's social-reforming eye, was almost a pleasure.

The effect on his serious work was all but unbelievable. Katie's em-braces were an intellectual as well as a physical aphrodisiac and the *Decameron* drawings acquired new depth, quality, strength. This was his first true love affair. The episode with the Creswick farmer's daughter and his other unimportant affairs had yielded nothing but passing physi-cal satisfaction. Now he was engrossed in an emotional adventure with a vital young woman who set his imagination teeming with gay and bawdy symbols. The feminine image had figured in his drawings ever since his pre-adolescent years; suddenly it became the central motif of his work and, taking possession, remained dominant for the rest of his life.

Then, one afternoon in May, his bright world crumpled and collapsed. Katie told him she was pregnant.

'How long?' he asked.

'Two months.'

'God Almighty', he said. 'Why didn't you tell me sooner?'

'I wasn't sure.'

'Are you sure now?'

'Yes.'

He told her not to worry. It was just a matter of getting a box of pills and in a week or two she'd be as right as ninepence.

He consulted a pharmacist who went away into the back of the shop and returned with an unlabelled bottle of whitish pills.

'One after each meal and one last thing at night', he said. 'They'll make her a bit sick in the stomach but don't worry. If she keeps at 'em they'll do the trick.'

Katie took the pills and, sure enough, they made her sick in the stomach; not just a bit sick, as the pharmacist had warned, but very sick. Her pallor alarmed Norman; he marvelled that sharp-eyed and bossy Mary noticed nothing amiss. Katie swallowed all the pills, but she was still pregnant. Norman gloomed through the Fitzroy Gardens, kicking his feet disconsolately on the asphalt walk and wondering what the next move should be. Then it struck him. He'd have to marry her— make an honest woman of her, as the saying went. He hadn't counted on that, any more than he'd counted on ever becoming a father. Well, there was no help for it, curse the rotten luck!

They were both twenty-one, and neither of them ever forgot their wedding day. It was Wednesday 23 May 1900, and the Victorian Government had declared it an official holiday so that the populace could celebrate the relief of Mafeking five days before. Although the weather was cold and foggy some 200,000 people flooded into the city to watch the march of the naval and military forces in the afternoon. Bands played, the streets were gay with bunting, and it was, as the *Argus* reported next day, 'an unparalleled display of loyal enthusiasm'. For all the atmosphere of popular excitement, Norman and Katie's wedding could hardly have been quieter. The only others present were the Reverend Cadwalader P. Thomas, the vicar of St John's Church of England in La Trobe Street, who performed the ceremony, and Jack Castieau and his wife, who had been invited as witnesses. Castieau justified his presence by drawing Mr Thomas aside after the ceremony and telling him the harrowing facts about the bridegroom's poverty; touched, Mr Thomas cut his fee from thirty to fifteen shillings. Norman was delighted. He had only eighteen shillings left after paying the first week's rent on a cottage in East Melbourne and buying a bed and a few pots and pans.

The wedding party caught a tram to St Kilda and walked to the Castieaus' house. While Mrs Castieau was busy in the kitchen Lionel Lindsay and Will Dyson arrived. Norman had intended waiting before breaking the news to them, but Castieau had been unable to resist inviting them. They kissed Katie, and slapped Norman on the back and told him he was a lucky devil. He did his best to act the joyful bridegroom but knew it was a lame performance. He felt he was trapped in an ignominious situation and looked rather an ass.

His money would just run to the hire of a hansom cab to East Melbourne. When he and Katie drove through the city that night the Mafeking celebrations were still at their height. Thousands of citizens were drunk, and rioting mobs were in possession of the streets. They bellowed patriotic songs, danced like whirling dervishes, and uncoupled the trailer-cars of cable trams and sent them hurtling into shop windows. Mounted and foot police were out in force trying to restore order, and the uproar was like the noise of battle. Norman itched to draw those scenes but he'd forgotten to put a pencil and sketchbook in his pocket when he'd got ready for his wedding. It was a chance he wouldn't have missed for quids! Blast marriage!

The *Hawklet* page was a sheet-anchor but thirty-five shillings a week went only so far. Norman bustled about picking up any and every commercial art job he could find but his income rarely seemed to cover his costs. He had little money sense and Katie was worse. If she saw anything she wanted—a scarf, a Brummagem bracelet, a box of bon-bons—she bought it. Being nearly as thriftless, Norman was on shaky ground when he reproved her. There were quarrels. The rent fell into arrears, bills came in and piled up. He thought with yearning of his bachelor days when he had been able to foil pressing creditors by stacking his things into a handcart and moving to another room. Now he had to pay up or face trouble—moonlight flitting was too troublesome when you had a wife, and a baby coming.

Melbourne had dozens of artists, all eager to earn a few shillings by turning out any kind of trade item. Norman got his fair share but had no time left for serious work. He looked at his *Decameron* drawings now and then, and sometimes added a stroke here or there, but that was all; the creative burst which had produced them was swamped by the struggle to live. He began muttering a new phrase: 'The curse of the coin'. He was never sure whether he invented it himself or picked it up somewhere but it expressed his sentiments. Money was a curse, especially when you had none. Ruff Tremearne had taken over a spare room in the cottage. His ten shillings a week was little enough but it helped; anyway it was all he could afford from his pay as a fledgling journalist. Luckily Katie liked him, and his presence eased the domestic tensions.

After the first shock the Parkinsons had forgiven Norman and Katie their runaway marriage. Or, being a realist, Mary had; and since she made the rules the rest of the Parkinsons also accepted the accomplished fact. Mary and her mother listened in silence to the story Norman and Katie told of their having been secretly married for nearly three months. This was Norman's idea. He wanted to explain why Katie was pregnant and make everything seem blameless, for his people as well as for hers. To give the unlikely tale some colour of truth, he paid for an advertisement in the Marriages column of the *Argus* on 24 May, the day after the wedding; this mendaciously recorded that they had been married on 3 March. It fooled nobody, but for a long time Norman prided himself on it as a master-stroke.

As the months went on and Katie's confinement drew near, Norman's anxiety to earn more money increased. He was not then, nor did he ever become, a conscientious husband, willing to jettison his dreams to support a wife and family, but he could not forget the looming medical bills, the cost of fitting the baby out with clothes, a cot and a pram, and the multitude of other expenses. He started looking for a steady job with a regular wage but nobody wanted him. Trudging home through the Fitzroy Gardens at the end of one more day of fruitless searching, he decided that potential employers were rejecting him because they distrusted his looks; they were more than likely writing him down as a harum-scarum art student, who wouldn't show up for work on time or even show up at all if he chose to stay away. Well, if it was simply a matter of making himself look sober and responsible he would attend to it. He bought a bowler hat and began to grow a moustache. Having taken a few days to practise with the bowler hat and let the moustache sprout, he set out once more on his hunt for a job. It was all in vain. After a week he subjected himself to a calm scrutiny in the bedroom glass and concluded that his failure was not really surprising. The bowler hat perched above his prominent nose and the straggling moustache made him look like nothing so much as a seedy pimp in need of a square meal. He threw the hat away, shaved off the moustache and resolved to make the best of things as they were.

Jack Elkington called in one evening and sat yarning for a while. Then he mentioned that he was leaving for Sydney in a day or two on a business trip and asked if he might borrow the *Decameron* drawings.

'I want to show them to some friends of mine in Sydney', he explained.

'Take them and welcome', Norman said. 'I'll be glad to get shed of the damn' things for a while. If they're out of the house I can't come on them and suffer an attack of bad conscience for doing no serious work.'

Some weeks later he was walking up Bourke Street after calling on four or five printeries and picking up a few pot-boiling jobs. He bought a copy of the Sydney *Bulletin* from a news vendor and, opening it while crossing Spring Street, ran his eye down the Red Page—at that time Australia's most commanding journalistic tribunal on literary and artistic matters. The Red Page's then editor, A. G. Stephens, could break a writer's or an artist's reputation; he could even go far toward making a reputation if he liked a writer's or an artist's work. Norman stopped dead at the sight of his own name embedded in a short item, unsigned but unmistakably by Stephens, at the end of the main article.

> For the imaginative illustration of books there is in Australia at present the least possible encouragement. One sees with surprise, therefore, the set of pen-drawings to illustrate Boccaccio's *Decameron* which Mr Norman Lindsay has executed, and which remain for the present at N.S.W. Society of Artists' rooms in Sydney . . . His incomplete series of some 30 or more drawings contains the finest examples of pen-draughtsmanship of their kind yet produced in this country. Indeed, one might almost venture to say that, in its kind, no better work than Lindsay's best is being done anywhere. The series is unequalled, but some of its pages are masterly . . . The way in which he realises the texture of stuffs, the rotundity of flesh, the contour and poise of bodies seen nude or under a robe is a delight to the eye . . . He succeeds least in his faces, which are usually too posed, too stiff, too monotonous in expression; and in his total result, which does not seem to disengage sufficient spirit, sufficient life . . .

Norman stood in Spring Street, oblivious of the late afternoon traffic and the curious stares of one or two pedestrians, reading about himself in the *Bulletin* of 18 August 1900 with a sense of unbelief. He experienced a rush of gratitude to Jack Elkington but as he walked on he did not guess that this was a turning-point in his life; it was to be some months before that became plain. Meanwhile the penny-grabbing workaday grind left him little time for himself. His only regular diversion was the fortnightly dinner of the Ishmael Club, which Randolph Bedford had founded among his familiars who were all young men of gay, sceptical and irreverent mind. The Ishmaels never numbered more than a dozen or so. Ruff Tremearne, Jack Elkington, and Ted and Will Dyson were naturally among them; so also was Percy Lindsay, who had grown tired of rustic peace and moved down to Melbourne. Relaxing in such company, Norman forgot his domestic cares for a few hours; but they always rose again when the wine was finished, the lights were turned out and the Ishmaels went home.

Seeking ways of making extra money as the birth of the baby drew near, Norman hit on a promising idea. He had a sober card printed announcing that he was 'prepared to execute Book Plates, Music Plates and other works in Decorative Design'. His charge for a book plate was four guineas, for which he supplied the plate, the drawing and five hundred copies on fine paper; for a music plate he charged £1 11s 6d, for the plate, the drawing and a hundred copies. He sent out his cards early in October and after a week or two the first orders came in. This was heartening because Katie's baby arrived on 20 October, rather earlier than she and Norman had reckoned on. Either Katie had miscalculated or, more likely, the birth was premature. They named him John. Norman registered the baby as the child of a marriage which had taken place on 3 March, and this fictional detail was duly and solemnly recorded on young Jack Lindsay's birth certificate along with the indisputable facts.

Norman did not feel any swelling of the heart when the Commonwealth of Australia came into being on 1 January 1901. He was too busy providing for his family. Nor was he stirred by the knowledge that the Duke and Duchess of Cornwall and York were to come from England so that the Duke might, with Royal magnificence, open the first Federal parliament in Melbourne on 9 May. Then he found a practical reason for seeing merit in all this ferment: it put some money into his pocket. The Government commissioned two artists to design a card of invitation and a printed programme. One was John Longstaff, an established oil painter of solid and growing reputation; the other was the unknown Norman Lindsay. Longstaff was the older by nearly twenty years but the two collaborated well. Their decorative designs made free use of lions, unicorns, kangaroos, emus and similar patriotic fauna.

At it turned out, 1901 was made unforgettable for Norman by events which had nothing to do with the launching of the Australian Commonwealth. These originated when a letter reached him soon after the *Bulletin* published its appreciative notice of the *Decameron* drawings. The envelope held a note from J. F. Archibald, the editor of the *Bulletin*, inviting Norman to illustrate two attached items; these were a short poem about a larrikin in love, and a clipping of a newspaper paragraph lamenting that while superannuated jockeys had some kind of provident fund superannuated poets had nothing of the kind. With John Haynes, another young working journalist, Archibald had founded the *Bulletin* in 1880, when he was twenty-four, and seen it acquire the most powerful, if also the most raucous, Australian voice of its day. He was the greatest Australian editor of his own time, and probably the greatest editor Australia has known. Although not creative himself, Archibald had a genius for recognizing the spark of talent in other people, coaxing it into flame, then fanning it until it blazed high and clear.

Norman worked hard at the drawings, pushing aside other commitments to put his best into them. Then he posted them off to Archibald. A reply came within a few days. It brought a cheque for five pounds—five pounds for two drawings which Norman had expected to net him fifteen shillings at most! The accompanying note was short. It merely said that Archibald would like to see him if he were ever in Sydney.

Almost at the same time Norman received another letter from Sydney. It was signed by a name as widely known as Archibald's: Julian Ashton. Ashton, an English-born artist, had settled in Sydney and become one of Australia's foremost art teachers and a man of unrivalled influence in the Australian art world. He was the chief driving force of the New South Wales Society of Artists and, believing that the *Decameron* drawings reflected a unique talent, he felt that Norman should go and study in Europe. He offered to raise three hundred pounds to pay fares and living costs—Australia had a few moneyed citizens who were willing to dig into their pockets to finance any young artist approved by Julian Ashton. Norman was touched but not tempted. He could not see himself trailing across the world with a wife and an infant son. Nor did Europe attract him much. He had formed the opinion that Europe devitalized the work of practically every young Australian artist who went there to study, smoothing its hard edges, softening its harsh tones, and impoverishing its national character, and he did not want that to happen to him.

But the possibility of working for the *Bulletin* excited him. The trouble was that Archibald had made no promise and Norman could not turn his back on his Melbourne work and go at once—he still had to hammer out the *Hawklet* page and the other bread-and-butter stuff. He was determined, however, not to miss this chance and, having charted his course toward it, he boarded a 700-ton coastal steamer for Sydney on a May day in 1901. The little vessel was overcrowded, and it was a dirty trip through wild and driving seas, but Norman was too exhilarated to feel frowsy or jaded when he stood on Circular Quay and looked out at the ships crowding Sydney Cove. They were mostly sailing-ships and his pulse quickened as he watched the sway and dip of their slim-fingered masts in silhouette against the sky. He had never before seen nearly so many tall ships at one time. He was to remember that spectacle all through his life.

Lugging his bag, he walked miles before finding a bed in a terrace house at Dawes Point, but he was too excited to relax. Next day he went along to the *Bulletin* office in George Street. Archibald swept him up and took him out walking. They were an odd pair—the boyish Norman, slight, eager, uncertain of himself, nervously garrulous, and the volcanic Archibald, bearded, effervescent, swift of eye, sure of tongue. It was a good meeting. It was also the beginning of a friendship which ended only with Archibald's death in 1919. Archibald offered Norman six pounds a week to join the *Bulletin* as a staff artist working on cartoons, illustrations for jokes, and decorations. This was more money than Norman had ever earned by a single week's work and nearly twice his average weekly income, and he accepted at once.

'When can you start?' Archibald asked.

'Now', said Norman.

He wanted to be sure of his place with the *Bulletin* before pulling up his Melbourne roots. He knew he would have to prove himself. And this was not the *Hawklet* or the *Tocsin* or the *Rambler*—he would be in talented company here. He sent a note to Katie telling her he intended staying in Sydney until he found his feet on the *Bulletin*; then he would come down to fetch her and joung Jack.

After his meeting with Archibald he called on Julian Ashton. The generous Ashton insisted that Norman must come and stay with him at Bondi. It was a friendly house. Ashton told him he must treat it as his home, and Norman settled in like a favourite son. At the office Archibald drove him hard and he liked it. He had plenty to learn but he was willing; he would cheerfully do a drawing two or three times if Archibald believed it could be improved.

At the end of three months he knew he was a fixture on the *Bulletin* staff, so he went down to Melbourne. Katie pouted about leaving her mother and Mary and the rest of the family and going to Sydney. Norman shrugged and said she'd soon get used to it—damn it all, didn't she know that at least they'd have enough money to live in decent comfort without worrying about the rent or next Sunday's dinner? He went off to find Lionel and Percy. They greeted him with cries of 'Good old Joe! You show 'em, Joe!' and there were drinks all round. Will Dyson and the rest of Norman's friends were equally warm. It was a wrench to leave them but when he boarded the ship for Sydney, with Katie and Jack and the luggage, he was counting the hours until he'd get back to work at the *Bulletin*. He knew he belonged there.

# 3

# Pagan At Large
## 1901-09

He was not one of the *Bulletin*'s black-and-white stars at the start. He had to make his own impact and win his own public. The *Bulletin* commanded a large and devoted readership which spread all over Australia and across the Tasman Sea to New Zealand; it even had some admiring subscribers in England and the United States of America. While the mere appearance in its pages of an artist's work was a kind of hallmark it was also a test—a newcomer had to show himself worthy of the company he kept. Ideally, a *Bulletin* cartoonist had to be able to make men not only laugh but also burn with anger or indignation or shame or compassion, and now and then he had to make them weep. Norman could do these things. He had the gift of reaching men's hearts and minds and bellies through their eyes. He could not have said how he did it—it was a feat of intuition, not intellect. Readers began watching for his drawings, discussing them, chuckling over them. So his *Bulletin* career took shape. With two intermissions of his own making, it was to last for more than fifty years.

Archibald raised Norman's salary to eight pounds a week. This was only the first of a number of raises which transformed the poverty-stricken battler from Melbourne into a prosperous Sydney artist-about-town. The knowledge that Norman was his discovery gave Archibald special satisfaction. He had done more than any other man to make the *Bulletin*, and in particular to persuade Australians that their own writers, speaking with an authentic Australian voice, were worth reading. But the *Bulletin* school of black-and-white artists had been created less by him than by William Henry Traill, and the thought piqued him. Traill had controlled the *Bulletin* for some years in the 1880s, in a period when Archibald temporarily lost the reins as a result of compli-

47

cated legal difficulties, and it was Traill who had engaged the English artist, Phil May, and the American, Livingston Hopkins.

May, one of the greatest caricaturists and cartoonists the world has known, stayed only about three years before going back to London but his contribution and influence were immeasurable. Hopkins, although less gifted, was an able cartoonist and his *Bulletin* work made him a figure and a force in the Australia of his time; it was also a big element in the range and intensity of the *Bulletin*'s political power. Now, in Norman Lindsay, Archibald had found a rich and idiosyncratic talent which would add something of lasting value to the *Bulletin*'s black-and-white tradition. Archibald's admiration of Norman's gifts never abated. Years later, when discussing the merits of celebrated *Bulletin* cartoonists, including Phil May and Livingston Hopkins, he told a friend, Henry Manning,* 'Though they were all great, Norman Lindsay was the real genius of them all'.

When Norman joined the staff, Hop, as Livingston Hopkins was known from the signature on his drawings, was a grave, spare and stately man in his middle fifties, who looked and dressed like a banker rather than a newspaper artist. He remained chief cartoonist until he retired from regular work shortly before the First World War, but by then Norman was equally well known to *Bulletin* readers and even better known to Australians in general. Hop, who was aloof and distant with his juniors when he deigned to notice them at all, never gave the smallest sign that he was disturbed by the rivalry of this puny youth. It possibly did not even occur to him that Norman was a rival at such an early stage in his career.

Archibald took Norman along gently, letting him find his feet as an illustrator of jokes and a decorator of verses and other short items, and occasionally giving him a small topical cartoon to draw. Norman did not like everything about the *Bulletin* but he had no quarrel with much that it did and, in particular, approved the 'euphoric nationalism', as one writer has charitably described it,† which was a dominant element in its policy under Archibald, and later. The contempt of *Bulletin* writers for people with black, brown or yellow skins, and for Jews, was no less offensive because it was expressed with a kind of hearty innocence. Negroes were 'niggers' and Chinese were 'Chows', even in the leading articles often enough; they and other coloured people were habitually represented by *Bulletin* artists, including Norman, as stupid, ridiculous, or grotesquely comical. Jews were equally derided. They were apt to be depicted as pawnbrokers, moneylenders or old-clothes dealers, with

---

* Manning was called to the New South Wales Bar in 1902 and took silk in 1930. He entered the New South Wales Parliament in 1932 and was Attorney-General and Vice-President of the Executive Council 1932-41. He was knighted in 1939.
† Godfrey Blunden, in *Norman Lindsay Watercolours*, p. 17.

exaggeratedly hooked noses and obsequiously cunning smiles, behaving in keeping with the mythology which Aryan prejudice has created for them. It was crude and ugly, and, whether Norman acquired his notions from the *Bulletin* or merely accepted a *Bulletin* outlook which happened to affirm his instinctive view, racist theories became a lifelong pillar of his philosophy.

As his confidence grew he began to develop a distinctive style. The *Bulletin* was publishing two full-page cartoons a week, one by Hop, and the other by Alf Vincent who covered the Melbourne scene, and often a third full-page spread of cartoonlets by Hop. On 15 February 1902 the cartoonlets were attributed to 'Hop's Understudy'; the style was similar to Hop's but some touches suggested Norman. In the next issue the chief full-page cartoon, a comment on the Anglo-Japanese Alliance, was signed by Norman. Although effective enough, it had none of the assurance of his later work. Hop did the cartoonlets that week and Vincent his usual Melbourne page. The pattern became established—three full pages of topical black-and-white nearly every week, with Hop more often than not doing two and Vincent the third, but Norman's signature appearing every few weeks either on the chief cartoon or the cartoonlets.

He scored his first major success less than eighteen months after joining the *Bulletin*. In September 1902 a woman named Selina Sangal and her lover, August Tisler, were sentenced to death in Melbourne for the murder of the woman's husband. It was an uncommonly brutal crime. Tisler battered the husband to death and then, helped by Selina, dumped the body down a well at the Sangals' Dandenong farm. Tisler was duly hanged one Monday morning in October, but Mrs Sangal was granted a little grace. She was pregnant and the Victorian Government decided to wait until her baby was born some months later and then hang her. Archibald's humanitarianism was wrung. He told Norman to do a cartoon showing Mrs Sangal, her face a mask of dread, cowering in a hospital bed under a barred window and throwing out a hand to her new-born babe while the Premier of Victoria, William Hill Irvine, stood by, watch in hand, telling off the seconds before he summoned the masked hangman waiting by the door, noosed rope ready. Norman's cartoon spoke louder than any words. The supreme touch was the expression of icy calm on Irvine's face.

The cartoon appeared on 25 October 1902 over the title *WAITING*. A few hours after the *Bulletin* reached the Melbourne news-stands Irvine was walking down Collins Street. He met a man he knew, who had a copy of the *Bulletin* in his hand and, flipping it open, said, 'Seen this, Irvine?' Irvine glanced at the cartoon, nodded and walked on, making no comment. After a face-saving interval of some five weeks the government commuted Mrs Sangal's sentence to imprisonment for the term of her natural life. A friend of Norman, who knew what went on behind the scenes in Victorian politics, told him that Irvine had, on his own admission, decided to reprieve Mrs Sangal because he could not get the cartoon out of his mind.

The affair had an ironic undertone. Norman did not believe that Mrs Sangal should have been spared. He never hid his belief that capital punishment was one of the essentials of an orderly society, and to the end of his life held that death was the only fitting penalty for premeditated murder. Sixty years after drawing the Sangal cartoon he said of capital punishment:

> Of course it is a deterrent. Criminals don't fear a prison sentence but in common with the mass of humanity they fear death. Look at the way imposing the death penalty on kidnapping in America put a stop to it. Hanging a criminal acts as a catharsis on the mass mind, lifting an emotional tension. The effect is one of relief and satisfaction.

Hop had a serious illness in June 1903 and was away for six months. Archibald had relinquished the editorship of the *Bulletin* at the end of 1902, after a difference with the manager, William Macleod, and his successor, James Edmond, decided that Norman was not yet ready for the cartoonist-in-chief's responsibilities. Edmond called Vincent from Melbourne to do Hop's work and engaged Ambrose Dyson to draw the Melbourne page. Norman contributed a few main cartoons and some secondary ones in this period, but Vincent usually did both pages. When Hop came back the earlier order was restored; he and Norman worked in Sydney and Vincent in Melbourne. These three were the *Bulletin*'s black-and-white stalwarts for years, with an outside artist like Ambrose Dyson or B. E. Minns contributing a topical page now and then.

Although Norman was never allowed to overshadow Hop, who was a highly competent artist and a public favourite of long standing, he was soon no mere understudy but a staff cartoonist in his own right. When he had been with the *Bulletin* nearly four years he scribbled out answers to questions on a form circulated to Australian artists and authors by an agency seeking information for the archives of public libraries. Under the heading 'Present Occupation' he wrote 'Purveyor of joke blokes to a disinterested [sic] public'. This gave a misleading picture of the scope of his work. The *Bulletin* was still making heavy demands on him as a comic artist but he was also by then a cartoonist of national stature whose pictorial comments on public issues could, and often did, rouse popular feeling and persuade governments to reverse or modify decisions on important matters. If the people who were swayed by his cartoons imagined that he was deeply moved by these causes they were wrong. He never managed to grow impassioned over routine political affairs; he believed that the masses were mindless, insensitive and stupid and, on the

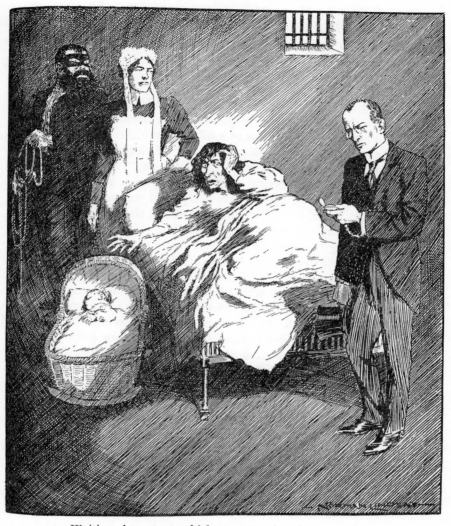

*Waiting,* the cartoon which won a reprieve for a murderess

whole, got pretty much what they deserved from those who governed them. Most of his cartoons, not only in his *Bulletin* days but at any stage of his career, were based on themes shaped in the editorial councils and handed to him in ready-made outline, as on the Sangal issue. In developing a central idea and presenting it in the most effective way he sometimes changed from a neutral into a partisan, but as a rule the technical problems were what drove his pen and his mind.

He could always submerge his own convictions when he was doing his journalistic tasks. He could never bring himself to take journalism quite seriously. He felt that even the *Bulletin* under Archibald wasted too much talent, paper and printer's ink on fugitive trivialities. As a result he did not think of cartooning as a facet of his life's work. It was only a means of earning a living.

It was a good living. He had money troubles now and then but nothing like those which had plagued him in Melbourne. Katie's extravagances and his own were apt to lead on to minor crises but there was generally enough money to go round; and, if necessary, the *Bulletin* counting-house would always make an advance. The frequent trips which Katie insisted on taking to Melbourne were a constant drain. Katie missed her family, particularly Mary, and yearned for a sight of them every few months. Like all the Parkinsons, she had grown to rely on Mary's leadership and was at sea without it.

Norman secretly resented Katie's dependence on Mary. He was possessive of those close to him; he liked them to look to him first of all, and his jealousy was easily roused although he took pains to hide it. He also resented the disruptions which Katie's comings and goings imposed on his life. The duration of her absences grew longer every time, so Norman took to surrendering the tenancy of each rented house when she went to Melbourne and putting the furniture into store until she came back—storage cost less than rent. And finding a bed for himself at these times was easy. Soon after settling down at the *Bulletin* he had rented a room near the office and fitted it out as a studio; after that he always had a studio with a wash-basin and a gas-ring somewhere in the city, and only a stretcher against the wall was needed to convert it into his idea of a home.

After a time he began to welcome Katie's truancies. It was a relief not to have to make daily journeys between the city and a house kept in slapdash style where Jack, now toddling, was for ever underfoot. Living in a studio, and eating in restaurants or running up a makeshift meal for himself, reminded him of the carefree Melbourne days, with the advantage that he was no longer penniless. He found this way of life a boon, because after a year or two in Sydney he began working once more at serious drawing when the demands of journalism let him. To be sure, his *Bulletin* work gave him little freedom but he found time to renew his struggle for mastery of the pen—in his own words, 'the most obdurate instrument of the lot to control with ease and assurance'.

His marriage to Katie was going to pieces, not in a spectacular way but with a slow and deadly inevitability. He told himself later that it had been doomed from the start because of the psychological differences between them. He was undoubtedly right. It was the result of the chance throwing together of two young people who happened to rouse each other's sexual desires, and if there had been no baby there would have been no marriage. Norman's great need was a wife who would relieve him of practical worries and set him free to work in his own way and his own time. The hopelessly unpractical Katie was no better equipped than Norman to do battle with the nagging and recurrent problems of every day. She did not understand his aspirations nor did he understand hers; they were rarely at ease with one another's friends and never in sympathy with one another's tastes. He had all the ego of the creative artist, all the blind selfishness of the man who resolves to follow his own path at any cost. No woman could deflect him from that purpose, nor could any man.

He did not let the flatness of his marriage bother him. Life in Sydney held so many compensations. For a man with Norman's feeling for ships, even so simple a thing as a ferryboat journey across the Harbour was an adventure. The golden age of sail had all but ended but many square-riggers were still in commission, and it was a poor day when three or four were not loading, discharging or lying at moorings. Norman began to learn about ships as well as to marvel at them. He became a dock-walloper and spent hours yarning with men who had sailed before the mast for most of their lives. He found his way on board dozens of sailing ships and, probing into the secrets of their construction and behaviour, discovered that every ship, like every man, has its own peculiarities which make it different from all other ships. He did not know, or care, what he was going to do with this knowledge; in gathering it he was feeding his love of ships, and for the time being that was enough.

He made friends both inside and outside the *Bulletin* office. He and A. G. Stephens took a liking to each other. Their friendship was to wither some years later, but it flourished at the start. Stephens, then in his late thirties and a pontifical figure behind an imposing beard and moustaches, was a perceptive critic, although his literary and artistic judgements were notoriously changeful. He revelled in his power as Red Page editor and liked to remind those whom he had raised up that he could, and if need be would, pull them down. 'It does these fellows good—keeps them in their place', he once said, in words expressing the critic's classic attitude to the creative man. He and Norman collaborated in producing and publishing a collection of his poems, *Oblation*, which appeared in a limited edition in 1902. The poems smacked of literary hard labour rather than inspiration, but *Oblation* helped to strengthen Norman's reputation as an illustrator.

After a year in Sydney he was hardly recognizable as the shabby and underfed young man who had come from Melbourne. He never gave much thought to clothes but, having no longer to dress out of second-hand shops, he acquired an unobtrusive elegance. His slim body was naturally graceful and, as he hurried through Sydney at a brisk walk, he looked every inch a well-to-do young artist, in his casual but well-cut jackets and trousers, set off by the wide-brimmed hats he favoured at that time. His face, with the delicate yet resolute jaw, the rather sensual mouth, and the alert and nervously darting bright blue eyes which took in everything about him and stored the images away in his memory, was arrestingly handsome in an unconventional way. His nose, although still prominent, was less of a beak, and the height of his forehead seemed to be emphasized by his habit of combing his hair down over it in a fringe. Although only a splinter of flesh and bone, he stood out in a crowd. This was a product of something inside him, some kind of force generated by his spirit.

At times that spirit could throw off violent sparks. He had packed his boxing gloves in Melbourne and taken them to Sydney. As before, they hung on a nail behind the door of his studio and he boxed a few rounds whenever possible. His best sparring partner in his early Sydney days was a male model named Nat (Norman never knew Nat's surname) who was a master of every legal and illegal trick in the pugilist's book and, although nearing his fifties, was still a superb and smoothly muscled figure, tapering from wide shoulders to narrow hips. Nat, a former professional boxer, towered five or six inches over Norman, and for some months they put the gloves on at the studio nearly every day. One morning, fresh from sparring with Nat, Norman was walking along Pitt Street when he passed a group of roughs idling on a corner. One of them catcalled and shouted a few muffled words. Glancing round, Norman saw the others leering after him and laughing. He started to walk back. He had not taken two steps when he regretted it, but he could not turn tail because half a dozen pedestrians had stopped to watch and a cabman, perched on the high dicky of his hansom at the corner, had a grandstand seat. Remembering a trick of Will Dyson's, Norman hooked his thumbs into the waistband of his trousers, walked up to the man who had called after him and asked:

'Did I hear you pass a remark about me?

The lout sneered down at this challenging cock sparrow. He was lounging against a fluted iron veranda post and did not even trouble to straighten.

Norman brought his left fist up in an upper-cut. It took the lout on the point of the chin and smashed his head against the post. His eyes glazed and he slid to the footpath and keeled over on his side, out to the world. Somebody whooped and the cabby vaulted down from his dicky shouting, 'Good on you, lad! Get into 'im!'

The success of the punch astonished Norman. He had no intention of pushing his luck too far.

'That's good enough for him', he grunted and strolled off with the air of one who felled hulking bullies every day.

Norman was not physically pugnacious, however. Given time to think, he would always go out of his way to avoid a street fight. If fear of a hiding did not deter him, the thought of his hands did. They were too precious to risk.

He suffered recurrent attacks of what he called 'bad conscience' in his early years in Sydney. To him, bad conscience did not mean remorse for conventional failings; it meant the sense of guilt he felt when he turned out no serious work or only a thin trickle. It was another name for his Daemon, which was always at his elbow, whispering in his ear and giving him no peace.

The files of the *Bulletin* while he was a staff artist teem with the evidence of his journalistic industry. Most men would have felt they were justifying themselves by producing such a volume of work, but Norman's conscience kept goading him. Cartoons, illustrations for jokes and other such items were well enough in their way but he could not persuade himself that they had any lasting value. If he were content to stop there he would be denying his *raison d'être*. He knew he was merely flirting with his life's work. And there was so much to do. Detesting the aesthetic intolerance of the time, he longed to topple the walls of cant and hypocrisy which hedged the artist in and denied him free expression, and to attack and scatter the army of taboos which weighed on his hand. The missionary spirit which he had inherited from Grandpa Williams was clamouring for an outlet. While Grandpa Williams would have been pained by Norman's worship of the naked human body and his contempt for Christian ethics and teachings, he would have understood the fire which raged in his grandson's blood. A similar fire had raged in his own blood when he had wrestled with the pagan gods of the Fijians.

One day in 1903 Lionel and Norman came together again. Lionel had left Melbourne and spent a year in Spain, painting and drawing and beginning an everlasting affair of the heart with Spain and its people. Now, having fallen in love with Jean Dyson, a sister of the Dyson brothers, he was back in Australia intent on carving out a career which would enable him to marry. He had decided that Sydney offered better prospects than Melbourne and Norman agreed with him.

Norman and Katie gave him their spare room at Lavender Bay.

'Great to have you, Joe', Norman told him. 'Stay as long as you like. It will be like old times.'

It was like old times in many ways, with the difference that Lionel was no longer the vagabond of the Melbourne days but a devout lover with a consuming purpose. Jean Dyson, who was travelling in Europe with the Bedfords, had promised to follow him to Australia within the year and he was determined to have a home ready when she arrived. He had always been a man of huge resolve and, working from Norman's city studio, he accepted any and every journalistic and commercial job on offer. His stamina was inexhaustible. Hearing that the Sydney *Evening News* was looking for a cartoonist, he submitted specimens of his work and was appointed. He held the post for more than twenty years, turning out three topical cartoons a week while doing other money-earning work, and at the same time developing his talents as etcher, wood-engraver and water-colourist, and writing prolifically on art and artists.

He was good for Norman. Their talks helped to clear Norman's mind of confusions and uncertainties. Lionel, who had long been an un-grudging and vocal admirer of his brother's skill with the pen, saw a clear advance in Norman's drawings. The Mediterranean warmth of Sydney was in them; they were also strengthened and enriched by the study Norman was making of Petronius in particular, as well as of Horace, Plautus and Catullus. His reading, then and all his life, was wide rather than deep. He was never a student like Lionel; nor like his first-born son Jack, later. Lionel and Jack always wanted to know and be able to quote their authorities; Norman was content to know largely by intuition. Sometimes he went wrong because he had not gone far enough, or on occasion gone any distance at all, but at others he glimpsed soaring peaks which Lionel or Jack never saw.

Although he felt that the few drawings he had done since coming to Sydney—few by his standards, that is—were a meagre yield, his spirits lifted under Lionel's boisterous enthusiasm. He put his head down and worked with restless energy. It was astonishing that this seemingly frail young man could work with burning intensity until nearly dawn, then snatch a few hours' sleep and, going back to his drawingboard, once more throw himself into the task with undiminished zest.

The preference for literary men's company which he had shown in Melbourne became more marked in Sydney. He and Julian Ashton shared a deep reciprocal liking, but otherwise Norman tended to be the odd man out among his professional brethren. His ideas on art and the way he asserted them exasperated many artists and sometimes led on to quarrels. On his side, he held that most artists were verbally inarticulate, and unable to contribute anything worth hearing to a philosophical dis-cussion. Hence he could never find much in common with them; and, be it said, few of them could find much in common with him.

He carried some weight in the Royal Art Society of New South Wales, however, both as a talker and an exhibitor. Drawings which he showed at the annual exhibition in 1903 attracted some notice. Then at the 1904 exhibition, in September, he showed a group of works one of which scandalized the righteous, pained many normally broad-minded laymen, and split the artists into two angry factions. Its title was *Pollice Verso*. Norman said of *Pollice Verso*:

> It was the first affirmation of my credo, which is that the Greeks and Romans established all that the word civilization can mean, while Christianity, that communist uprising of the underworld, sought to destroy it and very nearly succeeded in doing so. All through my work I have maintained that theme, and that is the reason why it was attacked, although the attack took the crude device of denouncing it as indecent and immoral, because I took the nude human body as my symbol of the freed spirit of man.

*Pollice Verso* depicts a man crucified on a gloomy hillside. Emaciated and forsaken, he hangs in an attitude eloquent of hopelessness and defeat. The foreground is a crowded mass of figures, mostly naked—men and women, a jovial Bacchus astride an ass, a Roman soldier, a bearded merchant, a child leading a leopard, and a peacock. Many are leering back at the crucified man with derisive grins or with arms outstretched and thumbs turned down in a gesture of rejection. The figure on the cross is not identified, but most of those who saw the drawing interpreted it as a repudiation of Jesus Christ and his spiritual teachings in favour of a hedonistic and sensual world.

The daily newspapers led the outcry. They disliked the moral implications of most of Norman's exhibition drawings but settled on *Pollice Verso* as the focus of evil. The *Sydney Morning Herald* critic wrote: 'Mr Norman Lindsay may ultimately make a name as great as Phil May's, but the preference which he here manifests for depicting only the bestial types of humanity is difficult to understand'. The *Daily Telegraph* critic said:

> In the black and white class, Mr Norman Lindsay's work is beyond praise, regarded merely as pen draughtsmanship. It is positively wonderful, and that is probably why the selection committee could not make up its mind to reject the work. But the subjects suggest an artist with an imagination in an advanced stage of decomposition.

Even Norman's own special patron, Stephens, who gave the exhibition a review running to more than three columns in the Red Page, disliked some aspects of *Pollice Verso*, including 'the excessive belittlement of the ascetic figure on the cross'. But his closing words were balm to Norman's soul:

> The labour in the drawing is very great; the talent that is exhibited reaches genius; and the ambition of the ideal that Lindsay has set before himself, the power of his effort toward it, are a reproach to local slackness and unworthi-

ness. His faults are faults of virile youth; his merits are a master's. We look to him to bring lasting honour to Australia that bred him.

The newspapers published many letters from readers damning or extolling the moral qualities of *Pollice Verso*. On 14 September the *Daily Telegraph* printed one from Julian Ashton. Under the headline 'A Work of Genius', Ashton wrote:

> I have been waiting for an abler pen than mine to point out that at last a great work has been produced in Australia. But no; again all our critics are dumb . . . In years to come, when English and foreign critics shall have placed Norman Lindsay's work in the niche where it belongs, it will be a matter for regret that the trustees of our National Gallery did not earlier encourage a talent so brilliant and so original.

The war of words at least ensured the popular success of the exhibition. Hundreds of people who would not have known an oil painting from a woodcut went along to see *Pollice Verso*, like sensation-seekers going to gape at a two-headed calf. Some art patrons acted as if Norman had personally affronted them. A society lady marched up to Julian Ashton and launched into a tirade against Norman. Stemming the flow of her words at last, Ashton said:

'Allow me to introduce you to Mr Norman Lindsay.'

Norman, standing beside him, acknowledged the introduction and assured the lady that he had no intention of corrupting anyone—he merely wanted to tell the truth about life as he saw it.

He fought down the temptation to retort to his critics in public although among friends he damned them with scathing words.

'Forget them, Joe', Lionel told him. 'You ought to thank them. It means you've hit them where they live.'

It was weeks before the heat went out of the controversy, and echoes of it were heard for months. The *Bulletin* felt the backlash. Readers and advertisers wrote in expressing horror that a respected weekly should continue to employ a ribald and coarse blasphemer like Norman Lindsay. A parson composed a denunciation in the form of a long poem. Each stanza ended with the same two maledictory lines:

> Never since Man saw the face of the Devil
> Have been such creations of absolute evil.

Norman considered having it framed. As a rather belated gesture of appeasement to indignant readers, the *Bulletin*, on 16 February 1905, published a two-column reproduction of *Pollice Verso* above an editorial comment which said:

> There is no intention to represent *the* Crucifixion. The crucified figure is the symbol of Asceticism; the rout of revellers of Epicureanism . . . the picture represents the challenge of Pleasure to Asceticism, but not necessarily Pleasure's victory. The joy of life is set in bright light . . . against the pangs

One of Norman's anti-wowser cartoons, published at a time when some churchmen were agitating for 'a quiet, squashless, bananaless, gloomful Sunday'

of death. Yet, for all that is said by the work to the contrary, the palm may be with the stubborn figure in the gloom.

Norman's opinion of this grovelling attempt to conciliate the antagonists of *Pollice Verso* without offending its admirers is not on record.

It is necessary to step forward three years in time to tell the end of the story. Norman showed *Pollice Verso*, with other of his drawings, at a

Melbourne group exhibition by Sydney artists in October 1907. A few days after the opening the National Gallery of Victoria bought *Pollice Verso* for 150 guineas; this was said to be the largest price ever paid in Australia until then for a pen and ink drawing. Apart from some minor rumblings, the response in Melbourne was wholly favourable. Every daily newspaper critic acclaimed the Lindsay works in the exhibition, particularly *Pollice Verso*. Yet a myth persists that *Pollice Verso* was loudly and stormily denounced in Melbourne, on moral and religious grounds. This appears to be founded on Norman's own statements and it has no basis in fact. As time passed he evidently telescoped the purchase of the picture in 1907 with the Sydney controversy in 1904, and in his mind these two distinct episodes became one. It was an example of his talent for editing events to accord with dramatic symmetry.


Norman's domestic affairs were not prospering like his professional career. Indeed they were not prospering at all, but a marriage does not usually end with a thunderclap, and Norman and Katie's was no exception. Some of the glow of the sexual passion which had drawn them together in Melbourne lingered on after the move to Sydney, and Katie, being a conventional woman who valued the proprieties, clung to the hope that if she were patient a calm and settled marriage would evolve. She supposed that Norman's obsession with work which made him a neglectful husband and an unsatisfactory father would in time burn itself out like a fever. There was never the smallest chance of that, but Katie could not know it because she did not understand the labyrinthine complexities of his nature. Nor, for some years, did she know about the growth of his feeling for Rose Soady.

Norman met Rose about a year after he began working for the *Bulletin*. She was sixteen and just beginning to make a mark as an artist's model when Julian Ashton introduced her to Norman. The daughter of an irresponsible Cornish carpenter and a little English woman, who was explosive, courageous and eternally ready to forgive her scapegrace husband's frailties, Rose was a girl of unswerving resolution. She had taken up modelling after her father had deserted his wife and family and gone off to New Zealand. It was the only way she could help her mother, who was struggling to hold together a family of nine, six of them younger than Rose. Nature seemed to have fashioned Rose to be an artist's model. Her figure, which would settle into statuesque lines later, was strong but graceful in her youth; her face was handsome, with a mouth, nose and chin which betokened the stubborn determination of her Cornish forefathers. She carried herself in a way which drew all eyes to her when she walked into a crowded room; all men's eyes anyway.

Although her schooling had been sketchy she was intelligent, and her mind was inquiring and her memory retentive.

Norman found her the best model he had ever known. She did her work in thoroughly professional style, never talking unless there was need. When he said anything which called for a reply she answered without wasting words.

One of the first times she posed for him was at Lavender Bay, soon after he brought Katie and Jack from Melbourne. Their relationship was purely that of artist and model—a deeper emotional link was still two years or so off. When she was leaving he escorted her to a flight of steps leading from the house to the street. As he stood there he became aware of Katie standing on the veranda and staring at Rose. Rose returned the stare, then went on up the steps. The impact on Norman of the spontaneous antipathy between the two women was almost physical. He felt like a swimmer caught in a cross-current.

He joined Katie on the veranda.

'That's a bold creature', she said with feeling.

Having a clear conscience, Norman did not protest. He cracked a mild joke and went inside to his work.

If Katie suspected that Norman and Rose were on terms of intimacy, she did not show it. At that time there was nothing for her to suspect. Norman was never a womanizer. He had done his share of girl-chasing when he was a sexually inquisitive adolescent and a sexually hungry young bachelor, but no more than any other healthy youth. As an artist, he had a lifelong rule proscribing love-making or even light flirtation with his models. This was a practical not a moral interdict; he believed that artistic concentration suffered if physical passion were roused. When any of his models flashed him a signal to treat her as a woman he pretended not to see it. He found this never failed. Presently the girl would give up and revert to her impersonal status as a model, and work would go forward without any threat of sentimental complications.

He did not have to pretend blindness to signals from Rose because she sent him none. She thought him a personable and interesting young man but nothing about him made her look on him as a possible lover. She had a large number of young men trailing at her heels eager for any sign of favour. Most of them, being single, were more eligible than Norman, but she gave none of them much encouragement; it was fun to keep them dangling and play off one against another but she did not wish to think about a husband and children and domestic ties for a long time to come. She was only too familiar with the quicksands of marriage; she had seen her mother struggling in them and did not hanker after them herself. She did not even let Norman see how much she admired his talents. Although a stranger to the artistic world until she began modelling, Rose had an eye for quality in a picture, and did not take long to decide that Norman was an artist not only of surpassing manual skill but also of phenomenal conceptual powers. She knew the work of all the Sydney artists of the day and had sat for many of them, but this man stood out. He seemed to carry a volcano inside him.

He had no romantic thoughts about Rose when Katie, who was pregnant again, told him in the middle of 1903 that she proposed going to Melbourne and staying with her people until her baby was born. He was not sorry that Katie wanted to go when he remembered all the fuss that had attended Jack's birth so he lost no time in making arrangements for them to travel to Melbourne. After seeing them off he walked away with the jaunty step of a free man, congratulating himself on having five or six weeks ahead when he need do nothing but suit his own convenience. He did not dream that he was about to embark on a love affair with Rose Soady.

He was renting a house at Northwood, on the North Shore. Lionel, who was chafing with impatience for Jean Dyson to arrive home from Europe and marry him, was staying there and he and Norman were doing for themselves while Katie was away; their wants were simple and they were both well experienced. It was a biggish house and when Will Dyson appeared, on a visit from Melbourne, he moved in with them. Being a foot-loose bachelor, Will wanted a girl to cheer his Sydney stay. Norman thought of Rose. She was leaving Julian Ashton's studio one afternoon when Norman hailed her and introduced Will Dyson. She liked Will's cool, mocking style and he liked her. A few days later she was invited to the Northwood house. It was the first of a string of visits and she enjoyed herself. The house ran itself and food was often short, because the shopping was done by guess and by God, but it was all relaxed and warm and cheerful. They laughed and frolicked and played the fool but nothing could have been more innocent. She tricked herself out in improvised costumes and joined with the others in acting out scenes, as Norman and Lionel and their friends had done in the kitchen garden of 'Lisnacrieve'. Norman took scores of photographs and developed them in the kitchen, splashing around in dishes of chemicals by the light of a ruby lamp and chirping with enthusiasm when a plate came out well.

He said later that he and Rose became lovers 'spontaneously and without premeditation', and there is no reason to doubt it. It happened soon after Lionel moved out of the Northwood house to concentrate on making his final preparations for marriage. Norman, who begrudged the time he had to spend travelling to and fro across the Harbour, closed the house up and went to live in the city. He took a large room in Rowe Street, five or six blocks from the *Bulletin* office, with another room next door which he turned into a studio. Will Dyson went to Rowe Street with him but stayed only a few days, then packed his bag and took himself back to Melbourne. He and Norman parted on outwardly genial terms, calling each other 'Joe' and swearing they'd meet again soon, but there was an underlying strain. Will had fallen in love with Rose, and Norman had suddenly discovered the intensity of his own feelings for her. He was not going to concede possession of her to Will Dyson or anybody else and when it came to the point he found he did not have to; Rose liked Will but by this time she had realized that Norman was the man she loved.

They knew there was awkwardness ahead. Katie would be coming back from Melbourne soon with Jack and the baby—Ray, born on 26 August. Norman could tell her the whole story and make a clean break at once, or he could let things run on and trust that time would provide a solution. He took the second course. He was never good at facing personal crises—his moral courage was always apt to crumble when he stood face to face with somebody he knew well and with whom he had an unpleasant account to settle. He welcomed Katie and Jack back to Sydney, gabbled a few words of self-conscious admiration over his new son, then whistled up a cab and piloted his wife and family to a house he had rented at Waverley.

He did not wish to sleep at the Waverley house but felt he must. He also gave up his room in Rowe Street and moved into another city studio; Katie rarely visited any of his studios but he did not want to take the risk of her calling at Rowe Street and lighting on evidence of his association with Rose. Although he had no intention of breaking with Rose he was anxious to defer the show-down with Katie for as long as possible. There was no reason, he told himself, to meet trouble half way.

As year followed year Norman steadily gained public acceptance. Every Australian who could read and a few who couldn't knew his work in the *Bulletin*, and nearly as many knew his serious pen drawings. Even those who deplored his 'pagan philosophy' granted the magic of his technique; many were repelled by the message of his 1905 work *Dionysus*, in which a mass of naked figures, laughing and wanton, whirl to a focal apex, but they could not deny the masterly workmanship. There was talk that he was working on a sequence of wash drawings for the *Memoirs of Casanova* and these were whispered to be so good as to eclipse anything else he had done. Some of his admirers said there were no heights he could not reach if he chose; they predicted that he might become another Dürer or Kley, Graf or Vierge. It was heady eulogy for an artist still some years under thirty but it did not upset his balance—praise of his work from one quarter was always tempered by attack from another and that helped him to keep a healthy sense of perspective.

One of the most persistent attackers for many years was none other than A. G. Stephens. Stephens left the *Bulletin* in October 1906 and after that, until his death in 1933, had to battle hard for a livelihood. As a freelance, he could not reject any grist that came to his mill; and Norman, with his knack of rousing the passion of his fellow Australians, was good grist. Some while after breaking with the *Bulletin*, Stephens published the first of many articles examining 'the rise and fall of Norman Lindsay'. After that a similar article by Stephens appeared in some magazine or newspaper every few years. The form and the words varied but the theme was constant: Norman's work was 'superficial and impermanent'; he was a mere adapter of other men's styles, who had 'become notorious for crude nudes and designs crowded with a fury of meaningless phantoms'. Stephens always protested that his purpose was not to damn his one-time protégé but to warn young Australian artists against the risk of imitating him. These attacks irritated Norman but he never let it be seen that they worried him. He said they strengthened and stimulated him.

Whether critics were friendly or hostile, work was his reason for being, and his personal life a mere aside. As far as he could tell, Katie had no inkling of his liaison with Rose. He often slept at his studio but that was nothing new; Katie might not like it but he had done it ever since their first few months in Sydney, so she had no reason to see it as a symptom of a new emotional interest. They lived in a succession of rented houses. Most of these were around the harbourside suburb they had liked from the start, Lavender Bay, and Katie either was, or pretended to be, incurious about what he did when he was away for two or three days and nights. Perhaps she did not wish to know. She had her home and her boys, and that was enough. Never a man to submerge his own aspirations, Norman could not bring himself to make any large personal sacrifices to bolster Katie's belief in the stability of the marriage but he made some concessions. As a result of one of these she had another son, Philip, who was born at Lavender Bay on 1 May 1906. This blessed but undesired event—undesired by Norman anyway—must have involved him in making some complicated explanations to Rose.

Katie possibly hoped that Phil's birth would save the foundering marriage, but Norman was home less than ever, and when he was there Katie and he bickered in front of the boys and sometimes quarrelled. Jack Lindsay remembered a New Year's Eve when his mother said that he and Ray might stay up until midnight. Norman came home about eleven o'clock and asked why they were not in bed. Katie told him and he went inside. When the New Year sirens sounded the boys

9 *The Crucified Venus,* one of Norman's early controversial pen
drawings, is in the National Gallery of Victoria

10   *Pollice Verso* (in the National Gallery of Victoria)

11   Norman with Jack Castieau at Heidelberg

exploded crackers, banged tin cans, blew whistles, and hallooed and yelled, adding their quota to the hooting of the boats on the Harbour and the joyful uproar created by other revellers at Lavender Bay.

Norman reappeared and suggested that the confounded children might stop their hellish noise and go to bed where they should have been long ago.

'Nonsense, they've got a right to enjoy themselves once a year. Everybody else is making a noise. Go on, boys.'

We beat our tins with enhanced glee. Against such a noise no human retort was possible. Without his hat Norman went off down the steps, retreating to the city and his studio.*

He was never close to his sons when they were young. He neither understood how to bridge the gap which separated him from them nor wished to bridge it. He had, in his own words, 'nothing of the parental urge in my make-up'. Jack, Ray and Phil were aware of him but only as a shadowy figure who came and went and took little hand in their lives. They did not miss him even when he stayed away for days at a time. Their mother was inefficient and indolent in practical things but she gave them comfort, companionship and protection, even if meals were sketchy and beds often went unmade. Although she was no match for Norman in mental stature or personality, her maternal instinct was strong.

Norman borrowed money from the *Bulletin* a year or two after Phil's birth and bought a house at Lavender Bay but this did nothing to close the widening gap between him and Katie; he only wanted to put an end to the moves from one rented house to another, which were a drain on his pocket and his time. They settled into the new place but nothing else changed. The part of Norman's life that mattered to him rarely touched Lavender Bay. Katie would have fitted into it no better than Norman did into the ambience of a suburban marriage. She could not understand that, to him, his work was more than the making of pictures which would bring in money. *Pollice Verso* or *Dionysus* or a drawing for *Casanova*, which he had laboured over with anguish and hope and passion, meant no more to Katie than a *Bulletin* cartoon. They were citizens of different worlds, and once the intimacies of the marriage bed failed them they were as far apart as two strangers. The inward links having broken, the breaking of the outward links was only a matter of time.

Katie was unhappy; Norman was not. He was too busy to mope. His work absorbed nine-tenths of his waking time. With two establishments to support and rising expenses in some other directions, he had to increase his income, so he joined with Lionel and together they poured out a torrent of commercial art works. They could not sit back, for

---

* Jack Lindsay, *Life Rarely Tells* (London, 1958), pp. 41-2.

F

as well as paying their own way they were sending money to Creswick. Doctor Lindsay's practice had dwindled under competition from a new generation of medical men, and the old man, now past his middle sixties and impoverished by unlucky speculations in gold-mining, was having a hard battle. Neither Norman nor Lionel wished to dodge their obligations to 'Lisnacrieve' but these added to the load each of them carried. As in their Melbourne days they scorned no commission, but there was a difference; they now commanded fees twelve or fourteen times as large as those they had gladly accepted five or six years earlier. Some of their most profitable commissions were large advertisements, among them a series for the *Bulletin* lauding the virtues of Cobra Boot Polish. The Cobra items each ran to a full page and, appearing every week for years, had a following which made them more popular than many of the edittorial features. The drawings illustrated jingly verses turned out by a short-story writer and journalist, Ernest O'Ferrall, which were based on the putative character, adventures and philosophy of a comic Indian snake-charmer, Chunder Loo of Akim Foo. Lionel drew most of them, but Norman took over sometimes when his brother was overwhelmed with other work. They were always ready to deputize for one another, so their partnership could not have been easier.

These labours did not impair the quality of Norman's work as a *Bulletin* artist. His regular salary was still the solid backbone of his income and he could not take liberties with it; anyway he was a perfectionist who was driven to do everything he attempted to the limit of his abilities. One of his reasons for disliking journalism was the compulsion to cut corners and do work which was less than his best, because the implacable deadline had to be met. While bowing to this harsh necessity he still tried with all his might to make his cartoons and other *Bulletin* drawings as artistically valid as possible; this had less to do with his desire to please the people who paid his salary than with the need to satisfy his own conscience. Now and then he succeeded in delivering a drawing to the *Bulletin* which nearly qualified as fine art but this did not happen often. As a rule he had to finish his drawings in a hurry and use the guile of the craftsman to hide artistic deficiencies. But he acknowledged the merits of his journalistic experiences along with the evils. While disliking the need to acquire a superficial facility, which enabled him to skate around technical challenges and ignore subtleties, he valued the discipline: work had to be done and it was done. He was no less grateful for the way journalism plunged him into the fast-moving and oftentimes murky world of men and affairs; not always admirable men and rarely savoury affairs, but priceless background material for any artist concerned, not with polite society, but with what Norman called 'the human loony-bin' in all its crazy manifestations.

An abiding curse of his *Bulletin* work was the incessant quest for subject-matter. He kept a notebook in his vest pocket and jotted ideas down in it whenever they occurred to him, on boats or trams or trains, in the midst of a talk with a friend, even in the small hours of the morning. He assembled a reference library which, growing steadily larger and more cumbrous, had to be packed and taken along whenever he moved to a new studio. It consisted largely of photographs and drawings clipped from newspapers—thousands of photographs and drawings of animals, birds and reptiles, ships, buildings, fashions in men's and women's clothing down the ages, trees, mountains, bullock waggons, Salvation Army meetings, locomotives, bridges, and other animate and inanimate objects. And politicians. Especially politicians. Norman held nearly all politicians in contempt, as vainglorious and self-seeking lime-lighters or cynical and infamous crooks. To him, they were, with very few exceptions, 'just blown-up bladders of wind, and when time pricks the bladder we see that there was no real substance in them'. One of the few politicians for whom he ever admitted a grudging regard was Randolph Bedford, the gay and irrepressible crony of his Melbourne years. Bedford was elected to the Queensland parliament as a Labour member in 1917, and Norman delighted in telling the story of his first appearance at Parliament House, in Brisbane. Buttonholing a solemn patriarchal legis-lator he asked in a stage whisper, 'Where is the Bribery Department?'

For all his success as a topical cartoonist, Norman preferred other facets of his *Bulletin* job. He always clucked with pleasure when he in-vented or came on a joke about small boys. He loved drawing small boys. He modelled them in every essential on himself and his mates at Creswick, supplemented by his adult observations. Lionel presented him with a telescope in Sydney, and he sometimes sat with it for hours at a window, or behind a hillock or a clump of shrubbery, spying on unsus-pecting people, especially children. Children at play always fascinated him; their rompings were precious material. His small boys were greedy, lawless, selfish, graceless, profane, but true to life; little monsters, per-haps, but fearsomely authentic. They pleased him and pleased the *Bulletin* but they did not please everybody. Whenever one of his small-boy jokes was published it brought letters of protest from sentimental adults who objected that little children were not like that. Were Norman Lindsay and the *Bulletin*, the writers demanded, trying to peddle the wicked idea that children were not sweet and innocent and guileless? Now and then an indignant father or mother came raging into the office shouting that Norman should be sacked.

But even those who smelt evil in all Norman's other work granted him a clean bill on one subject: the koalas, bandicoots, kangaroos, wombats and other native animals which his pen sent frolicking through the pages of the *Bulletin* (and, later, the *Lone Hand*) were admitted to be above reproach, sexually, spiritually and zoologically. Nothing else he ever drew nearly equalled his native animals in popularity, with his koalas far in advance of the rest. Not that he ever called them koalas; to him, as to most Australians, they were always native bears. A claim put forward in a newspaper article* by Lionel Lindsay's son, Peter, that Australia 'owes the discovery of her animals' to Norman is probably true. In the same article Peter told how Norman held a show of pictures at Angus & Robertson's gallery, in Sydney, before his first trip to Europe in 1909. The offering included a selection of fine pen drawings and some early water-colours but nothing equalled his koalas in popular appeal. Peter Lindsay wrote:

> . . . his pictures of native bears sold like hot cakes; the demand being such that Fred Wymark [a director] of the Firm had Norman installed behind a screen churning out bears as clergymen, bears as lawyers, bears in top hats; in fact bears as everything—until finally the artist went on strike and refused to draw another 'blanky' bear.

No matter how Norman rigged out his koalas and other bushland creatures in human clothing, or put human words in their mouths, they never degenerated into human beings in fancy dress but somehow remained animals. Perhaps that was the secret of their charm.

Naturally many of his artist contemporaries sneered. The common gibe was that Norman Lindsay was 'climbing to fame and fortune on koalas' backs and women's tits'. He did not let the taunt get under his skin. He despised most of the Sydney artists of the time as daubers incapable of producing anything but genteel landscapes and overwrought sunsets suitable to hang on suburban sitting-room walls. None of them could see his visions or dream his dreams. His mind was never bounded for long by the Sydney streets and the Sydney skyline; his spirit, as often as not, was away in eighteenth century Europe with Giovanni Casanova and the unscrupulous Venetian's merry and dissolute associates. He spent five years working on his hundred illustrations for *Casanova*. Lionel Lindsay said: 'Like a diver he went down into the careless depths of the Eighteenth Century to bring up its scandalous treasure, and Casanova and his connections lived with him more nearly than his shadow. The Eighteenth Century was for him no affair of powder, patch and clouded cane; but a world more real than the actual.'†

Now and then Norman wondered what he would do with the Casanova drawings when they were finished; but never for long. He always drew what he wanted to draw first, and only afterwards thought about turning it to practical account.

* *Smith's Weekly*, 3 January 1948.
† Introduction to *The Pen Drawings of Norman Lindsay* (Sydney, 1918).

Small boys fighting, one of Norman's favourite subjects

Norman had to relax sometimes or go stale, so he turned to horse-riding. Although he had last ridden as a boy at Creswick his old assurance quickly came back. Machines were multiplying in Sydney but they had not yet taken possession, and Norman hoped they never would. To him, the sight of a fine horse cantering or galloping was akin to great poetry. The rhythm and beauty of it stirred and excited him.

He and Rose took to riding on Wednesday and Saturday afternoons, and were soon members of a group who shared their passion for horses. One of the others was 'Banjo' Paterson, at that time a Sydney newspaper editor, who was known to every Australian for *The Man from Snowy River* and his other bush ballads; a superb horseman with an uncanny knowledge of the way horses think and act, the lean and muscular Paterson lived behind a wall of patrician reserve, and was one of the few men of whom Norman ever stood in awe. Another of the riding coterie was Douglas Fry, an English artist who painted horses well but rode them better; immaculate in perfectly cut riding clothes, he became one with the horse the moment he swung into the saddle. Frank Fox, the assistant editor of the *Bulletin*, although a flashy and mediocre horseman, was also a regular rider, and sometimes he and Norman would jog out into the country on a Saturday and, putting up at a hotel for the night, stay away until the Sunday evening. It was on these excursions that the *Lone Hand* was conceived.

Norman and Fox did not call it the *Lone Hand*; the name came later. Their talk centred on Australia's need for a general magazine which would encourage sound literary and artistic standards yet steer clear of highbrowism; they agreed that it should be modelled on the best English popular monthlies but remain wholly Australian in outlook and purpose. Their motives were not altogether altruistic, nor even mainly so. Fox, who was to forsake Australian for English journalism a few years later and win success and a knighthood in London, was an ambitious man in his early thirties and wanted a magazine to edit. Norman, on his side, wanted an outlet for his growing skill as an illustrator. He and Fox spent some time thinking and talking about the project. Then they took it to the *Bulletin*. Or, more specifically, they took it to Archibald.

Although no longer the editor, Archibald was always about the office looking for something to occupy his restless mind. He owned a quarter share of the company and, having stayed friendly with Macleod in spite of their professional disagreement, still wielded an appreciable influence. For Norman, there never could be another editor like Archibald, and there never was. James Edmond was a powerful and courageous writer with a precious gift of humour but he lacked Archibald's inspired flair. He did not try to change the *Bulletin* pattern, and under him it went on much as before and held its place as the supreme Australian weekly, but some subtle essence—the outfall of genius perhaps—was missing. Norman liked working under Edmond but the mere possibility of again being linked with Archibald made his pulse leap.

Archibald caught fire when Norman and Fox put their suggestion to him. This promised to be the very thing which would engage and test his capacity for high-grade journalism. He strode up and down, tugging at his beard, pouring out ideas in a glittering stream. They'd put out a magazine such as Australia had never had and sorely needed, he said. It would capture and express the richness, the adventure and the gaiety of Australian life. It would be big like Australia; it would breathe out the very spirit of Australia.

'By George, we'll bring it off!' he enthused. 'Just see if we don't!'

Macleod had to be convinced, but Archibald overwhelmed him. It was hard for anybody to resist Archibald once he set his heart on something and Macleod, having raised one objection after another and seen them all demolished, gave in. Anyway he was less reluctant than he pretended. As business manager he felt obliged to play the devil's advocate but he was not blind to the possibilities. It might be a failure and lose money but, with Archibald as the driving force, it might well become a huge success. So Macleod, an astute manager, having weighed the chances, agreed to gamble.

Archibald chose the name. The *Lone Hand* had an authentic Australian ring which fitted the kind of magazine he aimed to produce. He flung himself into the preparations with cyclonic energy. Fox, a skilled and able journalist, was the editor, but Archibald was the man with the creative flame. Lionel Lindsay, who called on him at the *Bulletin* office, found him

> . . . all lit up with an amazing prophetical enthusiasm for the new venture which was to transfigure Sydney life. He read, or rather declaimed his famous manifesto, conjuring up a picture of *cafés chantants*, bands in the park, red umbrellas and a gay people taking its aperitifs—its light wine and Pilsener— in a hundred cafés or in the open air.*

He worked with all his old-time intensity and something extra. Norman marvelled to see it. 'I've never known Archie like this before', he told Fox. No one realized that Archibald was sickening for the mental breakdown which eighteen months later was to lay him aside for some years. They saw him only as an inspired man; which, at that early stage of his illness, he was.

The first issue of the *Lone Hand* appeared on 1 May 1907. There were a hundred-odd editorial pages and sixty or seventy pages of advertisements. Henry Lawson, Louis Esson and G. B. Lancaster headed the short-story writers, and Hugh McCrae, Victor Daley and Roderic Quinn the poets. Norman contributed a number of drawings, notably a full-page romp in which two of his koalas fought a boxing contest with a troubled penguin as referee. George Lambert, who had begun to make a name in Europe and was to make a much bigger one, did a striking humorous drawing, and Lionel Lindsay, with illustrations to a short story, to an article on Sydney, and to an article on Australia, was well to the fore.

There were some controversial topical articles—inevitably so, with Archibald as the power behind the editor. One, headlined '*Wren and His Ruffians*', was a cool and scathing piece on the Melbourne adventurer, John Wren, and the dubious fortune which he had founded on profits yielded by his illegal totalisator in Collingwood and his manipulation of big sports events. Norman read it with glee. In the *Hawklet* days he had heard stories of Wren's barefaced doings, but he now saw these recorded in print for the first time. One episode described by the *Lone Hand* writer concerned a betting coup by Wren on the 1901 Austral Wheel Race. Wren had backed a rider named 'Plugger' Bill Martin to win. And, of course, 'Plugger' Bill did win. Wren saw to that. It cost him a large sum in bribes but the profits were many times larger, and Wren collected thousands. Norman knew this story already. He had heard it in intimate detail from one Harry Gordon, better known as 'General',

* Lionel Lindsay, *Comedy of Life* (Sydney, 1967), p. 227.

who at that time was coming to his studio every morning to spar a few rounds and massage him. 'General', an ex-boxer who bore many honourable scars and owned, in Norman's words, 'the largest ears in Australasia', had little liking for 'Plugger' Bill Martin and less for Wren. He had been 'Plugger' Bill's trainer and was with him when he paid over the Austral Wheel Race bribes to other riders in a Melbourne hotel bedroom under Wren's instructions. Norman showed 'General' the *Lone Hand* article. He read it through in his slow way, lips moving as he puzzled out each word, then nodded his approval.

'That's right what it says here, about the Austral', he said. 'That's the gospel truth, son.'

Norman thought no more about it for some days until he walked into the *Bulletin* office and went along to Frank Fox's room. Macleod was there. He and Fox looked like two condemned men waiting for the hangman.

'What's the trouble?' Norman asked.

A copy of the *Lone Hand* on Fox's desk was open at the article about John Wren.

'Wren's sent in a writ for libel over what we say about the Austral Wheel Race', Macleod said. 'It could cost us thousands.'

'The article is true, isn't it?'

'It's true', Fox said, 'but proving it could be damn' difficult. All this time afterwards it will be next to impossible to dig up witnesses we could put into the box.'

Norman remembered 'General' Gordon. 'Would a witness who was there when Bill Martin paid over the bribes be any use to you?'

'Do you know one?' Macleod almost shouted.

Norman explained. '"General" is probably sweeping up my studio at this moment', he added.

They summoned 'General' Gordon and he told Macleod and Fox what he knew. Macleod put him on the payroll at £2 10s a week and arranged for somebody to leak the information to Wren. Some months later Wren dropped the case and 'General' Gordon's retainer came to an end. He had no complaints. He told Norman it was the easiest money he had ever earned.

Norman was glad he had been able to save the *Lone Hand* from a crippling financial blow. He wanted to see it prosper. It was an excellent medium for his work and paid him well. He also thought it could go a long way toward laying the solid foundations of a national culture. He believed with all the passion of his nature that Australia must rise above what he called its 'colonial cultural status'. He aspired, first of all, to see his own work recognized and the survival of his own name assured, but close behind came his dream that in his time Australia would take its place among the older nations in all the artistic fields. Throughout his life he never ceased looking for young Australians of exceptional talent, particularly poets and prose writers. Four or five times he persuaded himself that he had discovered a literary genius and, although he had to discount most of these judgements, disappointment never discouraged him; he was always ready to try again. His quest was the symptom of something verging on cultural xenophobia but, however extravagantly it made him think and talk and act at times, it was one of the most admirable and selfless expressions of the man. He was prodigally generous with his time and advice to all the chosen, and to some of them also by supplying illustrations which enabled them to get their books published and make a little money.

Hugh McCrae was the earliest beneficiary. Norman and McCrae never lost touch with one another after their first meeting in Melbourne, although sometimes for long periods their only link was an occasional scrawled note. A year or so before Norman left Melbourne, McCrae had gone off to the country to live in carefree poverty, writing an occasional poem and loafing in the sun. Then, soon after Norman settled in Sydney with Katie and Jack, McCrae, as handsome and gay as ever, arrived with a wife. The Lindsays were in a two-storey house at Lavender Bay and Norman rented the upper floor to the McCraes until they were ready to move into a place of their own. They stayed for six months and the friendship between the two men touched a new height. They 'often sat together until dawn when the first ferry would tumble the water under the window . . .'*

Norman was enchanted with McCrae's poetry. It was like sunlight on a bird's wings, like the music of mountain streams. It had first laid a spell on him in Melbourne. One day McCrae had carelessly tossed a sheet of paper to him bearing a poem entitled 'We Dreamed'. Norman had read:

> And we—we dreamed of love and stars, and waters deep,
>   Of shining gleam-kiss'd waves and tears,
>   Of fallen worlds, torn from a wilderness of lights . . .

The poems that McCrae was writing in Sydney seemed to Norman even purer and richer. He believed that here was a great lyric poet, among the greatest in the English language. For him, the best of McCrae's poems— 'Colombine', 'Rake's Song', 'Ambuscade', 'Camden Town', 'Joan of Arc', 'Song of the Rain', 'June Morning', so many more—held their witchery to the end.

Delighting in satyrs, nymphs and fauns, McCrae shared Norman's paganism and expressed it in his poems. Otherwise the two had little in common. Norman envied McCrae's talent for idling; or said he did. McCrae had the gift of being able to sprawl in a canvas chair on a

* Hugh McCrae, *Story-Book Only* (Sydney, 1948), p. 72.

sunny lawn for hours, perhaps with a book open on his knees but only pretending to read and in reality letting his mind gallop off in pursuit of mad and exuberant fantasies. Norman could never bear to sit and do nothing even for a few seconds; his Daemon was always at him, prodding him into action and making him writhe with bad conscience. McCrae had one infirmity of character which Norman found it hard to pass over; this was a readiness to censor his verses under puritanical pressure —to barter a bit of his soul for a quiet life. In Norman's eyes such perfidy was disgraceful, and if the traitor had been almost anybody else it would have ended their friendship. Yet, while deploring McCrae's frailty, Norman could not cast him aside. The man's charm was too strong. His laughing innocence somehow excused the inexcusable.

At the best of times it was a mystery how McCrae contrived to live on his earnings from poems, articles and other odds and ends of journalism, and an occasional fee for one of his joyously idiosyncratic drawings, but for some years after going to Sydney he found life a shade easier. Norman sang his praises to Archibald, Edmond, Fox and others, and a week rarely passed that the *Bulletin* or the *Lone Hand* or some other journal did not publish something he had written or less often drawn. Norman's illustrations helped to build the popular appeal of McCrae's poems. Norman was all the time growing in effectiveness as an illustrator. He never limited himself to making a pictorial transcription of a writer's words; his illustrations had a revelational character. When McCrae's first book, *Satyrs and Sunlight*, came out in 1909 it was bought and admired for the imaginative daring of Norman's decorations no less than for the limpid and fragile beauty of the poems. Norman permitted himself a chuckle of pride, particularly over the satyrs he had drawn for it. He liked their air of lecherous geniality.

Some of his friends were perplexed that he could be enchanted by McCrae's poems and yet turn to the professional boxing ring and revel in its sweaty brutalities. One of his intimates was Hugh D. McIntosh. They had met and taken an immediate liking to each other when Norman was drawing for the *Hawklet* and McIntosh was managing sports meetings in Melbourne. The showy and spendthrift McIntosh, who had an exceptional business brain, was burly, muscular, and ready with his fists, and it was his physical toughness that had first roused Norman's admiration. Norman loved listening to McIntosh's stories of his rise to affluence and notoriety from his modest business start when, with a tray slung about his neck, he had hawked pies and pasties to Sydney racecourse and prize-fight patrons. Norman saw his two-fisted friend as the very model of a man of action, a buccaneer born two centuries out of his time and none the worse for that.

McIntosh promoted the world heavyweight title fight in which Jack

Johnson, the Negro challenger, beat Tommy Burns, the white champion, in Sydney on Boxing Day 1908. Norman made a series of studies of Burns to illustrate an article in the *Lone Hand*, and Lionel drew Johnson for an accompanying article. Norman also did a large drawing showing Burns and Johnson facing up to each other; McIntosh had hundreds of copies printed as posters to advertise the fight and spread them all round Sydney. Norman loved being in the thick of it. His racial prejudice made him hope that Burns would win, but he knew the chance was slender. While disliking Johnson, he thought he had never seen a more perfect specimen of the human male.

The widely publicized enmity between Burns and Johnson was no press agent's invention. They never met to discuss any detailed arrangements for the contest without all but coming to blows. McIntosh contrived to keep the bickering from ever turning into a brawl, but now and then it was touch and go.

One day Norman was in McIntosh's office when he picked up a rolled sheet of music lying on the desk. It concealed a lead bar.

'What the devil is this for, Hughie?' he asked.

'It's for that black bastard if he tries any funny business', McIntosh replied.

Norman's eye fell on the title of the music: 'Sing Me to Sleep, Mother'. The discovery confirmed his suspicion that McIntosh's rugged head and chunky body housed a poet's soul.

Time never dragged for Norman. Between the demands of the *Bulletin* and the *Lone Hand*, his work on the *Casanova* drawings, his exploits as a horseman, his friendships with men as disparate as Paterson, McCrae, Ashton, Archibald, Fox and McIntosh, and above all his love affair with Rose, he had little time to play the husband and father. It is hardly to be wondered at that he was more successful as a public and professional figure than in the private and domestic sphere.

# 4

# *Time of Exile*
## *1909-10*

Norman was restive. He turned thirty on 22 February 1909 and, although he never bothered much about his own birthday or anybody else's, this one loomed up like a dolorous milestone on his personal road. He believed he was in a rut and likely to stay there unless he took determined steps to hoist himself out. It was true that his work was known throughout Australia, but he felt that his fame was hardly more substantial than a bubble. He wanted to underpin his reputation as a serious pen draughtsman and could see no way of doing this in Australia. Much as it went against his nationalistic grain, he decided he would have to go to Europe.

It was not the first time he had thought of Europe. More than a year earlier he had told a newspaper interviewer that he intended going to England in 1908 to supervise the publication of a new edition of the *Memoirs of Casanova.** That proposal lapsed but Norman did not forget it. He had done a hundred full-scale drawings and 300 smaller illustrations for *Casanova* and hoped to see these used as the foundation of a de luxe edition. No Australian printery could have produced a work of the size and elegance he envisaged; England offered the best hope. He saw *Casanova* merely as a beginning and believed that, once launched, he might find a steady market for higher-grade illustrations with English publishers.

The decay of his marriage was an added incentive. He gave Katie the money she needed to keep the home going and never let more than a few days pass without seeing her and the boys; he even slept at Lavender Bay every second or third night but that was simply a matter of convenience. Rose was discontented with her status or lack of it, and her

* Melbourne *Herald*, 29 October 1907.

patience did not increase as time went on and Norman dodged the issue with Katie. He could find no rational answer to Rose's questions why he did not ask for a divorce or a legal separation, but he let himself hope that if he and Katie were apart for a year or more with the breadth of the world between them it would be easier to engineer the break. Or so he chose to pretend at least.

Whatever was said or left unsaid when he told Katie he was preparing to go overseas, each of them must have known that the marriage was in a bad way. She had surmised for a long time that Norman had another woman in his life, and for many months before he mentioned England she had been in no doubt of it. Will Dyson had told her about Norman and Rose, saying he thought she should know because the affair had become 'a settled relationship'. Katie was troubled; although no longer in love with Norman, she disliked upheavals and valued the security which marriage gave her and her sons. She had a helpless feeling, a sense of aloneness. Years later she told her son Jack that Will Dyson was her one true friend at that time. She always carried in her handbag the last letter he wrote her. It was a long letter in which he urged her to think of him if she were ever in difficulties. She also cherished a water-colour portrait which Will had done of her wearing a blue suit and a hat decorated with a single upstanding feather.

How close their friendship was is a matter of conjecture, but Norman had no doubt that for a time they were lovers. He believed that they first became intimate while he was on a visit to Creswick and Will happened to be in Sydney. If Katie turned to Will, it is hardly to be wondered at. She had been a neglected wife for a long while, and he was not only a good-looking and vital young man but also a sympathetic one. Long afterwards, Norman told a convincingly detailed story of a triangular confrontation on his return from Creswick; this ended, he said, in Katie and Will admitting their guilt. Norman knew he had no ground for acting the wronged husband, since his association with Rose had long before absolved Katie from any wifely obligations; but perhaps the discovery assuaged his conscience.

The mystifying thing is that the episode did not shake Norman's friendship with Will. At least neither ever admitted that it did. What hidden cross-currents it set in motion can only be surmised, but on the surface there was no change. They still called one another 'Joe'. When Will was in Sydney or Norman in Melbourne they met, talked, laughed, argued, and sometimes dined together. The occasional letters they exchanged were as undemonstratively warm as they had always been.

Nothing altered for Norman and Katie. There were no recriminations. They spoke of Will now and then but only as a family friend. Their lives went on as usual with Katie going her way and Norman his. Then he took his decision to go to Europe, and the tempo quickened as he made his preparations. He had much to do.

Money was the big obstacle. He had no talent for accumulating money. He had never thought of opening a bank account. What he earned he spent, knowing that his skill with pen or brush would replenish his pocket when it was empty. The idea of putting money aside and investing it in shares or lending it out at interest never crossed his mind. This had nothing whatever to do with moral or political scruples. Using money to make more money was just something outside the range of his thinking.

He worked out a rough estimate of his needs. It would be substantial, even allowing for anything he might earn in England. He would have to find enough for return fares for himself and Rose—he intended going on ahead and letting Rose follow him. Then there would be their living expenses for a year or more, and the cost of supporting Katie and the boys in Sydney. On top of everything else he would have to leave something behind to help keep the pot boiling at 'Lisnacrieve'. The size of the figure sobered him. He was determined to get away before the end of 1909, and to earn a thousand pounds or more over and above his settled income by then would take some doing.

The *Bulletin* people were not anxious to see him go. Both the *Bulletin* and the *Lone Hand* set big store by his work. His topical cartoons, his native animals and his joke drawings commanded a strong public following and he'd be missed. Worse, if he went overseas, he might not come back. It was a worrying thought for the *Bulletin* editor, James Edmond, and also for Arthur Adams, who had taken the *Lone Hand* chair when Frank Fox had gone off to try his luck in London. Even Macleod was downcast. He had disliked Norman's early *Bulletin* work and had kept at him to imitate Phil May's style instead of developing his own. Norman had refused to be jockeyed into becoming an echo of anybody, and as time went on Macleod had changed from a carping critic into an admirer. Resigning himself to the inevitable, and hoping the pilgrim would soon grow tired of Europe and come home, he made the best of things by offering to buy all the comic drawings Norman could turn out before he went. Norman thanked him and meant it. He knew he could do at least a hundred drawings and the money would be a big help, but he would still have to find another seven or eight hundred pounds somewhere.

There was only one way. He would hold an exhibition. Or two exhibitions, one in Sydney and one in Melbourne. He detested exhibiting and never learned to like it—it was, he said, 'like trying to draw with someone jogging one's elbow', but he accepted it as an unpalatable necessity. Time was the trouble. Friends—mostly writers, journalists, artists and horsy people—were forever dropping in at his city studio to pass an hour or so. He liked seeing them but soon realized that he could not afford these interruptions, so he packed his stuff and moved across the Harbour to a house at Willoughby. Rose looked after him there and, with no callers bursting in and distracting him, he poured out more journalistic and commercial work than ever before and steadily built up also a stock of serious pen drawings and water-colours. He had accepted a challenge in deciding to give two one-man exhibitions with only a few months to make ready, but as the middle of the year drew near he breathed easily. He had produced enough pictures to give each exhibition a solid core of serious work and would pad them out with originals of his *Lone Hand* illustrations; and of course with drawings of koalas—scores of koalas, which would sell if nothing else did.

He had not contemplated having company on the journey to Europe but then his sister, Ruby, and Will Dyson told him they wanted to join him and make it a honeymoon trip. Their decision to marry was no great surprise. They had been constantly together in Melbourne for some months. As far as Norman knew Will had not seen Katie for a long time, and anyway he took the view that other people's emotional entanglements were no business of his. Will and Ruby were old enough and intelligent enough to work out their own lives.

Will's anxiety to find a footing in London was his motive for resolving to go abroad. Australia did not seem to want him. He had struggled for years as a freelance, contributing superb caricatures and an occasional cartoon to the *Bulletin, Lone Hand,* Melbourne *Punch* and one or two other Australian journals and counting himself lucky to be paid ten shillings for a drawing. He would have seized any offer of a salaried job worthy of his abilities, but for some reason editors went on ignoring him and he had grown sick of hope deferred.

Norman was delighted that Will and Ruby would be with him. He always found Will stimulating and original, and since they had tacitly agreed to forget the awkwardness over Katie there were no hard feelings between them. He also had a warm brotherly liking for Ruby, a shy and reticent young woman of exceptional beauty. She was twenty-four and had been living in Melbourne for seven or eight years, first with her brother Percy and later alone, while studying art and making do on what she could earn by commercial and journalistic work, supplemented by a few shillings from home whenever there was anything to spare at 'Lisnacrieve'. Percy had inherited the *Hawklet* page from his brothers, and now and then Ruby did it for him in the best Lindsay style. She also drew anything else that would earn a fee, including occasional illustrations for the *Lone Hand,* but her driving purpose was to develop her talent for fine pen and ink work. Like Norman, she was consumed by an almost religious passion for the thing she wanted to do. Her Daemon, like his, never let her rest or be content with what she accomplished.

Norman held his Sydney exhibition at the beginning of September and his Melbourne exhibition a few weeks later. If his pictures had not sold it would have played havoc with his plans: at the least he would have had to postpone the trip—he had paid his fare but he could not go off either empty in pocket or leaving nothing behind. But Sydney and Melbourne responded well. Both exhibitions sold out and he netted well over eight hundred pounds.

Will and Ruby took the train from Melbourne to Creswick near the end of the month and were married on 29 September in the Wesleyan church. They were back in Melbourne in time for the closing of Norman's exhibition on Monday 4 October, and all three of them boarded the Orient liner *Osterley* at Port Melbourne next day. Norman found a deck chair and sat watching the low and rather drab shores of Port Phillip Bay slide away into the afternoon mist. He had been working for months without lifting his head and he needed a spell. He had even kept on doing topical cartoons for the *Bulletin* until a week or two before sailing day. Now that the pressure was off he felt exhausted, almost light-headed, but a few days would put him right. The sea always worked wonders with him. The moment the hawsers were cast off he felt his anxieties slide from his shoulders.

The *Casanova* drawings, crated and packed to withstand the sea air, were already on their way to London. They would be waiting there when he arrived and then he would go out and try to find a publisher. Meanwhile he wanted to breathe the sea air and argue a thousand different points with Will Dyson. He also wanted to re-read at leisure a translation of the *Satyricon* of Petronius—for him, from the first time he read it, 'the greatest of novels'—which he had tossed into his bag at the last moment. It was a pleasant prospect.

Even on shipboard Norman could no more loaf than the world could stop turning. After a few days his fingers were itching for his pencil and sketchbook, and presently, unknown to themselves, scores of his fellow passengers became his models. The artist-critic Blamire Young once wrote that Norman's hands were 'so highly functioned that incessant occupation must be found for them'. Young went on:

> To compare great things with small, the case has something in common with the knitting needles of the tireless old lady that needs must be clicking no matter what happens. The stockings may do for John or for Willie—that's not the point. So long as there is no idle moment she is content.*

* Melbourne *Herald*, 27 December 1930.

12   Norman's studio in Sydney with 'General' Gordon, Norman, Rose, Doctor Lindsay and 'Creswick's fattest pub-keeper'

13   Norman in Bond Street, Sydney      14   Norman in his Sydney studio

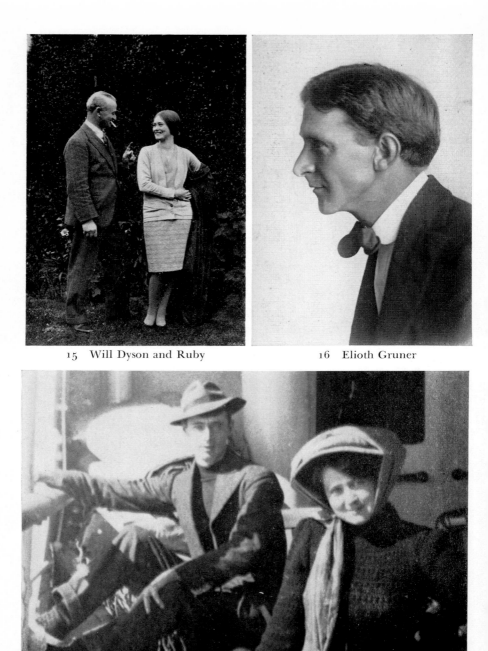

15  Will Dyson and Ruby          16  Elioth Gruner

17  Norman and Ruby on the ship going to England

When Norman went ashore at Colombo the colour of the place and the indolent grace of the people fired his imagination. He was very fast with the pencil in those days, through working at high speed to meet the demands of pictorial journalism, and could complete a full figure sketch in five minutes or less. This was invaluable when he took his stand in a Colombo street and set to work to sketch some of the wealth of material before his eyes. Dazzled and excited, he quickly discovered that, in return for the smallest silver coin in his pocket, any of the thronging natives would stand and pose for him. This was good, but word spread that a madman was giving money away and within a few minutes he was surrounded by a clamouring horde all willing to be sketched and demanding silver coins. Hemmed in by the press of would-be models, none of whom paid the smallest heed to his pleas to them to stand back, he was on the point of giving up and making his escape when George Meudell rescued him.

Norman had boarded the *Osterley* intending to dodge social entanglements but the ship had hardly left Port Melbourne when Meudell hailed him. To his own surprise, Norman, who remembered Meudell as a boon companion of Randolph Bedford but hardly knew him, found the noisy, boisterous, bouncing little man irresistible. A prosperous Melbourne stockbroker with international interests, he was equally at home in Boston, Madagascar, Paris, Cairo, Lisbon, London, Rome, Port of Spain, Berlin, Buenos Aires, Honolulu, and fifty other places. He was making his ninth or tenth world trip in the *Osterley* and was on jovial terms with everybody on board long before the liner left the Australian coast. A lively friendship sprang up between him and Norman. Perhaps it was the attraction of opposites, for Meudell was nearly twenty years older and the two had little in common beyond the accident that each had been born and had spent his early youth in a Victorian country town; or perhaps Norman responded to the quicksilver brain and the genuine warmth of heart behind Meudell's pushfulness, and Meudell to the defiant unorthodoxy of Norman's views.

Seeing Norman about to be overwhelmed that day in Colombo, Meudell went into action, somehow quieted the jostling mob, and brought order out of chaos in a few seconds. He was like a magician stilling the waves of the sea.

'Leave this to me, my boy', he said. 'Now which of these chaps do you want to sketch?'

In obedience to a word from Meudell any native chosen by Norman would step forward, take up any required pose, and patiently stand to be sketched, while the onlookers held back, chattering and chuckling, but never attempting to break ranks and disturb the work in hand. When the sketch was finished Meudell would pay the model off with a small

G

coin and a cheerful quip, then beckon forward the next subject for Norman's racing pencil.

'Anything special you'd like?' he asked.

'Yes', Norman said, on a wild impulse. 'I'd like to see a dwarf.'

Meudell's eyes travelled over the seething crowd, Grunting, he dived in among them and returned in a few seconds leading a tiny misshapen man by the elbow. Norman, who had never dared to hope for so perfect a specimen of a dwarf, sketched the poor little freak in a series of attitudes. Over the years he used variations of the Colombo dwarf in hundreds of pictures.

The ebullient Meudell's performance convinced Norman that here was no ordinary man. He had some power which cast a spell over illiterate natives speaking only a few words of English as readily as it conquered the men and women of his own world.

It worked no less well at Port Said. While Meudell acted as entrepreneur, Norman half-filled a sketchbook with studies of Egyptians picked out at random in the street.

'You know, George', he said, 'I'd like to make some nude studies'.

'Simple', said Meudell. 'Give me a minute.'

He came back with the address of a select brothel. Norman and he found their way to it and were ushered in and presented to the Madam, a massive and embellished lady who greeted them with regal dignity. Having supposed them to be clients for the recognized services of her house, she was taken aback when Meudell explained that they came in quest, not of sexual entertainment, but of subjects for his friend's artistic skill. Won over by Meudell's eloquence, she summoned three or four shapely girls and bade them parade in the nude while Norman made studies in his sketchbook. It was a cheerful interlude, with Meudell playfully slapping the squealing girls' bottoms and exchanging badinage with the Madam.

Norman and the Dysons left the *Osterley* at Naples. They wanted to see something of Italy and then go on to Marseilles by train and rejoin the ship there. Norman had been through and through the *Satyricon* since leaving Melbourne and the characters and atmosphere had captured his imagination as never before. A year or two earlier he had done a few experimental pen drawings based on episodes in the story, but he had packed the book for the journey to Europe only with the idea that it would be cheerful reading on the long lazy days at sea. Now, in Italy, he saw its possibilities as the medium for a major series of illustrations.

He had begun to lose some of his earlier enthusiasm for the *Memoirs of Casanova*. While recognizing it as a good racy tale by an impenitent rascal, he no longer considered it a work of genius; indeed he had reluctantly admitted to himself that Casanova's writings revealed a second-rate mind. While Norman had no intention of jettisoning the *Casanova* illustrations after all the work he had put into them, and especially since many of them were excellent of their kind, he knew that Petronius offered deeper and richer inspiration.

From Naples he and the Dysons made the short train trip to Pompeii and, as Norman explored the excavated city, studying the relics of a civilization which Petronius had known, he resolved to go to work on the *Satyricon* at once. Will and Ruby were soon tired of Pompeii and decided to move on to Rome. Norman told them he would join them there in a few days and, happy enough to be alone for the time being, got out his sketchbook and, leaving the Grand Hotel early every morning, prowled the ancient streets, making studies of the public baths, theatres, temples and villas until his wrist ached. Although the glory of the *Satyricon* lay, for him, not in the time and place of the events but in the doings and misdoings of Trimalchio, Encolpius, Ascyltos, Giton and the rest of Petronius's characters—so little different, in human essentials, from the people Norman knew in Sydney, Melbourne, and Creswick—he saw it as his duty to reconstruct the setting of their lives with absolute fidelity to truth. He had to be certain that the detail of his drawings was exact, from the fluting of a column down to the design of the tiles in a tesselated pavement.

It was hard labour. He did not find it inspiring. To stand in an amphitheatre over two thousand years old or to walk a street worn by sandalled feet in Nero's time gave him no sense of kinship with the storied past. Any page of Petronius could all in a moment transport him back to the great days of Rome but these ancient stones had no power over him. Tourists wandered through the excavations, guidebooks in hand, touching and exclaiming and marvelling. Norman would have liked to share their excitement, but he could not. He valued what he saw as indispensable and tangible reference material, and took copious pictorial notes of it, but it woke no sense of wonder in him.

He was working under another handicap also. He mentioned this in a letter to Lionel who had his hands full back in Sydney looking after Norman's affairs as well as his own. Having said how much he wished that 'dear old Joe' were there, Norman remarked that he had 'the most bloody attack of piles, and can only walk the ancient world in a feeble and decrepit manner'. He believed that sitting around on the cold hard stones of Pompeii while he sketched had brought on his trouble.

Norman reached London in the middle of November. Winter was little more than a month off and the air was dank and chill. He and the Dysons found rooms in Bloomsbury, and Norman shivered as he stood at his window looking along the street of identical grey narrow-gutted houses. An icy wind always seemed to be blowing when he went out. He was cold and miserable, and often wet. He wondered why the devil he had come.

After a few days they moved into a furnished studio flat at Hampstead. Although an improvement on Bloomsbury the flat was small for three people, and Norman had to sleep on an improvised bed in the studio. He did not mind that, but after a week of the meals Ruby cooked in the tiny kitchen he began to fear that he would starve to death. Ruby, who had trained herself to eat sparingly in her penurious Melbourne days, was determined not to spend a needless farthing on food and her idea of a dinner was half a small fish topped off with bread and jam. Norman was never a big eater and one of his maxims was 'No one can think clearly on a full belly' but Ruby was overdoing it. He wrote to Rose in Sydney telling her to hurry up and join him, then settled down at Hampstead to make the best of things until she arrived, eking out Ruby's spartan meals with an occasional lunch or dinner at a restaurant.

As soon as he found his bearings he called at George Meudell's office. The beaming little man pumped his hand, stopped work for the day, and led him out to see London. Wherever they went Meudell had friends and one turned out to be a director of London *Punch*, who knew Norman's *Bulletin* work. Norman was bidden to dine with Owen Seaman, the editor, E. V. Lucas, the assistant editor, and other *Punch* luminaries, and afterwards given the text of three jokes to illustrate. Although secretly irritated by the *Punch* people's attitude of condescension 'to a hireling from the colonial slums' he did the drawings which, according to Meudell, 'shone like a phosphorescent watch among a lot of grandfather's clocks'. The reward was not commensurate. Norman went along to Meudell's office and burst in on him, waving a *Punch* cheque for three guineas.

'This microscopic offering must be spent quickly', he chortled, 'before it goes bad'.

They telephoned Will Dyson and another Australian, Ernest Buley, who was editing one of Lord Northcliffe's newspapers, and the four met at Pinoli's restaurant, in Wardour Street, and, as Meudell put it, 'knocked down the cheque amidst loud and prolonged applause'.* Norman had not come to London to break into pictorial journalism, and the miserly *Punch* cheque fortified him in that resolve.

He was pushing on with the *Satyricon* illustrations and wondering how best to seek a publisher for them when he had a piece of luck. The

* The details of this episode are from Meudell's book *The Pleasant Career of a Spendthrift* (London, c. 1929), p. 234, supplemented by information from Norman Lindsay.

One of Norman's popular animal cartoons

*British Australasian Weekly*, which specialized in news of Australians and New Zealanders visiting Britain, printed a paragraph about him in its issue of 2 December. This mentioned his interest in the *Satyricon*. Within a few days he had a visitor: one Ralph Straus, a young man of substantial private means who was already making a reputation as an author and literary critic. They had met two years before when Straus was visiting Australia, and now he told Norman that he had a hand-press in the cellar of his home and intended publishing de luxe editions as a hobby. Might he see any of the *Satyricon* drawings? Norman produced all those he had ready. Straus was greatly taken with them and said he would be delighted to go ahead. He would need a hundred illustrations.

'When can you have the rest finished?' he asked.

Norman made a rapid mental calculation. 'In five months', he said. 'Perhaps less.'

'I'll get it under way', Straus said and they sealed the agreement with a handshake.

Norman disliked most Jews and in later years his anti-Semitism grew into an obsession, but his respect and liking for Straus never waned. There was good reason for it. Straus not only produced a handsome edition of the *Satyricon* but also went to some trouble to see that Norman met London's literary and artistic élite.

When Rose reached London in March 1910 Norman met her at Tilbury. He piloted her to a red-tiled studio cottage he had found in the Hampstead region, and she took over the housekeeping while he slaved away at the *Satyricon*. He was working at top pressure and Petronius ruled the days and nights. It was not only a matter of sitting and drawing; now and then he had to spend days in the British Museum or some other storehouse of information checking a seemingly insignificant fact. He had a hard search to settle the pattern of the razor used in Petronius's day. In the end he unearthed evidence that it was a direct ancestor of the modern safety razor, with the blade so poised that it lay flat against the barber's palm, which acted as the guard. Straus was well satisfied with the progress but Norman found the going hard. Unhappy in England and homesick for Australia, he lacked inspiration or any real desire to work, and had to flog himself to keep at it. He felt the *Satyricon* illustrations were second-rate compared with his best Australian pen drawings, and writhed under the sense that he was doing less than justice to the greatest novel he knew.

He could not complain that the Dysons interrupted him. They were living hardly a mile away but a fortnight after Rose's arrival they had still not noticed her presence. Norman took her to call on them one Sunday afternoon. The atmosphere was bleak, and Norman and Rose soon left. They understood. Will and Ruby, being now legally and respectably married, were fearful of compromising themselves in the eyes of their English friends by consorting with a pair of reprobates living in sin. Their disapproval was ironical, since they had been lovers before they married, but Norman did not laugh. When he and Rose got home he sat down at once and wrote Will a scorching letter, then hurried out and posted it. Norman wrote more letters barbed with defamation, mockery, sarcasm and insult than perhaps any other man of his time— it was his way of assuaging spiritual wounds. Only a few of these ever reached their destination because, when Rose understood him better, she always tried to lay hands on any particularly explosive letter and keep it out of the mail. Norman was happy so long as he believed it had gone; indeed catharsis was achieved once he had written his fury down. Rose always said she intended making a book of these missives and publishing them one day under the title *Norman Lindsay's Unposted Letters*. It would have been a shattering work.

Will Dyson called on Norman and Rose full of self-righteous indigna-tion. The meeting was stormy, with Norman hurling recriminations and Will hurling them back. It finished with Will gritting, 'Oh, yes! Every-thing's got to go your way! You're a completely selfish and self-engrossed bastard. You haven't any use for people unless they serve your ends.'

He strode out. It was years before he and Norman met again, and neither ever quite forgot the bitter words spoken that day.

Even when winter passed and the trees burst into leaf Norman found London drab. The great city went into mourning when King Edward VII died in May, but Norman hardly noticed it—he was too busy with his own affairs. His feeling of not belonging, then or later, went deep and formed the basis of an opinion which he held for the rest of his life. This was that any creative man's powers shrink if he is transplanted from his native environment to a different one. Norman's undoubtedly shrank in London.

He almost envied his brother Bert, who arrived from Australia in a later ship and at once took London to his heart. Bert had gone to Europe hoping to work as a dress designer, but how or even where he lived was never clear to Norman and Rose; Bert had a secretive streak and all he ever told them was that he was sharing a flat with a man who designed women's hats. More or less overnight he blossomed into a sartorially impeccable man-about-town. He had the right clothes for any and every occasion, an unobtrusively aristocratic air, an irreproachable accent. It was an astonishing transformation for a man in early middle age who had spent all his working life as a bank clerk in Australian country towns, where the most fashionable social event of the year was the Country Women's Association Ball or the Cricket Club's Whist Drive.

The Lindsay boys had always known that Bert, with his delicate airs, precise manners, sharp tongue and dandyism, was an alien among them. London emphasized the immensity of the difference.

Norman was glad to see him. He was unbending by nature, but Norman suspected that the heart beating under the modish waistcoat was warmer than most people guessed. Bert did not hide his pleasure in having Norman and Rose's studio cottage as a place of call, but he screwed up his nose in distaste at the sight of Norman's casual jackets and careless trousers.

'This will never do, my dear chap', he said. 'London isn't Sydney or Melbourne. You can't dress like a tramp here and hope to be accepted by people of standing. They'd send you to the servants' entrance.'

Norman said that he didn't care a damn what they did—they could take him as he was or go to the devil! This was not altogether true, because he was trying to make a good impression on publishers and literary people, and he submitted when Bert, insisting that he must fit himself out in decent style, led him to a Savile Row tailor. The wardrobe included, among other things, a cutaway coat, striped grey trousers, spats, gloves, a walking stick, a bowler hat, and a top hat. Norman managed everything else with aplomb, even the bowler hat, but the topper was too much. Bert declared that it was an indispensable passport to London Society but when Norman tried it on and looked in the mirror what he saw there reminded him of an organ grinder's monkey. He never brought himself to wear it. Whenever he was invited to some formal affair he arrived and left by cab carrying the topper in his hand and hoping he looked fairly nonchalant. 'My head', he once said, 'is not adapted for the wearing of belltoppers, but it is perfectly adapted for the wearing of a fez'. On this score, he regretted that England was not a Moslem country.

People, not clothes, were the real trouble. To him, most Englishmen seemed to be hedged about by innumerable social inhibitions which discouraged any close approach. He was almost tempted to wonder if the fault was in himself when his father arrived in London as a ship's doctor and, without trying, made a small army of friends in a few days. Doctor Lindsay, whose Creswick practice had all but faded away, had taken the job for the sake of the trip—his love of the sea was no less strong than Norman's. He had the faculty of engaging total strangers in conversation and winning their liking at once. His ability to sweep aside barriers of class and nationality was the fruit of an effortless and spontaneous spirit of amiability. Norman longed to be able to duplicate it but couldn't, any more than his father could have duplicated *Pollice Verso*. Norman had a rich and compelling charm but, like other of his talents, it worked better in his own country than anywhere else, while his father's charm took oceans and continents in its stride.

Norman met scores of celebrities but found common ground with only two or three. Men as disparate as the poet Henry Newbolt, the artist William Nicholson, and the best-selling novelist Robert Hichens woke no glow in him; nor, it was plain, did he in them. At the Fabian Club he heard Bernard Shaw speak but did not meet him or wish to; Norman thought Shaw 'a buffoon, spouting about himself in terms of exhibitionistic self-laudation'. On another visit to the Fabian Club he heard Sidney and Beatrice Webb forecasting the Socialist Utopia. Being a confirmed believer in the doctrine of individual responsibility, he found it hard not to spring to his feet and denounce them; he thought them 'snake-blooded'. He was never tolerant of ideas which ran counter to his own, nor at pains to hide his impatience of those who voiced them.

Max Beerbohm was one of the few pillars of the English aesthetic Establishment with whom he formed a warm friendship. He had long admired Beerbohm as a caricaturist and writer, and when somebody introduced them at the Savile Club he discovered an equal liking for Beerbohm as a man. Beerbohm evidently reciprocated Norman's good opinion, and the two had several meetings. When Beerbohm went off to Italy, for a stay which lasted until 1912, Norman felt that a brilliant light had gone out in London.

His sorest disappointment was the discovery that, intellectually, England was even narrower and more straitlaced than Australia. The reek of prurience was everywhere. Thomas Bowdler, the purifier of Shakespeare and Gibbon, had been dead for eighty-odd years but his soul went marching on and free expression was a purely relative term. Norman was soon convinced that publishers, librarians and booksellers either approved the apparatus of repression and its destructive influence or were too craven to fight it. It was true that Ralph Straus had not rejected or questioned a single illustration for the *Satyricon*, although Norman had done some which were startling by the standards of the time. But Straus was only one bold man among a host of timid ones, and anyway Norman could not look to him to provide a regular and adequate publishing outlet. Being a mere amateur in the field of de luxe editions, Straus had his hands full with the *Satyricon*.

The *Casanova* drawings had travelled well. Having uncrated them and found they had suffered no harm on their long sea journey, Norman began making the rounds of the publishers. They were all cordial. They praised the drawings, and fairly marvelled that an artist who had spent all his life in Australia should have succeeded in capturing so faithfully the atmosphere of Casanova's world, with its swagger, knavery, profligacy and violence. But did Mr Lindsay understand what he was asking? No publisher would dare to issue an edition of the *Memoirs of Casanova* in England. Why, it was only a year since a privately printed translation had been seized and destroyed! Any publisher who so flouted public opinion would most likely find himself serving a term in prison. And, my dear Mr Lindsay, the artist who drew the pictures would in all probability be in the next cell! John Lane, whom he disliked, lunched him and dined him and offered him commissions. So did William Heinemann, whom he liked—the short, squat, thick-lipped Heinemann, with his bald head and eternal cigar, had an engaging directness of manner and speech. While proposing that he should illustrate *Othello* and Homer's *Odyssey*, Heinemann had some reservations about the quality of his work. He saw Norman as 'an interesting young fellow with a great deal of talent', but thought that 'in order to do anything which is going to count he certainly wants a few years at a first-class Academy—the sort of training he can't get in Australia'.* Nothing came of it in the end. For Norman also had reservations; he believed he would have to make too many concessions to public prudishness.

The problem of *Casanova* continued to plague him. Despondent, telling himself that he might as well tear the damned drawings up and throw the pieces in the Thames, he was walking along the Strand after an abortive interview with yet another publisher when a familiar voice hailed him. It belonged to Hugh D. McIntosh, who, having set up as a fight promoter in London and Paris, was more prosperous than ever. Norman told him the story. McIntosh had never published a book, nor read a word of Casanova's *Memoirs* or seen the drawings, but those were insignificant details—he always worked by intuition and he was more often right than wrong, even though some of his bad guesses were disastrous. He considered Norman the world's greatest black and white artist and believed that any book he illustrated must be a hit.

'I'll publish it', he said. 'We'll show these Pommy bastards how it ought to be done. Now, where do we start?'

He was like a huge wind. Norman's spirits soared. He even began to like London, or at any rate to find it tolerable. When McIntosh saw the illustrations he blazed with enthusiasm. He'd publish editions in French, German, Italian and Spanish, as well as English, he said. It would be a bigger money-maker than the Burns-Johnson fight. He strode up and down his office juggling with promotional ideas which would sell tens of thousands of copies. Norman found himself believing it. McIntosh had the gift of hypnotizing those about him as well as himself.

He whisked Norman and Rose off to Paris and talked with French publishers and printers and block-makers. He had to use an interpreter because neither he nor Norman spoke French. Norman had worked at the language for some months under a teacher in Australia, in preparation

* Letter to T. C. Lothian, at that time Norman Lindsay's Melbourne agent, 7 February 1911.

for his European travels, and from London he wrote letters in passable French to Lionel for practice. But he was almost gawkishly shy of trying to speak French in France, nor could he understand it as the French spoke it, and in Paris he never uttered a French syllable. Lionel, seemingly without much effort, could master any language in a few months; he taught himself to speak, read and write in Spanish, French and Italian, as well as to read in German. Norman could only marvel at such linguistic wizardry.

Norman liked Paris no better than London. He believed that, artistically, both cities were degenerate. The weight of the Post-Impressionist movement was being felt, and the names of Cézanne, Van Gogh and Gauguin were being spoken in the hushed tones hitherto reserved for Norman's artistic gods such as Rubens, Titian and Rembrandt. It made him splutter curses. His first encounter with Post-Impressionism had occurred in Italy, on the way to England; Will Dyson and he had both been baffled and unbelieving at what they had seen. Now, in Paris, he went to another Post-Impressionist exhibition and was horrified. 'I could smell the human jungle in it', he said. To him, the Post-Impressionists were 'a mob of modern Hottentots', striking at the very heart of his aesthetic creed. For he was not an art rebel in any technical sense. While in revolt against nonconformist puritanism and the code of written and unwritten laws which forbade the artist to take his subject-matter from any aspect of life, he was remorseless in his antipathy toward technical revisionists. The licence which the Post-Impressionists claimed to distort, enlarge, condense or otherwise edit the forms of nature to suit their purpose was, to him, blasphemy. He believed that art must be based, for subject, on what he called 'the whole drama of life', and, for technique, on hard-won craftsmanship. He saw the English academic painters of his childhood and youth as stodgy frumps in what they painted but admired the skill with which many of them painted it. He held that the best of them—Solomon J. Solomon in *Ajax and Cassandra*, for example—were excellent craftsmen, and that to craftsmanship of that order painting must return or give up the ghost. Although lamenting the Victorians' sexless nudes and other evidences of surrender to moral taboos, he acclaimed them for mastering the technique of their trade.

Perhaps nothing else about Europe so shocked him as the realization that art standards which he had always taken for granted were being discounted. At that time he refused to believe that Post-Impressionism was more than a passing fad, but the discovery that it had gained even a temporary footing riled him.

His distaste for London hardened as the year drew on. In September,

while in the grip of a cold which had plagued him off and on for
months, he wrote to Lionel saying 'I do not require to live in this land'.
He then went on to describe how, looking out of his bathroom window
that morning, 'I saw the filthy grey fog creeping over the house tops, and
I felt the chill in my bones and I said "Let me get out of this place
quickly" '.

The weather was only part of it, and not the greater part; the roots
of his antipathy went deeper than the shortcomings of the English
climate. Impatient for success, he was disappointed by what he saw as
London's indifference to him. He had done not badly for a comparative
newcomer—all 250 copies of the *Satyricon*, beautifully printed on hand-
made paper and each numbered and signed by him and Straus, sold
out in a few days and the response of connoisseurs was flattering—but
recognition on the scale he had hoped for was slow in coming. At least
he thought it slow, and told himself that England would never accept
the kind of work he wanted to do, or 'the concept of life that was then
maturing at the back of my mind'. Since he had joined the *Bulletin* in
1901 his technical skill had called forth almost nothing but eulogy in
Australia, even from those who thundered against the sexual frankness
and pagan spirit of his serious work. Now, like many another talented
man, he was discovering that London takes its own time about choosing
favourite sons or stepsons. He found it hard to accommodate his mind
to the notion that he might have to spend years proving himself before
he won a solid reputation. It was one of the paradoxes of his nature
that he had a capacity for limitless perseverance in working out any
technical problem of self-expression but little in conquering apathy or
antagonism to him and his work. The sense of rejection left an
indelible scar; he never openly admitted as much, but it was the root
of his implacable lifelong hostility to England and the English.

Although he was no longer seeing the Dysons he knew that Will,
while selling drawings here and there and earning just enough for a
breadline existence, was having an even harder struggle for recognition.
This knowledge gave Norman no comfort on his own account. If Will
wished to settle down to an endurance test that was his affair; Norman
had no intention of doing it. After all, Will had no real alternative. His
Australian reputation was hardly worth mentioning, except among a
handful of perceptive people; if he were to pack up and go home he
would have to  knuckle down once more to the ill-paid freelance grind,
so for him London spelt make or break. Norman was under no such
handicap. He could go back to Australia and pick up his career where
he had put it down—his Australian reputation, both as a fine artist and as
a pictorial journalist, was intact. Or so he hoped. As time went by and
he heard nothing from the *Bulletin*, he became less sure. Macleod,

Edmond and the others seemed to have forgotten him. What the devil did it mean? At any rate he could not stand another European winter. McIntosh was pushing on with arrangements to publish *Casanova* but even his cyclonic spirit could hasten operations only so much; having put the finished drawings into his hands, Norman could do nothing to help and he had no inclination to hang about London in the months which must pass before production was under way.

Determined to quit this, to him, benumbing and strangulating corner of the world as soon as possible, he hesitated only over where he should go. He was damned if he would cable the *Bulletin* and ask for his old job back. How the dull, stolid and stodgy Macleod, as Norman thought of him, would gloat over that! It would have been different if Archibald had still wielded any influence, but he had ended all close relations with the *Bulletin* after suffering a breakdown which had put him in Callan Park mental hospital for a time. Anyway, Norman reminded himself, he did not need the *Bulletin*. He had an open invitation to go to America and work for *Harper's Magazine* on terms which would bring him, by Australian standards, a princely income. A *Harper's* editor on a visit to London some months earlier had commissioned him to do two drawings. *Harper's* had liked them—particularly a typically Lindsayesque decoration for the lyric of an old ballad, '*Ladies of Spain*'—and paid him fifty pounds each for them; they had also urged him to move to New York and work for *Harper's* at the dollar equivalent of £100 a drawing.

This was flattering but his eyes and mind were fixed on Australia. After some agonized soul-searching, however, he concluded that the *Bulletin* did not want him, and was on the point of booking passages to America for Rose and himself when a letter reached him from Macleod. It had been lying in London for many weeks but a silly mischance had kept it from reaching Norman. All his resentment and anxiety melted away when he read it. He could forget America. Macleod pressed him to come back as soon as possible. His salary would be only a fraction of the money he could earn as a *Harper's* artist but that was of no consequence— all he asked was enough to pay his way. And, in his heart, he doubted that he would have been any better contented in America than in Europe.

Exile had taught him one thing: he could never be happy as an ex-patriate, cut off from his most vital sources of inspiration. He knew that the sensory and mental impressions which he had absorbed into his being in childhood and youth were the life-blood of his creative faculty, and away from the Australian environment he was no more than a competent journeyman. He hurried off and booked passages in the *Osterley*, leaving for Australia in the middle of November. Now he could bear with fog, rain, sad skies, and even a chronic cold in the head.

His one deep regret about leaving London was that he also had to leave the Science Museum, in South Kensington. He moved Rose and himself to rooms at South Kensington and spent nearly all his time at the Museum in his last weeks, studying the wonderful Ship Model collection and making copious pictorial notes on the fine points of marine architecture down the ages. He even succeeded in having himself admitted to the technical workshops where specialists built new ship models and refitted old ones to go into the museum's showcases. Whatever his strangeness among English intellectuals he was at home among these men; they accepted him as one of themselves and made him free of their world and its lore. To him, a sailing ship had always been one of the most inspired creations of man's mind and hands. Any wind ship—an East Indiaman, a Tudor galleon, a Greek galley, or any other—was a magical thing endowed with a beauty all its own which, having reached perfection in the clipper ship, perished when steam ousted sail.

In the Science Museum his love of sailing ships gained a new height. He did not go to the museum to amass knowledge which would equip him to build ship models; the idea did not even cross his mind then. Ships often figured in his drawings and anything he could learn about them was valuable, but it was his sheer love of ships, above all, that set him delving into the inexhaustible mysteries of the subject. He revelled in what he was doing for its own sake. If London had given him nothing else, this would have made everything worth while.

He could have spent years in the museum but November came and he had to be off. Cold rain was sifting down out of a grey sky when he and Rose boarded the *Osterley* at Tilbury, but he was in cheerful spirits; the time of exile was over. Before leaving London he had got out the top hat which he had never succeeded in wearing and stood it on the floor, then jumped on it. It was his way of saying farewell.

# 5

# Retreat to the Mountains
# 1911-14

The *Osterley* tied up at Port Melbourne on a cloudy morning which threatened to turn showery. Norman was a little disappointed. Since it was the second day of January he had hoped for a hard blue sky and air pulsing with summer heat, perhaps with a faint tang of bushfire smoke borne from the hinterland by a north wind. He believed that was what he needed to restore his lost energy. The trouble was that he felt tired all the time; when he thought of it, he seemed to have been tired for months. Anyway, he told himself, he would soon find health again now that he was home. It was only a matter of getting the damned English fog out of his lungs and the damned English damp out of his bones.

He got off the ship at Port Melbourne and left Rose to go on to Sydney alone. The ever-helpful Lionel had rented a cottage for them at Artarmon, and Rose could move in there at once. In Melbourne Norman saw Ted Dyson and other old friends, and caught an afternoon train for Creswick. The little town had not changed. He met two or three acquaintances on the short walk from the railway station and stopped to shake hands and pass the time of day, then went on to 'Lisnacrieve'. They gave him a fond welcome there but thought he looked—even for him who never carried any spare flesh—haggard and wasted.

'You need feeding up, old man', Mary said. 'Couldn't you stay for a week or two?'

'I wish I could, Mame', he told her. It was not true because he was longing to get to Sydney and go to work again, but he said it to please Mary and his mother. 'I'll be as fit as a fighting-cock once I get some sunshine and clean air.'

He believed it but he was wrong. To be sure, the excitement of his arrival in Sydney was a powerful stimulant and buoyed him up for the

95

first week or two. The *Bulletin* team were overjoyed to have him back; even Livingston Hopkins unbent and shook hands with an arid kind of warmth. Lionel (who was once described by Sir Robert Menzies as 'a master of the art of divine and disordered conversation') submerged him in a flood of talk, interrupted only by cries from one or the other of 'Good old Joe!' and 'Wonderful to see you, Joe!' But once the emotional flurry died down Norman again felt slack and listless. Damn it, what was the matter with him? He'd have to do something to lift himself out of it!

He was spared one worry. Soon after he had left for Europe Katie had let the Lavender Bay house and, gathering up her three boys, gone to live in Brisbane. Most of the other Parkinsons were already there and Katie wanted to be with them; she needed some kind of substitute for her broken marriage. Jack Elkington had found a senior medical post with the Queensland Government, and he and Mary led the way from Melbourne, taking old Mrs Parkinson with them and drawing the others in their wake. Katie, lonely and unhappy, had nothing to bind her to Sydney, and in Brisbane she was under the shadow of the imperious Mary, which gave her a sense of being protected. Sometimes she and the boys lived in a rented house, sometimes in a boarding-house. They never seemed to be long in one place before Katie packed up and moved on to another. The routine of their existence was restless, makeshift and purposeless but in time it became a settled way of life.

In Sydney Norman, refusing to admit that he was ill, plunged into work at once. His first *Bulletin* cartoon after his homecoming appeared on 19 January and showed he had lost none of his journalistic verve. Over the title *Sleeping At His Homework*, it depicted Australia as a small boy slumbering with his head on his study table while the menacing figure of a sword-wielding Asian loomed above his chair. In the next issue of the *Bulletin*, on 26 January, Norman did the cartoonlets as well as the main cartoon. Hop, who had carried the burden of the topical cartooning while Norman was overseas, was ready to take life easier; he was nearing his middle sixties, financially comfortable, and no longer driven by professional ambition. Although he went on turning out cartoons with some regularity until seven or eight months before the First World War broke out, his gradual act of abdication dated from soon after Norman's return.

The well-planned arrangement for Hop to step aside would probably have moved faster if Norman had not fallen ill; or, more precisely, if he had not surrendered to the illness which had attacked him in London and steadily strengthened its hold. He clung as long as he could to the illusion that Australian sunlight and air would cure him. Always fatigued, constantly battling against feverish colds, and often racked by pain, he yet drove himself to work. His cartoons and other drawings for the *Bulletin*

18   *Witches' Sabbath* and the next Plate, *Port of Heaven*, are included
to illustrate Norman's remarkable line technique. In the Preface
to his *Selected Pen Drawings* he said of this:

> Putting draughtsmanship aside as understood, the major difficulty
> in pen drawing is tone. Most pen artists have sought a solution to
> it by the crosshatch, a slovenly device, destructive to all textures but
> its own. From my earliest years I detested it, seeking to substitute

(cont. on next Plate)

19   *Port of Heaven* (cont. from previous Plate)

for it pen strokes running in unison, thick or thin, as the tonal
value dictated. One may handle that method well enough in small
spaces while the arm rests on the table, giving free play only to
the wrist, as in writing. But it limits the stroke to a radius of only
about four inches. To cover a wider space, one must lift the arm
from the table and swing it from the elbow. This I accomplished
after hard practice.

But the disadvantage here is that this method keeps one too close
to the drawing to oversee its whole tonal mass; and to accomplish
that, it was necessary to work at arm's length when the drawing was
a large one. With practice, I acquired an equal control over my
shoulder muscles as those of wrist and elbow.

Finally, to make a tonal unity of a pen drawing, it is essential to
pay as much attention to the white line as to the black line. By the
white line I mean the space between the black lines. Even the
deepest blacks must have either hair-thin white lines, or minute
white dots, spaced in them, else the black will become opaque, as
when laid on with a brush.

and his illustrations for the *Lone Hand* bore no stamp of a sick man's hand. Nor did his serious work At that time he finished a pen drawing, *The Argument*, one of a set of illustrations to his beloved Rabelais; seen either as a re-creation of the French Renaissance atmosphere or as a tribute to the rollicking irreverence and bawdy wisdom of the immortal work, it is among his best pen drawings although he was miserably ill when he did it. A less stubborn man would have called for medical help weeks earlier but he refused to heed either Rose's urgings or the promptings of his body. While he could climb out of bed, hold a pen, and stumble from one room to another he would not give in.

Seeing doctors as the inheritors of a medieval cult of sorcery, he had no faith in their power to cure, or even to relieve, the ills of the flesh. He insisted that only people whose bodies were worn out by age ever died of disease—younger men and women died, not of disease but of the depression of mind which disease caused. The essence of his belief was that the mind could command any disease except syphilis and that most ailments ran their course and went away if left to themselves. Convinced of this, he struggled on until his weakened body forced him to collapse into bed and stay there. Rose was distracted with worry, and suddenly Norman found the Artarmon cottage swarming with doctors. Too weary to resist, he let them do what they would. One diagnosed appendicitis, another pleurisy. There was no escape for him. He was whisked off to hospital and operated on to free his lungs of fluid.

'He's about as bad as he can be but don't let him know', the specialist heading the medical squad told Rose.

Within two or three days he was demanding pens, ink and paper and, while serious drawing was out of the question, he went on with his *Bulletin* and *Lone Hand* work. The doctors knew it was a strain but concluded that enforced idleness would be worse for such a man. He was in hospital for three months and nearly every week he drew a full-page cartoon as well as a stream of illustrations for jokes, articles, stories, serials and verse, an occasional bush animal feature, and miscellaneous oddments. None of these items looked as if it had come from a sick-bed; even one full-page cartoon which he drew when his temperature was hovering around 105° lacked nothing of zest and assurance.

He was in danger for some weeks and Katie was summoned from Brisbane. Leaving Ray and Phil with the Elkingtons, she hurried to Sydney with young Jack. Her first visit to Norman's bedside emphasized the distance between them. They had not seen each other for eighteen months but Jack, who went to the hospital with his mother, remembered long afterwards the deadly flatness of that meeting.

'Hello, Katie', Norman said.

'Hello, Norman', she replied. 'How are you feeling?'

H

There was nothing between them but the surface amiability of acquaintances. It was like that all through the week that Katie and Jack stayed in Sydney. They did not meet Rose; she went to the hospital in the afternoons, and Katie and Jack in the mornings. When Norman was out of immediate danger they took the train back to Brisbane. To linger would have been pointless.

Rose had to play a part as the time for Norman to leave hospital approached. The doctors had told her that he was threatened with tuberculosis and might not live. They thought the humid air of Sydney would be dangerous to his enfeebled lungs and recommended her to take him to the Blue Mountains, the rumpled upsurge of highlands, gouged and furrowed by the rains of countless winters like an old man's face, which bars the way to the west. Rose found a cottage at Leura and rented it, then told Norman they were going to live there for six months. She did not mention tuberculosis; she feared that if he knew of it he would let go his hold on life. His old friend Archibald, who had completely recovered from the mental breakdown which had laid him aside some years earlier, called at the hospital in his chauffeur-driven Daimler and took Norman to Leura. The seventy-mile drive tired him but his eyes lighted when he looked about the cottage and saw all his things—his drawing-table, his pens and brushes and inks, his reference books, even a half-finished ship model which he had started at Artarmon. He was, for him, tractable even when Rose came with a hypodermic syringe to inject mysterious substances into his blood-stream. It was just some medical nonsense, he supposed, and would probably do no harm even if it did no good. The injections were against tuberculosis but he did not press Rose with questions. If he had, she would have found some way of putting him off.

He settled down at Leura supposing that he would be in the mountains only until he recovered his strength, but except for a few years in the 1930s they were to be his home for the rest of his life.

The doctors had told him to do no work. They might as well have told the grass to stop growing. For him, the daily quantum of work was a sacramental offering to his Daemon. He had the common sense to realize, however, that it would be some months before he could again charge forward at the old reckless gait, and by an effort of will he put a curb on himself.

The weekly cartoon for the *Bulletin* laid no great weight on him; James Edmond sent him an outline by letter and he would finish the cartoon in a morning or an afternoon, then put it on the train for Sydney. The rest of his *Bulletin* and *Lone Hand* drawings involved little manual and less mental effort. There were still many empty hours, and he finished his ship model and, feeling reasonably pleased with, it, started a new one, this time of Captain Cook's *Endeavour*. He did not count ship models as work, either then or later. Where other men went fishing or played bowls or climbed mountains, he modelled ships. He once said, 'I really made them for the same reason that Harold Skimpole ate roast lamb. Because he liked roast lamb.' Modelling ships was a way of relaxing his mind and nerves, and at the same time of paying his tribute to a vanishing age of maritime history.

He spent many hours at Leura in a secondary and less exacting but also highly skilled pastime: playing marbles. His opponent was Rose's young brother, Ben Soady, who was making an extended stay with them. Although Ben was an expert either at Big Ring or Little Ring, Norman held his own. He had not played marbles since his small-boy days at Creswick but he soon recovered his touch. When he finished a session holding more marbles than he had started with, he knew hardly less satisfaction than when he put the last pen-stroke to the *Bulletin* cartoon of the week.

The lease of the Leura cottage ran out after six months and Rose found a house at Faulconbridge, fifteen miles nearer Sydney but still high in the Blue Mountains. Mountain air and the meals Rose cooked had already worked wonders with Norman. He was eighteen or twenty pounds heavier than when he had left hospital and—although still a lean man as nature had made him, mostly sinew, bone and muscle—no longer tight-drawn and cadaverous with the stamp of early death on him. Luckily, he liked the mountains and did not hanker after Sydney; if need be, he could catch a train and be in the *Bulletin* office two hours later, and back home the same day.

There was plenty of land around the Faulconbridge place and he brought two horses up from Sydney, and Rose and he started riding again. He soon same to know the country near Faulconbridge well, and nothing drew him like the neighbouring township of Springwood. It was small and sleepy, just Honeysett's general store, a blacksmith's shop and a huddle of cottages, perched twelve hundred feet above sea-level on the eastern face of the Blue Mountains. He fell into the habit of riding that way, and one day, perhaps two miles from the township, he stumbled on a low one-storey cottage with bow windows and a red-tiled roof, standing in the bush beside a dusty rutted track made by the wheels of woodcutters' carts. There was no other house in sight.

Tethering the black mare, Mary-Ann, he climbed the post-and-rail fence and walked up to make a closer inspection. The four-roomed cottage was empty and the blinds were lowered, but the weather-beaten walls were sound, and as far as he could see there was nothing wrong that could not be put right. He strolled around the forlorn and unkempt garden, which was heavily overgrown, then tramped all over the rest of the grounds. The more he saw the better he liked it. Most of it was unspoilt bushland, harsh and gaunt and unyielding but beautiful to his eye. The scrub was as tall as a man in places and would take some clearing. Hundreds of native trees and shrubs—bloodwood, orange gum, grass-tree, juniper wattle, Sydney peppermint, red honeysuckle, grevillea, Sydney red gum, tea tree—were scattered over the grounds, their leaves rustling in the afternoon wind. They had the deceptively indolent air of slouching bushmen, and he felt at home among them, like one who finds himself among old friends. Walking on, he came to a deep, yawning gully, well back from the cottage. He stood on the edge of the plunging cliff, looking out across the bush which marched away into the blue haze, ridge after ridge rolling into the distance like an endless procession of long wind-tossed ocean swells. It came to him that this was what he had been looking for without knowing it, and that here he wanted to make his home.

That evening he told Rose about the place by the woodcutters' track and said they ought to try and buy it. He had no idea if they could afford it—he did not even know what their savings amounted to or if they had any savings at all. He had always detested bank statements and business affairs, and since returning from England had pushed everything of that kind into Rose's lap and made it clear to her that she had better not bother him with it. It was a piece of luck that, although Rose had no more commercial training than Norman, her business acumen was hardly less remarkable in its way than his artistic talent.

They rode out together next day and looked at the cottage. A sombre and eccentric Irishman, Paddy Ryan, had built it and given it the strength of a small fortress so that the wildest mountain storms would not shake it. Rose liked the place and, seeing its possibilities, wasted no time in clinching the purchase of the cottage and the forty-two acres on which it stood. The price was £500. This was fantastically low, but it was all they had. The timber floors turned out to be riddled with white ants and had to be ripped out and replaced before Norman and Rose could move in. They did not grumble about that. They knew they were never likely to make a better bargain.

Norman grew stronger as each month went by. By the time 1912 was half gone he was telling himself that he had never felt fitter, and was once again working as hard as ever. Although Springwood was less than fifty miles from Sydney, the city seemed nearly a world away. That suited Norman. He had no wish to go back and bury himself in that human rabbit warren. He missed the Harbour and the ships, but little else, and his friends knew where to find him when they wanted him. His mind was clearer here; there were no conflicting currents to muddy one's train of thought. And when some piece of work he had set his heart on went wrong he did not mope over it. He simply thrust it aside and pressed on with something else.

He lost no sleep even over *Casanova*. He had left England never doubting that Hugh D. McIntosh would produce a de luxe edition worthy of the illustrations. As a boxing and theatrical promoter McIntosh was flamboyant and showy, but he was a man of rare if untutored intelligence. All his preparations for publishing *Casanova* had revealed unfaltering good taste; Norman had been able to find no flaw in them. Then, without warning, the enterprise collapsed. An ill-advised stock exchange venture brought McIntosh to the verge of bankruptcy and sent him hurrying home to Australia to rebuild his fortunes. He handed the illustrations back, saying that *Casanova* would have to wait until the financial sky cleared. Norman told him not to worry—there was plenty of time. Indeed Norman was not deeply disappointed. For the time being he was a little sick of *Casanova*. For one thing he had been jarred by an English critic writing on the *Satyricon*, who had dismissed him as merely an accomplished illustrator. He chafed under the implication that he was no more than a portrayer of other men's ideas, a begetter of pictorial echoes of Petronius, Rabelais, Boccaccio, Nietzsche or one or another of the great imaginative or philosophical writers. He did not agree that most of his serious pen drawings were illustrations in any narrow sense; he saw them as creative works in their own right, not subordinate but complementary to the writings which had superficially inspired them. The best of them appeared to him to constitute a statement of his personal creed: his worship of the human body, his antagonism to Christianity, and his militancy in the cause of individualism. Although he had no intention of changing his course under pressure from any critic, he yet decided that it was time he produced a new work which, like *Pollice Verso*, would demonstrably owe nothing to any concept of life but his own. An idea had been nagging at his mind for some time and he settled down and worked hard over it. The result was *The Crucified Venus*. It showed a tonsured monk nailing a naked woman to a cross silhouetted against a dark and foreboding sky, while a mob of ranting ecclesiastics and leering sensation-seekers jostled below.

This was Norman Lindsay the Evangelist in full cry, affirming his contempt for the mob and his admiration of feminine beauty in the person of his Venus nailed to the cross 'by the Christian hatred of all gay and freed imageries of a love for life'. It was the kind of picture that once made his easy-going brother Percy ask him, 'Why do you make a goat of yourself trying to tub-thump sense out of all that damned rot? It's Grandpa Williams coming out in you.' Percy, who had inherited not one

drop of Grandpa Williams's missionary blood, was inclined to think
that Norman had inherited rather too much of it. So were some of the
staunchest admirers of Norman's skill with the pen. He never seemed
to understand that when he let himself go in this way he was preaching
like any thundering pulpiteer. He once hotly objected when twitted on
the point. 'One thing I utterly reject', he said, 'is that I ever entertained
the fatuous proposal to convey in my work anything in the nature of a
message. The only driving impetus I had was to do the thing I wanted
to do, and if mankind at large didn't like it, it could bloody well lump
it.' He clearly did not see pictures like *The Crucified Venus* and *Pollice
Verso* as sermons in ink, flinging their message in the face of the be-
holder. Others did.

*Pollice Verso* had been damned on the ground that it was blasphe-
mous; *The Crucified Venus* not only gave off a strong reek of blasphemy
but for good measure took a naked woman—and a beautiful one, for
Rose was the model—as its central figure. In a time when, to the consciously pure, any unclad human body was automatically impure, *The
Crucified Venus* could not fail to outrage the pious.

Sydney first saw it at the Society of Artists* Spring exhibition in
November 1912. As well as other examples of black and white, Norman
showed some of his earliest oil paintings and his model of Captain
Cook's ship, *Endeavour,* and the critics were more interested in these
new expressions of his industry and versatility than in *The Crucified
Venus.* While the *Daily Telegraph* regretted that he had employed his
abilities 'as he so often does in exploiting the grotesque and repulsive',
the *Sun* made no comment on the theme of *The Crucified Venus* but
found the technique 'wonderful' and added, with some expansiveness,
'One can understand Mr Lindsay's excursion into oil painting—he has
nothing more to learn as a black-and-white artist'. The *Sydney Morning
Herald* concentrated on praising his oils and studiously avoided mentioning *The Crucified Venus* at all. The *Bulletin* critic called it 'the most
striking conception in the show' and also lauded his oils but noted that
two of his nude studies were 'likely to arouse little enthusiasm, especially amongst those who pursue Lindsay's work with the sandbag of
prejudice. One of the models, it must be admitted, could more appro-
priately have been hung on a hook in a butcher's studio.' *The Crucified
Venus* horrified some prudes, but the only result of their objections was
to whet the curiosity of people who rarely worried about art and to
swell the number of visitors to the gallery.

Melbourne did not see *The Crucified Venus* for nearly a year. It went

* The Society of Artists, originally formed in 1895, amalgamated with the Royal
Art Society of New South Wales in 1902, but was re-formed in 1907 by a breakaway
group.

on show there in September 1913, in the art segment of the All-Australian Exhibition—'the greatest, most varied and most representative exhibition of Australian industries ever gathered together', according to one enthusiastic journalist. The Melbourne newspapers devoted columns to the industrial exhibits cramming the large and draughty Exhibition Building, but only the *Age* found space for detailed comment on the display of some 250 pictures by New South Wales and Victorian artists. Although voting Norman's group of works 'the most striking and powerful' of all, the critic remarked that his inventiveness was 'seen perhaps in its most repulsive form in several scenes from medieval times . . . and in one or two nudes'. The critic did not name *The Crucified Venus*, but the picture excited many disapproving as well as many admiring words on the opening day, Saturday 13 September, and when the protests continued on the Monday it was taken down. After standing for a while with its face to the wall it was carried off and locked in a storeroom while the managing committee of the great exhibition pondered the next step. Julian Ashton, as president of the Society of Artists, which had provided the New South Wales pictures, was irate. He sent the committee an ultimatum: *The Crucified Venus* must go back on the wall or the whole New South Wales collection would be withdrawn. The picture was re-hung after five days. It had been taken down, the committee explained in a press statement, only because 'it might give offence to a section of the community'. The committee itself 'took no exception to the picture as a work of art'. After that practically everybody who visited the exhibition in the eight weeks it was open made a point of seeing *The Crucified Venus*.

The Melbourne rumblings were only a gentle foretaste of what was to come in the future, but they were plainly audible to Norman in the Blue Mountains. They did not deter him, even though the telepathic impact was frightening. Many years afterwards, in an essay on Byron, he wrote 'When a man has been through Byron's experience of mass hatred, he will never get rid of that phantasm', and in framing that sentence he was drawing on his own knowledge. He never grew indifferent to such attacks, but never shrank from them. His refusal to make any concession to those who condemned him as a moral leper and a corrupting force was a measure of his moral courage in defence of artistic liberty. It revealed also a vocation for martyrdom which matched his evangelistic zeal.

The Norman Lindsay legend had lost some of its edge while he was in England, and when illness had for a time reduced to a trickle his output of serious work after his return. The contention over *The Crucified Venus* revived and invigorated it. He seemed to have an unequalled knack of generating storms of what he called *dementia puritani*. The way he portrayed women had much to do with it. An Australian who did not know that 'the Norman Lindsay woman' was strapping and voluptuous, with generous breasts, lusty thighs and massive buttocks, was a rarity. 'I've got no use for these starved hawks, you might call them', he once told an interviewer. '. . . All the old masters—they're all the same. You don't find any bones sticking out of their ladies—they're all beautifully modelled.' If a model was not of adequate proportions he magnified her to fit his requirements. A visitor to Springwood was present one day when a slim-bodied model aged seventeen or eighteen looked at a series of studies of her which Norman had done.

'Oh, Mr Lindsay,' she exclaimed, 'surely I don't look like that?'

'You will, my dear,' he said, 'you will'.

When the visitor saw the girl some years later he had to concede that Norman's prophecy had been amply fulfilled.

Australians who had never seen him, or seen any of his drawings except a *Bulletin* cartoon or a *Lone Hand* illustration, were able to tell intimate stories of the licentious life he lived in the mountains. Sightseers sometimes stationed themselves outside his fence hoping to catch a glimpse of wanton revels. Now and then their peerings were rewarded by the spectacle of a slender little man walking alone in the sunshine, head bent while he wrestled with some stubborn problem. They had to make what they could of that.

The transformation of the Springwood cottage had begun as soon as Norman and Rose took it over. As time went on it became an extension of their combined personalities. Seeing no reason to disturb what Paddy Ryan had built so well, they let it stand as the core of the large and restful colonial house which grew up around it. Norman planned the new place and built much of it with his lean-fingered and delicately muscular hands. The cottage expanded into a home of generous flowing spaces and lofty rooms, with French windows opening on to a broad veranda shaded by a roof supported on graceful cement columns. There was, of course, a studio for Norman, and a great sweeping living room, a drawing room, and a wide high-ceilinged kitchen, as well as bedrooms and guest rooms and other essentials of a country residence.

Norman tamed the wild garden but not too much. He added a covered walk sheltered by a trellis covered with a riot of wistaria and yellow roses; in summer it was murmurous with the droning of bees and the shadows were dark and cool. He treated trees like sacred beings. He revered trees—the pagan in him doubtless explained his affinity for them—and disliked seeing even some scrawny old bushland warrior fall to the axe. When he built a second studio some distance from the house he altered the plan rather than let one gaunt and rawboned eucalypt be chopped down. He needed the detached studio as a retreat in which he could work undisturbed, or read, write, sleep, and live a monk's life if and when he felt the need to escape and be alone with himself. He was particularly proud of the doorway. Unaided, he cut the stone for the massive side pillars and lintel from a rock face higher up the slope. He liked showing the scarred rock face to visitors. It attested his skill as a stone-cutter.

For relaxation, he turned to sculpture, and nymphs and fauns and other creatures of his imagination began to appear on the lawns and in the greenery about the house. He modelled these nearly life-sized figures in cement which set as hard as rock; a strong man with a sledge-hammer and a day to spare might have been able to smash one to pieces, but it would have been heavy work. Norman said they were 'harder to break than make' and never took them seriously—they were just a way of decorating Springwood and at the same time finding exercise for his muscles. His method was to build a basic skeleton of iron rods and wire netting, then dab on the wet cement, moulding and modelling as he went. Once as he dabbed away he chuckled, 'Damn it all, I'm like a swallow who's gone mad and taken to building statues instead of nests'. Each of these pieces usually weighed half a ton or more and needed three or four men equipped with pulleys and chains and crowbars to swing it up and seat it on its pedestal. They were not remarkable works of sculpture but they enlarged the charm of the place. On a moonlight night the figures had an eerie semblance of reality. It was easy to believe then that they were breathing, sentient beings.

The titanic appetite for heavy work of the man who had been desperately ill a few months earlier staggered everybody who came to Springwood. It lent force to Norman's conviction that the mind was the body's master. Archibald, who was there pretty well every second weekend, was never done marvelling. 'That fellow!' he exclaimed one day. 'What's he up to now? He hasn't built a cathedral yet, has he? If it occurred to him he'd do it.'

Visitors were plentiful. Some—like the artist Harley Griffiths, who persuaded Norman to do his first experimental oil paintings—were always welcome to come and stay. Others—like the writer J. H. M. Abbott, a handsome man, tall and powerfully made, who carried a black demon inside him which woke to dangerous life when he drank—were not. The door was always wide open for Archibald. Although still a substantial shareholder, he had taken no hand in the running of the *Bulletin* or the *Lone Hand* since his release from the mental hospital but his brain had not grown slack from disuse; it moved with unerring swiftness and precision.

For Norman, there was never anybody else like Archibald. He was a unique human being, a man with a gift of striking fiery particles from the mind of anybody except an irreclaimable dullard, and Norman found him ceaselessly refreshing, endlessly stimulating. Perhaps nothing else linked them so closely as their Australianism. Archibald's faith in Australia and its intellectual possibilities never flickered and was strongest when he was raging, either in talk or in print, against Australia's failings. Norman was an enthusiastic disciple, and at Springwood he was just beginning to evolve his theory that Australia could become the centre of a great renaissance which would rejuvenate Western culture. He was also—and nothing he did at that time had farther-reaching effects, in view of his later influence on the growth and enrichment of Australian literature—taking his first deliberate and calculated steps to follow his bent as a novelist.

He had dabbled in imaginative writing since his early Sydney years. One of his experiments had yielded a play, *The Pink Butterfly*, set in ancient Rome. Then, about 1904 or 1905, he had leapt twenty centuries forward and amused himself by scribbling out a cheerful and discursive tale based on his and Lionel's experiences in Melbourne. He called it *A Curate in Bohemia*. Peopled with characters taken straight from life, including himself, Lionel, Max Meldrum and other art student contemporaries minimally disguised by changes of name, its author saw it as a free experiment in autobiography rather than a novel. He had no thought of publishing it and when it was finished threw it into a drawer and more or less forgot it. After that, whenever he had time on his hands and a few sheets of blank paper handy, he was apt to fiddle with a story, often based on memories of his childhood. One of these was called *Saturdee*. Its publication in the *Lone Hand* on 1 July 1908 marked the first mention in print of the town of Redheap; this was the name under which Creswick was to figure in a number of Norman's novels, sometimes to the accompaniment of anguished wailings from citizens, who believed they identified themselves behind the flimsy masks worn by libidinous, hypocritical or otherwise dubious characters.

But those early occasional gambols with the written word had meant little more to Norman than his later games of marbles with young Ben Soady. It was only when he had lain in hospital, slowly convalescing after medical skill and his own spirit had dragged him back to life, that he had begun to think about the novel as a useful form of intellectual exercise. Always a fast reader, he was getting through two or three books a day in hospital. These were all popular English novels of the time and he found little merit in any of them—they seemed to him to be based on false values, to ooze sentimentality, and to be written to a rigid formula designed to avoid giving offence to the most blue-nosed puritan. One day he opened a novel called *Jonah*. The first sentence gripped him and he soon found himself deep in a story about a Sydney larrikin. Its atmosphere was as stridently authentic as the cry of a back-alley bottle-oh, and it brought the seamier side of Sydney to pulsating life. Norman finished it, then at once read it through a second time, more slowly. He had never before heard of the author, Louis Stone, which was not surprising: *Jonah* was Stone's first novel. And a remarkable novel it was, Norman decided, written by a man who knew and understood Australia, and particularly Australian city life, whereas most Australian writers appeared to know and understand only the bush. Ironically, as Norman discovered when he became friendly with Stone later, the author of *Jonah*, who earned his living as a school-teacher, was English-born and had been brought to Australia by his parents in 1884 when he was twelve.

Norman's impatience with the English novels he read in hospital and his admiration of *Jonah* combined into a kind of yeast which kept working in his mind when he went to the mountains. As his vitality returned he began toying with the idea of writing a novel for his own diversion. Three of his friends, Ralph Stock, a writer of popular fiction, Stock's sister Mabel, and another man set off from Sydney to sail the Pacific in an eighteen-foot boat, and wrecked themselves on a reef off Norfolk Island.* This gave Norman the idea for a comic tale about the adventures of three men and a young woman cast away on an uninhabited Pacific Island. Although *The Cautious Amorist* is one of his more trivial novels, it ultimately became the most financially profitable piece of writing he ever did. His son Jack said that Norman wrote it 'in part to assuage his unending hatred of curates [one of the characters is a curate, the Reverend Fletcher Gibble] and in part to parody de Vere Stackpoole's *The Blue Lagoon*†. If so, it succeeds on both counts and also as a rollicking piece of slapstick.

Writing never came easily to Norman and he wrote three drafts of *The Cautious Amorist* before he was satisfied. It took eight or nine months, because the task was a mere pastime and had to yield first place to cartooning and serious drawing. The story ran smoothly and when it was finished he put the manuscript aside but never quite forgot it. Sometimes when a friend was staying at Springwood Norman would bring it out after the evening meal and read a chapter or two aloud. He could never get through the more comical scenes without chortling over the antics of the castaways and—a spontaneous mannerism if his sense of fun was roused—clapping himself on the leg. These readings were not only a symptom of the vanity which every author secretes; he liked having his novels liked, as he once put it, and never resented applause, but he also

---

* Ralph Stock, *The Cruise of the Dreamship* (London, 1921).
† Jack Lindsay, *The Roaring Twenties* (London, 1960), p. 91.

wished to test the responses of different people to his handling of situation, character and dialogue. Even while he seemed to be entirely absorbed in relishing his own words he was studying his listener with judicial detachment. This was not because he cherished an ambition to become a successful professional author; it was a token of his quest for perfection in anything he tackled.

For all his firm intention of merely playing at authorship as a private hobby he made his public bow as a novelist within a year. At the time the New South Wales Bookstall Company, owned and managed by an enterprising publisher named A. C. Rowlandson, was putting out Australian popular novels at a shilling a copy. Norman, who sometimes accepted a commission to illustrate one of these books, mentioned that he had written a farcical tale around the exploits of art students and their cronies and girls in Melbourne. Rowlandson asked to see it, and Norman unearthed the manuscript of *A Curate in Bohemia* and sent it along. To his astonishment, Rowlandson offered to buy it outright for £100. Norman, slightly dazed, agreed and the book was published. It had a cover design in colour and some thirty illustrations by the author. The cover depicted a confrontation between a shrinking curate and a buxom young woman half-hidden by a swirling drape but with invitingly uncovered breasts. Bombarded by protests and fearing prosecution, Rowlandson appealed to Norman who, grumbling but resigned, drew a new cover picture for later editions; this time all the lady's strategic areas were concealed. Thus launched, *A Curate in Bohemia* became a bestseller at the start and, holding its popularity over the years, ran through edition after edition. The outright sale was one of the worst business deals Norman ever made. He realized it when sales went on mounting and passed 10,000, then 20,000, then 25,000. He never again made the mistake of selling the copyright of any book.

At the time he suffered some heart-burning about the popularity of *A Curate in Bohemia*. He did not want to become known as a novelist. Wishing Australians to see him as an artist, to absorb his philosophy as an artist, and to judge him as an artist, he believed that if he were to go before them as an artist who was also a novelist he would confuse them and tend to lose the audience for what he considered to be his real work. He accordingly hoped that *A Curate in Bohemia* would sink out of sight and be forgotten as soon as possible. Instead it continued to sell and be read and laughed over, and, if critics did not rate it a literary *tour de force*, tens of thousands of Australians thought it marvellous entertainment. The book just would not fade away! Norman could have kicked Rowlandson for seducing him into letting it be published, and kicked himself twice as hard for being seduced. He made a private vow that he would take the lesson to heart and in future keep his novels to himself.

Although he did not stop writing novels for his own amusement he held to that resolve for seventeen years.

Life at Springwood went on with deceptive calm. That the most destructive war in history would break out within a year was unthinkable. Yet an atmosphere of menace was thickening over Europe as Germany pressed on with a naval building programme. Those few Australians who were students of international affairs knew that their country would be drawn in if a storm should come, but Norman was not among them. While owing his livelihood largely to his topical cartoons he was more or less blind to the political trends they reflected. His far vision was at times extraordinarily penetrating, but he rarely showed any gift of anticipating immediate or near events. In that sense he was not a political animal—a curious deficiency in a man who, for many years, was Australia's most influential topical cartoonist.

Even before Hop faded into the background about the end of 1913, to concentrate on making violins and violoncellos and playing bowls, Norman was doing more than any of his contemporaries to sway the political thinking of Australians in the mass. His pre-eminence among *Bulletin* black and white artists was never challenged once Hop dropped out except as an occasional contributor, but a formidable opponent was in the field; this was a twenty-year-old New Zealander, David Low, who had come from Christchurch in November 1911 to work as the *Bulletin*'s staff artist in Melbourne for six months. When Low's temporary job ended he wandered Australia for some months making portrait caricatures of local celebrities for the *Bulletin*; then he presented himself in Sydney and, taking possession of a room in the office, did anything the *Bulletin* or the *Lone Hand* asked of him. Although a fine draughtsman and gifted with rare political sagacity he had to strive hard for a footing, because the *Bulletin* was flush of staff cartoonists just then. Nearly fifty years later Low recalled:

> Sometimes Norman Lindsay would appear from his Blue Mountains fastness, a birdlike man of rapid speech with sharp intelligent eyes. This was Norman's heyday when he was busy proving that he was the best penman of his generation, his talent shining so bright as to dim lesser lights into insignificance. I could hardly speak to him for reverence.*

Hop's retirement from regular cartooning opened the door to Low and he was soon building a reputation as a major cartoonist. Prodigiously ambitious and pushfully intent on reaching the top, he disliked squatting in any other man's shadow, but Norman was immovably seated; he was well aware of Low's jockeying but did not let it worry him. He never cared for Low—'Like all ruthless go-getters', Norman once said, 'he was

* *Low's Autobiography* (London, 1956), p. 56.

not a likeable man'—but also never doubted his greatness as a journalistic artist.

Norman's mind was untroubled by thoughts of war, in that last year before the *Pax Britannica* ended. He felt he was on the brink of a rich and productive artistic period. It was all a matter of finding the right key. He knew he faced some formidable problems if he hoped to make any headway with serious pen drawing. After long self-questioning he had reached the conclusion that, for the pen, the nude was not the best form of expression; he believed it cut him off from too many valuable assets in the way of textures and, while useful as a subordinate image, could not be given a dominant place. He was in a state of indecision over the proper handling of the pen—torn between, on the one hand, reluctance to seek a new form of expression and, on the other, a growing belief that he must throw aside the conventions which were clogging his inspiration. He could take his time about looking for solutions. Only tenacity and patience were needed. Meanwhile, the road ahead ran straight and un-cluttered. So he supposed anyway.

He could imagine no better place than Australia in which to work out his artistic destiny. He never wished to be anywhere else. The news that Will Dyson had leapt into the forefront of England's cartoonists did not stir his envy or make him hanker to go back and try to like England and the English. After more than two tight-buttoned and discouraging years, Will had become cartoonist of a new Labour newspaper, the *Daily Herald*, when it was launched in April 1912. He started at a modest five pounds a week but his cartoons, savagely humorous and always with a razor-sharp cutting edge, quickly gained him the recognition in England which Australia had denied him; in a few months his fame spread to the Continent and America and he was being paid a salary to match it. Norman did not grudge Will his success. Time had softened the memory of their London quarrel and Norman would have been delighted to see Will come walking up the road from Springwood.

Norman's personal life was giving him more worry than anything else. It was four years since he and Katie had shared a night under the same roof, and it was plain that they would never again come together. He knew he was being unfair to Rose in letting their association meander on while he dodged the issue with Katie, yet the thought of seeking a divorce repelled him. It would involve him in a network of time-wasting legal chicaneries and he was damned if he would face that. Never having believed in marriage as a stabilizing influence in a union between a man and a woman, he saw no reason why he and Rose should spend time and effort clearing the way so that they might marry. It might be different if there were children, but he was adamant about that. Hadn't he made it clear to Rose that, his experience of fatherhood having convinced him of his total unfitness for the part, he wanted no more children? After brooding on it he decided to tell Katie he must have a legal separation. That would ratify the end of his marriage and relieve Rose's mind of any fear that he might discard her and turn back to his wife and sons.

Katie and the boys were living in Brisbane near the Hamilton racecourse. The Elkingtons were in a house near by. It was a gloomy time. Not long before, Ray Parkinson had died after a battle with tuberculosis and everyone had been under heavy strain. Then Norman's ultimatum arrived. It hit Katie hard. As her son Jack wrote many years later, she 'couldn't see why everyone shouldn't be happy'\*, and the final collapse of her marriage plunged her into misery. The two younger boys were scarcely aware of their mother's distress but Jack, now a live-minded thirteen-year-old, knew that she was sorrowing, and why, and was troubled by his inability to help her. She acknowledged defeat by divesting herself of any reminders of the marriage. She went around the house and made a collection of all Norman's pictures and drawings and gave them to Mary Elkington; she even gave Mary a notebook which Norman had filled with pen drawings in his Creswick boyhood. A woman of steelier purpose would have kept these items for their value in a salesroom, but there was nothing steely about Katie.

Norman's mother had not yet become reconciled to the breakdown of his marriage and his association with Rose, but his father and most of his brothers and sisters did not let it trouble them; they took the view that Norman's matrimonial affairs were his private concern. There were never any shadows between Doctor Lindsay and Rose. He had dined with Norman and Rose in one of their Sydney studios before they went to Europe, and visited them in London, and now he came to stay with them in the mountains. He was at Springwood for a month or two while making up his mind whether to go back to Creswick and take up the struggle to earn a living there or try to find a footing in a new place. It was a poor outlook. He was nearing his middle seventies and the years were showing. He still loved good company, and delighted in meeting any of Norman and Rose's friends who came up from Sydney. They delighted no less in meeting him. He had the indestructible charm of the man whose spirit never ages.

Norman and Rose were sorry when he told them he must be moving on. A doctor was needed on the opal fields at White Cliffs, nearly five hundred miles away in the far west of New South Wales, and he was going there. Janie, he said, would be better off in Creswick, for the time being anyway. It might be possible for her to join him later, but from all he'd heard White Cliffs was harsh country for a woman. Norman

---

\* Jack Lindsay, *Life Rarely Tells* (London, 1958), p. 43.

and Rose harnessed up the trap and drove him to the Springwood station and put him on the train. When he went something warm and joyous went with him.

Hugh D. McIntosh came bursting in one day like a great gusty wind. He had worked a series of financial miracles since his homecoming and was rolling in money again. In a week or two, he told Norman, he was off to London—'In the best bloody suite in the ship, my boy!'—with plans which would make the reigning boxing promoters and theatrical entrepreneurs look to themselves.

'And this time', he said, brimming with self-confidence, 'we'll get that old bastard Casanova between covers'.

Norman fetched the illustrations and made them up into a great parcel. He was glad to be shed of them. McIntosh bade his chauffeur load the parcel into the car, and went hurtling back to Sydney in a cloud of dust. Well, Norman told himself, the chances that those damned drawings would be published at last seemed good. McIntosh clearly meant business. It would take an earthquake or a volcanic eruption to stop him. Or a war.

Norman found himself wishing for an hour of Hugh McCrae's company in those last months of peace. But McCrae was ten thousand miles away in New York City. He had scraped together enough money for the ship fare to England and, after taking a hurried look at London, crossed the Atlantic to try his luck in America. It was no easier there than in Australia—he had a rich talent but lacked the commercial touch. He sent his drawings and poems around the magazines with little success and would have had to run for home if he had not fluked work as a minor actor. Although untrained in the theatre, his tall and graceful good looks and histrionic aptitude won him a lowly place in a British company headed by the actor-manager-playwright, Harley Granville-Barker, which was playing an extended season on Broadway. Once or twice he sent Norman one of his unique letters, exquisitely handwritten and illustrated with three or four crazy drawings. These never told much about his doings on an everyday level but they brought his spirit, shouting with laughter and strong with the joy of life, into the Springwood house.

Early in 1914 Norman's youngest brother Daryl stayed at Springwood while he was between jobs. Daryl—his brothers called him Dan, which Percy had dubbed him in childhood because he had had a long mane of yellow hair like Daniel in the Lions' Den in one of the Family Bible plates—had shown flashes of the Lindsay talent for drawing but did not think of making a career of it. A fine horseman, he liked the bush and, after leaving home at sixteen or seventeen, worked in Queensland, New South Wales and Victoria as a jackeroo, drover, boss of the board in

20  *The Embarkation*, an illustration to the *Satyricon* of Petronius

21 *The Apotheosis of Villon*

22 *Panurge meets Pantagruel*, an illustration to Rabelais

shearing sheds, and station overseer. Norman was eleven years older and at Springwood Daryl became well acquainted with his brother for the first time. He was fascinated.

> With his bright face, sparkling conversation, infectious laughter, sitting with one leg doubled under him in a large chair, he would tell some fantastic story about a contemporary or read aloud . . . hordes of people came to sit at Norman's feet, share his humour and the philosophy of life which poured from his agile mind. They were a heterogeneous collection of writers, poets, artists, musicians, ship's captains and prize fight promoters.*

It was heady company for a young bushman and when Daryl packed up and left for his new overseer's job on a Riverina station the memory stayed with him, vivid and shining.

Autumn went out in a flurry of tinted leaves, and winter settled over the mountains. The wind was raw and sometimes there was snow but Norman refused to have a fire in the house. 'No fires', he said. 'The damn' things give me colds.' To stay at Springwood in winter was a test of endurance and friendship; those who came had to be willing to shiver and suffer. Norman thrived on it. He was always busy, drawing or writing or sculpting, or cutting paths through the scrub with a mattock. One of his theories was that the more work one did the more one was able to do—like the beer plant, he said, one's capacity for work expanded with use. His own tirelessness seemed to substantiate it.

As July ran to an end and August came in, the Australian newspapers were printing long reports about the danger of civil war in Ireland. Norman barely glanced at the headlines. He had no faith in anything the 'newsrags' said; they were forever tracking down some new sensation and dishing it up under scare headlines, then dropping it and going on to something else. This happened with the Irish crisis. One day it was pushed into the background to make way for a lot of nonsense about tension in Central Europe, arising from the assassination of the Archduke Francis Ferdinand at Sarajevo a month earlier. It would, Norman expected, bubble for a while and then simmer down like all the other crises. It didn't. In the first few days of August what had been a minor incident in the Balkans exploded into war. The echoes went rolling round the world and Australia stood pledged to 'stand beside the Mother Country and help defend her to the last man and the last shilling'.†

The *Bulletin*, taken unprepared, acknowledged the outbreak of war in a chief cartoon on 6 August, drawn in obvious haste by Low. That week Norman, on the Federal election campaign then in progress, was rele-

---

* Daryl Lindsay, *The Leafy Tree* (Melbourne, 1965), p. 178.
† These were the words of Andrew Fisher (three times Prime Minister between 1908 and 1915), who was returned to power at the head of a Labour administration as a result of the Federal election campaign which was being fought when the war began. Labour's political opponents gave a no less binding pledge in different words.

gated to a secondary page. He caught up with the war a week later in a cartoon depicting a colossal figure of Mars, stripped to the waist, crowned with a horned helmet, carrying a dripping sword at his belt, and raising a hammer to strike a gong. A heap of dead lay at his feet and lurid flashes lit the sky behind him. In the foreground stood a small boy representing Australia, clutching a puny rifle and wearing a bandolier studded with cartridges. The title was *The War God of Europe Strikes His Gong*. It appeared on 13 August and many of Norman's admirers acclaimed it as the finest cartoon he had ever drawn. It was not, but it captured the delirious and frenzied spirit of the time, and newspapers and magazines in many parts of the world, even some in Germany, republished it. Norman thought it an effective cartoon but the theme filled him with despondency. It was an admission that the world he had believed in was being blown to glory.

# 6

# *War comes to Springwood*
# *1914-18*

Even sleepy Springwood felt the excitement. Young men in civilian clothes took the train to Sydney and came back wearing khaki and walking with a soldierly swagger. While Norman envied them with one part of his being he was, in his own phrase, 'basely glad' with another part that he was physically incapable of going off to fight on some distant battlefield. A few years earlier he might have scraped into the army, small and seemingly frail though he was, but after his illness any recruiting sergeant would have told him to be gone and not waste the doctor's time.

The meaning of the war came to him with a hard jolt one day when he opened a letter from his sister Mary. She wrote that Reg, a forester with a wide knowledge of trees and wild birds and bush animals, had joined up and was in camp training to be a gunner. Norman always pretended that blood ties meant nothing to him—he evaluated his brothers and sisters, he said, by their personal qualities and was never influenced because he and they were born of the same parents. Whether or not this was strictly true, his affection for Reg was boundless. Although Reg was eight years younger, Norman saw him with almost hero-worshipping eyes. While Reg had never shown any artistic leanings, he was many other things that Norman had always wished to be and never could be. Tall and muscular, and an effortlessly accomplished boxer, footballer, horseman and tennis player, he was popular among men, and his good looks and easy masculine charm ensured that he always had a dozen pretty girls drooping after him. Norman made a special trip home to say farewell, and they had some happy days together when Reg was at Creswick on final leave. Norman particularly remembered a day in Ballarat when he found that he counted for nothing; he was merely Reg Lindsay's older brother and nobody, least of all the girls who kept hailing them as they strolled along Sturt Street, cared twopence that he was the *Bulletin* cartoonist and an artistic celebrity.

With the war like a black cloud overhead, Norman found it hard to concentrate on work. The *Bulletin* cartoons and drawings posed no problem; he had schooled himself to do them almost automatically while most of his mind was on other things. Serious work could not be tossed off like that; it demanded all his mental and most of his physical resources. War or no war, the Society of Artists intended holding its usual Spring exhibition and Norman felt he must show something—he could not let Julian Ashton and the others down. He was still experimenting with oil painting and a few weeks before the date of the show had three large canvases all but ready. Then, quite abruptly, he could not bear them. Seen in a mood of detachment they seemed to him hopelessly wrong. He knew they would be hung, and would doubtless cause a stir, not because of their intrinsic worth but because he had painted them. People would wrangle over them, eulogizing or execrating, but it would all be sound and fury because the pictures were no good. He told himself he could not yet handle oils and might have to slave away for years before he could. Well, the fowlhouse needed a new roof. He took the three pictures out and nailed them in place. The hens scuttled about below clucking with indignation. Norman decided they knew as much about art as most of the professional critics and solemn connoisseurs; and more than some.

There was no hope of forgetting the war for long. It dominated all the talk and every letter. Norman fell into the habit of riding into Springwood twice a day and picking up the morning and evening newspapers so that he and Rose could keep abreast of the news. He could not suppress a wry smile at the thought that he of all people should have become dependent on the despised 'newsrags', lapping up every word they printed about the war and even studying their crude maps. All the young men he knew were going. Daryl enlisted in the ranks like Reg. Many older men were joining up, too. One was a close friend of Norman, the painter Elioth Gruner, in his early thirties and just beginning to make a name with his lyrical and sensitive landscapes. Norman found these 'full of the spirit of delight—a new, vital and lovely transcription of reality', and believed that Gruner might go on to take his place among the great masters.

He could not imagine the pale-faced and reticent Gruner, whose suits, shirts and bow-ties were always the acme of good taste, as a soldier, nor did he guess what hidden agonies the step of joining the army had cost his friend. It came out one day when Gruner was spending a weekend leave at Springwood. He and Norman went for a stroll in the bush. They sauntered along yarning. A silence fell and they walked for some distance with nothing to break the hush but the occasional snap of a dry twig underfoot. Suddenly Gruner spoke.

'One of the things I've most feared is an attraction towards my own sex', he said without preamble. He was terrified, he confided, that in the male community of the army he would succumb to his hidden weakness.

Norman could think of nothing to say. He had never given much thought to homosexuality. It had never crossed his mind that Gruner might have homosexual tendencies. Women clearly found Gruner desirable, and he had responded, Norman knew, by having affairs with some of them.

'Look', Norman blurted out at last, knowing how banal the words were but feeling he must say something, 'I think it's best to dismiss such a thing from your mind.'

Gruner nodded and they walked back to the house.

Neither of them ever again mentioned the confession but Norman sometimes wondered in after years if Gruner was a casualty of the war, maimed by something more subtle than a shell splinter or a machine-gun burst yet as deadly in its own way.

Nearly six months after the war began Norman was still groping for a serious artistic objective. Then Lionel suggested one. Why not, he asked in a letter, do a series of pen drawings illustrating the poems of Francois Villon? Lionel's admiration of Norman's gifts as a pen draughtsman was as ample as it was generous; otherwise he would never have suggested Villon, one of his poetic gods whose works he knew by long and devoted reading of them in French.

He deduced that his brother, sitting up in the mountains and brooding on the war, needed a powerful stimulus to get him back to serious work. Norman was so depressed about everything, both in talk when Lionel went to Springwood and in letters; he was forever harping on the theme that he could not feel justified in taking an interest in work other than as 'a cowardly means of distraction'. He had not long before written Lionel a letter full of gloom saying he had a feeling in his bones that Germany was going to win the war. 'Outside the French, who must fight or be wiped off the earth, Germany is the only nation who is really fighting with a fixed intention to sacrifice everything to one end', he said. Lionel hated to see Norman sunk in despondency, and he hoped Villon would effect a cure. Norman fairly bubbled over with gratitude to 'dear old Joe'. The suggestion was an 'inspiration', he declared. Had Lionel any works in English on Villon? What would be the best way to get a mental picture of fifteenth-century Paris? He was depending on

Lionel for guidance; they must meet and discuss 'this fine idea' at length.

Although Norman was already acquainted with Francois Villon and his poetry, his knowledge was superficial. When he went to England he had been trifling with the idea of illustrating Villon's poems, but his exertions over the *Satyricon* and the toll the English climate and his poor health had taken of his energy had made him drop the project; now it was resurrected, brilliant with possibilities. He had never altogether lost sight of Villon. After returning to Australia he had painted a large oil, *Villon at the Tavern of the Pomme de Pin*, which had roused widespread interest at the Society of Artists' 1912 Spring exhibition. This canvas glowed with Norman's feeling for the character of the poet and the atmosphere of medieval Paris, and he found himself itching to go to work on a major series. He saw Villon, the scapegrace student whose poetry had come down the centuries like a wild and living voice from the Middle Ages, as one of the most gallant figures in literature, charging the adventure of life with reckless gusto and wringing the last drop of experience from it. Villon was not only a superb poet but also a man of action, and as such Norman loved him. It was true that he had been a brawling, drinking, whoring, gambling, thieving scamp, but he had accepted life for what it was, and remained unvanquished and impenitent in the teeth of the worst that men could do to him, even in the shadow of the gallows. Norman was fascinated too by the mystery of the poet's end when, having left Paris under a sentence of ten years banishment in 1463, he had vanished from history, as completely as if the earth had swallowed him up. Norman felt an affinity with Villon. Each was a rebel in his own way, and to each women were the most wonderful of all creations. They laughed at the same things, gloried in the same things, and Norman believed he understood and could find his way through the intricate fastnesses of Villon's rich, lustrous and tormented mind.

He was absorbed in Villon as 1915 opened. That was all to the good. It helped him to ignore the bleak winds blowing from the battlefronts. After hard thought he had decided to build his drawings less on the poems than on Villon's life and times. Perhaps he could see too little in the poems suitable for illustration; or perhaps the 'merely-an-accomplished-illustrator' gibe still rankled and he longed to negate it. At any rate he wanted to produce a series of drawings which, while taking Villon as the central figure, would express his own concept of life. He asknowledged how much it meant to him when he wrote to Lionel, 'I pin my hopes of resurrection to this new work'.

The quest for light on Villon and the Paris of his time proved to be harder than Norman had foreseen but it uncovered some lively information, particularly about the beggar students of the period and the riots in which they had joined battle with the forces of law and order. Norman neglected no detail which might help to re-create the atmosphere of Villon's Paris. He had one special bit of luck. Lionel owned some twenty large photographs, probably taken about 1850, of Paris buildings dating back to medieval times. Lionel, who had an uncanny knack of lighting on such treasure trove, had picked up the photographs in Paris on his first visit to Europe. He intended leaving them to the University of Sydney's school of architecture but was delighted to lend them to his brother. Having studied them, Norman threw them aside and they went out of his studio with the rubbish. Lionel was dismayed when he learned they were lost for ever but smothered his annoyance under a shrug and the thought 'Oh, well, that's Norman!'

The whole operation was typically Norman. He built streets of miniature medieval houses about three feet high so that he could draw them in exact perspective. He modelled figures of Villon, Fat Margot, and other characters from the poems and the poet's life, and arranged these like a stage director grouping his players. In his mind he lived among men and women and scenes of five centuries before. He worked at the series for two years off and on, and the choicest of the drawings are among his best pieces of penmanship. While Villon's poems provided the original inspiration and suggested the medieval atmosphere which saturates them, they extend far beyond the scope of his writings. Norman's own 'bedraggled youth', as he phrased it, was equally potent, for their concern is with human beings above all else. The finest of them—perhaps the finest of all Norman's pen drawings—is *The Apotheosis of Villon*. This depicts the cadaverous poet, haggard of face, raising haunted sidelong eyes to the feet of hanged men dangling from the gallows above a rabble of beggars, prostitutes, cripples, thieves, soldiers, and worthy burghers, against an impressionistic background of the towers and battlements of old Paris. To many, it is probably no more than a vivid re-creation of a grisly but commonplace medieval scene, to others, an unforgettable revelation of the aloneness of the creative man in a brutal and materialistic world.

Norman upset some of his admirers, Lionel particularly, by not finishing the Villon series. For some reason he grew tired of it while it was still far from complete, and, abandoning any thought that it might become the basis of a de luxe edition, sold the drawings piecemeal. His fascination with Villon as a poet and a man never waned, but the desire to use him as an artistic subject was dead. Perhaps the war was partly to blame. It was no time to be thinking of de luxe editions. They belonged to the days of peace and plenty, and who could tell when, if ever, those would return? Even Hugh D. McIntosh did not pretend to know. He had come back to Australia bringing the *Casanova* drawings with him. He drove up to Springwood and dumped the parcel into Norman's arms.

'There's a jinx on those damn' things', he growled. 'First they send me broke. Now they've started a war.'

McIntosh hated to admit that any of his pet schemes ever went awry but he had to accept defeat over *Casanova*. His disappointment must have put a damper on Norman's hopes for Villon.


Norman's attitude to the war was ambivalent in the early stages. While dazed to account for such a monstrous calamity and abhorring the accompanying death and destruction, he believed that any war had two elements which did something to justify it and that this one was no exception. First, he saw it as an immense stimulus to artistic creation and liked to point out that the Greek and Roman civilizations had flourished with the rumble of war as a constant accompaniment. Second, he believed that courage in battle was the supreme expression of human dignity, and that war therefore served a valuable end by giving men the chance to prove themselves as warriors.

He had to modify these falsely romantic notions as the young men of the warring nations went down to muddy death by tens of thousands in the senseless battles on the Western Front, but he never wholly discarded them. His stubbornness made him want to close his eyes to the difference between war as it is and war as the poets and storytellers of his childhood had told him it is; having always thought of it as heroic, he went on for as long as possible ignoring the evidence that it is a foul, cruel and dirty business. He could not, however, disregard the casualty lists. They appalled him far more than the news from 'Lisnacrieve' of his father's death in September 1915. Although the thought that he would never see the old man again was saddening, he could not agonize over it. After all, Doctor Lindsay, who had gone back to Creswick gravely ill as a result of night-long exertions helping men trapped in the flooded underground workings of a White Cliffs mine, had lived seventy-six good years, while most of the men dying in the war were still pitifully young.

Norman found the daylight hours not so bad; then he could hold the ugliness and horror at bay by drawing, painting, cartooning, or working up to his armpits in wet cement to make a piece of sculpture for the garden. It was harder to forget the war at night, and that was how he came to write his tale for children, *The Magic Pudding*, never deaming that it would become the best-loved and most enduring of all his writings. It was born of a casual conversation with a bookish journalist friend, Bertram Stevens, a kindly and sympathetic man, who spent many wartime weekends at Springwood. Yarning after dinner one night, Stevens and Norman drifted into an argument about children's stories. Stevens said he believed that fairies made the strongest appeal to the child mind.

One of the many anti-war cartoons which Norman drew
for the *Bulletin* during the First World War

'Not on your life!' Norman answered. 'The belly rules the infant mind.
The adult mind too, if it comes to that. Anyway, for kids, a story based
on food would win every time.'

He had formed that opinion when he was seven or eight, on his first
reading of *Alice in Wonderland* and *Through the Looking-Glass.* He
loved the Lewis Carroll classics but objected to the episode in which the
Red Queen introduces Alice to the leg of mutton and will not let her
eat it because etiquette forbids one to 'cut' people to whom one has been
introduced.

'Damn it, Bert', he said, 'for the sake of getting in that joke, which
most children wouldn't understand anyway, Carroll did the kids out of
the pleasure of banqueting with Alice. It always made me wild. It still
does.'

That would probably have been the end of it if Stevens had not called
to see George Robertson at his Sydney offices a few days later. Robertson,
a tall and powerful Scot with a fierce temper, was head of Angus and
Robertson, for many years Australia's premier book publishing and bookselling firm. After talking business, Stevens casually mentioned Norman's
view about children's books.

Robertson tugged at his curling black beard and grunted, 'Get him to
write a book for kids and you're on a fiver'.

When Stevens made the suggestion on his next visit to Springwood

Norman said, 'I wouldn't dream of it. I'm not capable of writing a book for kids. If I implied that I could, then I was talking hot air.'

Stevens said that George Robertson liked the idea.

'To hell with George Robertson!' snapped Norman, who believed that Robertson took an intolerably straitlaced view of life. 'He's a black Calvinist and I don't care for the breed.'

Although Norman had drawn covers and illustrations for several Angus and Robertson books and been treated fairly, he looked on all publishers as natural enemies. 'There's a blood feud between your tribe and my tribe', he once told Robertson. 'The road that leads to publishers' counting-houses is paved with the bones of artists and writers who have starved on the track.' He gave no more thought to Bert Stevens's urgings until weeks later when he was sitting in the studio one night with nothing to do. He could not steer his thoughts away from the war and how badly it was going. A vision of Reg and Daryl and other young men, who might even then be lying dead or wounded, kept flickering back and forth before his mind's eye. Looking for any means of distraction, he picked up a writing pad and pencil and began to scribble a tale about a koala, Bunyip Bluegum. In essentials it was the same koala that had figured for years in Norman's bushland drawings in the *Bulletin* and the *Lone Hand*.

The story was pure nonsense, interspersed with frothy verses, but once started it began to take on a crazy kind of coherence. Norman let Bunyip Bluegum come upon Bill Barnacle the Sailor and Sam Sawnoff the Penguin lunching off Albert the Puddin'—a walking and talking steak-and-kidney pudding which was magically renewed no matter how often a slice was cut and eaten. He grunted when he read over what he had written. He was doing exactly what he had told Bert Stevens he couldn't do and wouldn't do: writing a story for children. But he was also—and this pleased him—making food the motif. He determined to keep at it and finish the tale, if only to make Bert Stevens admit that a kids' tale about food was better than one about fairies.

It did not come easily after the opening. Nor was he by any means sure that it would amuse children, so he turned to his eight-year-old nephew Peter, Lionel's son. He sent the first forty-odd pages to Lionel, who read them to Peter. Peter, as Lionel reported to Norman, was enthralled. He adopted *The Magic Pudding* as his personal Bible and liked to go about reciting long passages from it to himself. After the first reading he was forever pestering his father for more and it was a bright day for him whenever Norman sent along a fresh set of pages. In his middle sixties Peter still remembered the 'ecstatic feelings it generated', even though his early hero-worshipping veneration of the uncle who wrote it had long since decayed and fallen into ruins.

Writing and drawing the illustrations filled most of Norman's spare time at night for nine months and called into play all his powers of imagination and inventiveness. He had not gone far with the tale before discovering that it demanded no less effort than any piece of writing on an adult level which he had ever attempted; if anything, rather more. And when it was finished he had no high opinion of it. He had a habit of decrying his own writings when talking with friends, but most of them knew his tongue was in his cheek. 'It might interest you to glance at this rubbish I've written', he would say, tossing the typescript of an unpublished novel to a house guest at Springwood, but he never showed much relish for the opinion of anyone who agreed that it was rubbish. Yet he genuinely questioned that *The Magic Pudding* was worth printer's ink. He sent the text and the drawings to George Robertson as he finished each of the four parts, or 'slabs' as he chose to call them in keeping with the pudding theme. Robertson never had a moment's doubt of its merit but, because wartime restrictions imposed delays, the book was not published until 1918, nearly a year after Norman finished it. It came out at the then dizzy price, for a children's book, of a guinea and sold well from the start; it was still selling well fifty years later, after a total of some 100,000 copies had been printed in Australia, apart from editions in Britain and the United States.

Whatever his later thoughts, Norman regretted in 1918 that he had agreed to publish *The Magic Pudding*. He was 'not at all proud of having produced this little bundle of piffle'. He was also worried that the public would think he had 'put forth this rubbish in all seriousness'. He was, however, no less grateful to it for having taken his mind off the war when things were going badly. It had carried him over a particularly black patch early in 1917 when Reg was killed on the Somme. Some months later Norman received a small package from Creswick. This contained a slim notebook which the army had shipped home among Reg's personal belongings. Norman had given his brother the notebook at their last meeting, bidding him record in it any salient impressions of his war experiences. The book was stained with blood and Reg's jottings were indecipherable.

Two young South Australians were idling away a few hours in Melbourne late in 1917. One was a twenty-five-year-old war veteran, Leon Gellert, and the other a writer named Charles Rodda. They had reached Melbourne that morning by rail from Adelaide, and Gellert was going on to Sydney by express the same evening to meet Norman Lindsay and stay at Springwood.

Gellert had been a school teacher before the war. Enlisting as an infantryman, he had landed on Gallipoli with his battalion, and, after seeing hard service and rising to sergeant's rank, been invalided home in 1916 and discharged as medically unfit. He was a little nervous about his coming meeting with Norman. He was not used to celebrities and hoped he wouldn't be out of his depth. His book, *Songs of a Campaign*, was his link with Springwood. This was a collection of poems which he had published as a modest paperback in Adelaide. It had taken George Robertson's eye and he had put it out as a well-made hardback with illustrations by Norman.* Both the critics and the public liked it, and Gellert found himself being hailed as Australia's outstanding soldier-poet of the war.

For want of anything better to do in Melbourne that day, he and Rodda found their way to the grey and heavy building housing the Victorian National Gallery and National Museum. They had been dawdling through the galleries for some time when, in the ceramics section, they saw two men coming toward them. One, silver-haired, ruddy-faced and sparely built, was in his middle fifties; the other, a mere wisp and probably twenty years younger, was doing all the talking in a tumble of eager words.

Gellert, who recognized him at once from his photograph, walked up and asked, 'Are you Norman Lindsay?'

The man eyed him as if expecting to be touched for a loan. 'Yes', he said. 'Yes. I'm Norman Lindsay.'

'I'm Leon Gellert.'

It was like pressing an electric button. Norman, his face alight, seized Gellert about the waist and danced him around that staid and hushed place, twittering with glee. The dance ended and Norman presented Gellert to the other man who turned out to be Sir Baldwin Spencer; Spencer, a senior trustee of the Gallery and Honorary Director of the Museum, was one of the most respected anthropologists of the day and a world authority on the Aborigines. Gellert introduced Rodda, and then Spencer led the party to his office and ordered tea. It was a golden moment for Gellert when he counted eight copies of *Songs of a Campaign* arrayed like soldiers on a shelf behind the desk.

Norman and he travelled to Sydney by the night express, with Mary Lindsay for company; Mary, who was going to Springwood for a holiday, was delighted to learn that a good-looking young Anzac, with intelligent blue eyes and fair hair, was to be a fellow guest. Rose was in Sydney at the Wentworth Hotel, and after a short stay there the four took the train for Springwood. When Gellert went to pay his hotel bill he found that Norman had settled it. That was his first experience of Norman's

* Two Adelaide editions published by G. Hassell and Son, and the Angus and Robertson edition, all appeared in 1917.

prodigal open-handedness toward any friend who was having a struggle to make ends meet.

It was night when they came to the house, driving in a horse and trap from Springwood station. Moonlight touched the house and grounds and bush with unearthly beauty. Gellert was bewitched. He stayed about six weeks, sitting at Norman's feet, talking a little, but mostly listening as opinions, theories, conjectures and fantasies streamed from the master's lips. At times, when alone and able to marshal his thoughts, Gellert shook his head over one or another sibylline utterance of Norman's which had seemed to be panoplied in truth while it was being delivered. Norman had a way of persuading listeners to assent, under the thrust of his enthusiasm, the spell of his voice and the lamp's glow, to hypotheses which were less tenable in the raw and revealing light of day. Gellert never felt strongly enough to challenge Norman at their next session and put forward his doubts about some scintillating assumption; he knew that to do so would only lead to an exhausting dispute and would be a waste of breath.

Two men whom he made friends with at Springwood were to exert some influence on his life. These were the amiable Bert Stevens, and Sydney Ure Smith, the artist, editor and publisher. They were producing a high-grade quarterly magazine, *Art in Australia*, which Ure Smith, actively encouraged by Norman, had launched in 1916 with himself as the editor and Stevens as co-editor. Stevens also carried some weight as the editor of the *Lone Hand*, which post he did not relinquish until December 1918. Norman and he had been friends since 1901, when he had been one of Julian Ashton's art students. He made a small income from etchings and water-colours but most of his energies went into an advertising and publishing company, Smith and Julius, in which his partners were a cartoonist and theatre caricaturist, Harry Julius, and a painter and commercial artist, Albert Collins. Fleshy, thick-necked and florid, Ure Smith was an enthusiastic *bon-vivant* and an entertaining talker, and no man of his time carried greater weight with Australian artists and art connoisseurs.

Norman was delighted to see how quickly Gellert found common ground with men like Ure Smith and Stevens. Norman always wanted his friends to like one another, and he had lost no time in electing Gellert as a friend. Hugh McCrae, who had come back to Australia and found work as, improbably, a wartime censor in Melbourne, was still one of Norman's poetic gods, but for a time Gellert overshadowed him. Here was a young man who did not write with the false heroics of the poet who has learned about war from books, but with the understanding of one whose mind and body has experienced war and who, in lines of his own, could

> . . . see paths and ends, and see
> Beyond some swinging open door
> Into eternity.*

Norman, who read aloud uncommonly well, liked reading Gellert's war poems to visitors while the embarrassed author sat back trying to hide his blushes. Sometimes Norman would interrupt a reading to announce with oracular certitude, 'Leon is the finest poet of the age'. For Gellert, who never thought himself more than competent, those declarations were hard to bear.

Nobody was indiscreet enough to remind Norman that a year or so before he had been lauding Christopher Brennan as the greatest poet of the war. The tragic Brennan, a hard-drinking and temperamentally erratic Sydney poet, scholar and intellectual, published a long poem called *A Chant of Doom* in the *Lone Hand* on 1 August 1916. Norman started by thinking it a masterpiece. He described it in a letter to Lionel as, the finest expression of a mighty anger against all that Germany meant' to appear since the war. 'I've been waiting', he went on, 'for such a piece, wondering where it would come from, expecting it from France, and never dreaming it was about to be born here . . . It is Homeric. A godlike expression of man's just wrath.' For some weeks after *A Chant of Doom* was published, no Springwood visitor could escape. Having settled the victim in a comfortable chair, Norman would take up the *Lone Hand* and, with all the considerable artifice at his command, read *A Chant of Doom* from beginning to end, not omitting even such unintentionally hilarious lines as

> Ring deliverance, ring the doom
> (Cannon, cannon, cannon, boom)!

He never read it to Leon Gellert. Indeed he quietly forgot it after once savouring the clean, sharp and soldierly tang of *Songs of a Campaign*. Norman sometimes made mistaken literary judgements, but he rarely erred in discriminating between the bogus and the authentic when he met them together.

Jack Lindsay once said that his father had 'a way of creating absolutes out of any experience or idea'. In that spirit Norman was given to saying that the First World War was, for him, a barren time in which he did little except journalistic cartoons and other drawings, and propaganda drawings to stimulate recruiting. This was an example of his gift of transmuting what had happened into what he wished to think had happened; it was not a conscious misrepresentation but a spontaneous revision which then became, for him, the reality. His output of serious

---

* 'These Men' from *Songs of a Campaign* (Sydney, 1917).

work in the First World War was smaller than in the 1920s, when he abandoned journalism entirely, but the volume was still formidable, even if one ignores the sculptures, writings and other items which he treated as recreational by-products.

Whatever the trials and exigencies of wartime life, he was yet so engrossed in work that he was able to say in 1916, 'The day is successful if one can go to bed anxious to get the business of sleep over in order to get to work next morning'. Julian Ashton left a picture of him at that time.

It has often been urged as a reproach against modern painters that the great Italians were not only painters, but sculptors, architects, engineers, and military experts in designing fortifications, while we are satisfied to follow one branch of our chosen calling, and make no excursion beyond its limitations. Lindsay has always lent a willing ear to the call of adventure. The catholicity of his taste is only equalled by the fecundity of his imagination . . . Walking with him at his home near Springwood I asked him if he did not tire of the monotony of the country and want to return to Sydney. 'I seldom go to Sydney,' he replied, 'and only when I am forced to do so. Here the days are never long enough for me.' I quite believe it. He rises early and works in pen and ink during the morning hours. For a change, in the afternoon he will begin a water-colour drawing or put in time out of doors getting ready the supports for a life-sized equestrian group he has designed for his lawn. In the evening he reads, retires early, and writes portion of his latest novel before he sleeps.*

Norman was working also in a field which Ashton did not mention: etching. He found it cruelly punishing but could no more resist it than a true mountaineer can refuse the challenge of an unconquered peak. He loved the results he could sometimes achieve although the agony of the task never ceased to harrow him.

His venture into etching placed the final seal on his partnership with Rose. To print from the etched copper plate calls for only less devotion and skill than to make the plate itself. Rose did Norman's printing from the start. She knew that he would never bring himself to print an edition of each of his etchings; after seeing a final print of any plate he at once lost interest in it and went on to something new. She also knew that he was not physically robust enough to do the heavy physical labour of operating the leverage wheel of the printing press; Rose was an exceptionally strong woman and managed the press without seeming trouble, but in doing so her splendid body incurred debts which it had to pay in old age. Like Norman, she was a perfectionist. No print she ever released was blemished by the most insignificant flaw. She would stop printing the moment a plate showed the first infinitesimal sign of wear. And once an edition was printed she destroyed the plate, scarring the face so that it could never be used again.

* Essay in *The Pen Drawings of Norman Lindsay* (Sydney, 1918).

Norman had hardly thought of etching until early in the war. Some years before, when he was making ready for Europe, he had done a few plates as an experiment, then dropped it. Staying at Springwood for a weekend in 1915, Lionel spent most of the time orating to Norman on the possibilities of etching, and urging him to try it again. It was a neglected branch of art in Australia. Livingston Hopkins and Julian Ashton had done a little etching but neither had persisted with it, and Lionel, having rediscovered the medium and done a number of plates, was in a ferment of enthusiasm.

'Etching!' Norman objected. 'It's not an art at all, Joe. It's only for artists who can't draw.'

'Is it?' said Lionel. 'Then what about Rembrandt, eh? And Klinger and Goya? They couldn't draw?' Norman looked thoughtful and Lionel, pressing his advantage, reeled off the names of six or seven other master etchers. 'You'd better have another think about it, Joe', he said. 'You seem to be getting into a rut.'

Norman hated that thrust. He always prided himself on his readiness to work in any artistic medium. And if what old Joe said was right—and it must be right, when you thought of Rembrandt and Goya and the others!—then etching could not be written off. He must take a new look at it.

Never one to procrastinate, he began as soon as he could get the materials and working tools. Lionel helped by throwing everything he knew at Norman's feet. His letters to Springwood were packed with advice based on hard-won knowledge, and Norman absorbed it like a sponge. He finished a plate a few weeks after Lionel's visit. Called *Lady and Parrot*, it was the first of a gigantic total of more than 200 published etchings. He probably etched no fewer than 700 plates in his lifetime, but only about one in three satisfied his exalted standards; the rest were scrapped. At one guinea a print the edition of *Lady and Parrot* sold out in a week or two. The price of his etchings quickly rose, from four guineas to six, to eight to ten, and then levelled off at fifteen. The bulk of every edition was bespoken by public and private collectors. At the height of his popularity speculators who bought prints for resale were asking and getting upwards of twenty and thirty guineas each for specimens of his more celebrated etchings after holding them for a few months.

Being the kind of man he was, Norman was not content to apply Lionel's, Rembrandt's or anybody else's methods without looking for something better. He detested most inflexible rules. Discussing the formulas and pontifical ordinances hedging etching about, in a letter to Ure Smith, he delivered himself of some ironic comments:

I confess that I know nothing of the religious ethics of etching, having with

23    Norman and Rose

24    Norman with Reg          25    Norman in his studio

26   An illustration from *The Magic Pudding*

great discretion taken care to read nothing whatever about them. As far as I might venture on a personal opinion, it seems to me that copper has a beautiful surface, and that upon it by a discreet use of certain chemicals, we may achieve the most delicate greys or the richest of blacks. Beyond that problem of its gamut of tones I have never troubled to go, and if one chooses to achieve the greys by scratching them with a feather, or the blacks by jumping on them with the feet, both methods may be considered holy, if the result justifies them.*

For himself, he tackled etching in the spirit of Ernest Moffitt's advice, 'Never take any notice of what people tell you you ought to do. Do the thing you want to do.'

He tested the methods evolved by his forerunners and, having studied the results, kept whatever seemed of value, then invented and applied refinements and variants of his own. His technique of using dots instead of fine lines for delicate tones of grey was his most revolutionary innovation. It was also the thing that more than anything else made etching, for him, a test of endurance. In seven or eight hours intensive work, sitting over the plate in a cramped posture and using a powerful magnifying glass, he could barely cover a square inch with dots; sometimes he worked on a single plate for as long as two or three months. The effort played hell with his eyes and worse hell with his gastric functions. After a day of it he had to soak his right hand in hot water to unbind the muscles.

He called etching 'the Black Art' and always said his studio was 'built over a hole in hell', but it fascinated him, and as a craftsman he was supreme among Australian etchers and arguably the equal of any etcher the world has seen. Whether the concept of life presented in his astronomical range of etched works—as diverse as *Enter the Magicians, Self Portrait, C Sharp Minor Quartet, Death of a Pierrot, Hyperborea, Allegro Vivace, Don Juan in Hell* and *Death's Mask,* to name a few at random—justified the technical mastery lavished on it is a matter of dispute. Opponents of what he stood for, and those who deny that he stood for anything more than an adolescent preoccupation with sex, dismiss his etchings, along with most of his drawings and paintings, as mere 'boudoir pictures', however technically accomplished, while his admirers see them as the expression of a unique vision of life. Time will decide who is right.

It was the need for some release from the mental and muscular tensions of etching that woke Norman's taste for music. He had never responded to any music except the marching tunes which Mary had played on the 'Lisnacrieve' piano when they were children. Now, in his late thirties, he discovered this new, and hitherto only dimly suspected, world. He was dazzled and bewitched. What joy, what consolation he had been missing all these years! Now he understood for the first time

* *Art in Australia*, No. 6, 1919.

K

why his friend Ruff Tremearne, who had been a talented violinist in their Creswick youth, talked of music in tones of rapture. Norman grew hot with shame at the memory of the way he had often cut Ruff short and pushed the conversation into some other channel.

As in so much else, Lionel broke the music trail and Norman followed. It began when Lionel bought a player-piano and pommelled Norman with esctatic descriptions of its capacity to produce music which could excite, soothe, uplift and captivate.

'It's the very thing for you, Joe', he urged. 'Damn it, shut away in these mountains you need music to keep your mind on an even keel. Look here, old man, you get a player-piano and you'll never regret it, I promise you.'

Norman had one and an assortment of rolls sent up from Sydney. Not knowing one composer from another, he was uncertain in the beginning but assurance soon came. Beethoven was the first of his musical gods—'the greatest, bravest and most joyous soul that ever dwelt on earth'. Although as time went on Norman formed a huge admiration for Mozart and Wagner, and a warm respect for some other composers including Bach and Rossini, Beethoven's seat on the pinnacle was never threatened. Norman had his musical aversions also; Brahms bored him, he detested Chopin ('He is trivial . . . a mean little mind, a self-sentimentalist'), and he could not bear Italian music.

He sometimes sat for hours playing Beethoven rolls, letting the music flow over his mind like a great cleansing river. He always said that if he had not lived in the era of the player-piano he would probably never have come to music. He could manage to make himself sit through an orchestral concert or listen to gramophone records but, even when it came to music, he liked to feel he was doing it for himself; he was never altogether happy as a mere listener. It was an unalterable element of his nature.


The puritans had hardly troubled Norman since before the war but they were dozing, not dead. He realized this in 1918 when *Art in Australia* put out a book of his pen drawings. Such a collection had been planned in 1914, then shelved when war broke out. When 1918 opened with the war dragging on, Ure Smith and Julian Ashton persuaded him to let them revive it.

'If we hold off any longer', Ashton told him, 'some of your best stuff will have to be left out. We've lost track of a few things already. They've vanished into private collections and we don't know where they are.'

Norman was reluctant because few of his drawings went even near satisfying him and none pleased him, but Ure Smith and Ashton kept at him and at last he said, 'All right. Do what you like with the damned stuff but don't expect me to have anything to do with it.'

They spent days rummaging through a big stand of drawers at Springwood crammed with black and white works of all kinds, and made their own selection. The book missed few of the drawings which had built Norman's reputation. The controversial pieces, notably *Pollice Verso* and *The Crucified Venus*, were in it; so were a number of morally uncontentious, and better, things, including *The Apotheosis of Villon, The Argument, Panurge Meets Pantagruel*, and three illustrations to Francis Thompson's *Tom o' Bedlam*. Ure Smith and Stevens expected him to be delighted but he was rather depressed; he was passing through one of the jaundiced periods which afflict every creative man and felt that the book only summed up and emphasized his shortcomings as a penman.

He became even gloomier when the Wowser hue and cry started—it seemed so piffling with the Allies and Germans still at death-grips and no certainty how long the war would go on or which side would win. He was denounced from sundry pulpits as a blasphemer and a peddler of immoral pictures. His mail brought many letters reproving or reviling him; whether signed or anonymous, they all went into the fire. Then, at the end of June, constituted authority took a hand. The Tasmanian Public Library in Hobart banned the book, on the ground that some of the drawings were obscene. The episode merely confirmed Norman's dislike of the Australian national ego—'a crude and bastardly conglomeration', he once said, 'of the basest contents of English Nonconformism, Scottish Presbyterianism and Irish Catholicism'.

He counted himself lucky that he was too busy to lose sleep over the antics of any library board. He was giving nearly all his time to a task which made him groan: turning out posters and cartoons for an army recruiting campaign. The Australian Government had twice tried and twice failed to carry a referendum in favour of conscription and, voluntary enlistment having fallen to a low level, determined measures were needed to bring in more fighting men. The recruiting organizers asked Norman to help. They knew his power. No other cartoonist had so much sway with Australians. At that time he and David Low were an exceptional cartooning team. Low, who had been sent to Melbourne as the *Bulletin*'s resident cartoonist soon after the war started, had won wide popularity; he was producing splendid work, distinguished by the gift of recognizing and deflating the pomposities of public men which was to make him internationally famous after he moved to London in 1919. But Norman was still unchallenged on the black and white throne. His 'dramatic and allegorical cartoons in the grand manner', as Low described them, forty years later, with a touch of derision,* were neither

* *Low's Autobiography* (London, 1956), p. 64.

subtle nor intended to be. but they breathed out a spirit of uncomplicated patriotism conspicuously well suited to the rather artless outlook of most Australians then.

Norman's feelings were mixed when he listened to the request that he should help the recruiting drive. He had qualms about exhorting other men to risk their lives in battle while he was safe at Springwood. Comforting himself with the reflection that he was unfit for any kind of active service, he agreed and flung himself into it, pushing aside everything but his *Bulletin* work. He induced Lionel, Ure Smith, Harry Julius and a few other artists to help, but his was easily the heaviest individual contribution. He gave four or five months to it. 'The stuff is not art', he said in a letter to Sir Baldwin Spencer in Melbourne, 'and its sole intention is to stir up the slack to a sense of what this war means, but it has been no end of toil'. His recruiting cartoons, many in colour, were deliberately and shamelessly emotive. Most of them exploited the theme of enemy frightfulness, depicting German soldiers as bloody-handed baby-killers, brutal rapists, and merciless barbarians in general. Seen today, these drawings are more laughable than horrifying but they must have been forceful arguments in the febrile atmosphere of 1918.

Other of Norman's propaganda drawings proclaimed the desperate need of the Australian soldier in the front-line trenches. One of the most striking was a poster bearing the title *The Last Call*. This showed three diggers lying dead and a fourth, with a blood-stained bandage round his head and one wounded hand grasping a rifle, blowing a rallying call on a bugle while spiked German helmets moved toward him against a funereal skyline. Working from a photograph, Norman had given his bugler the face of a young man named Jim who was serving in France with the Australians. He did it largely to please Jim's sisters, Fanny and Hilda, who were the cook and housemaid at Springwood. Fanny, tall, black-haired and black-eyed, with a touch of the gipsy, was a vital young woman and any healthy man of military age who was not in uniform did well to steer clear of her; if he came within earshot, she never failed to demand his reasons for skulking at home and letting other men fight his battles. Hilda, although younger and less fiery, was always at hand to second Fanny's outpourings of patriotic ardour. Together they were more daunting to stay-at-home Australians than a squad of recruiting sergeants.

Once the poster was printed and Jim, bugling his call to arms, began appearing on hoardings all over Australia, Fanny and Hilda were more energetic than ever in hounding the gun-shy into khaki. All unsuspecting, three young and stalwart stonemasons reported at Springwood one morning to build a courtyard wall. Before they had time to spit on their hands, Fanny, with Hilda at her elbow, appeared from the kitchen and loudly commanded them to explain why they were not in France helping Jim to stem the German avalanche. Two of the men stood their ground and went on working, pretending to ignore Fanny's thunderbolts, but the other, Tom, although the biggest and huskiest, could not stand it. He bolted and took refuge in a gully where he crouched, quaking. Having scourged the other two, Fanny and Hilda went after Tom. They cornered him in his gully and he stood, sweating and flushing, while Fanny raked him with scornful words. At last her vocabulary of insults ran out.

'Feel his feet, Hilda', she ordered.

Hilda pounced on the shrinking Tom and, stooping, ran her hands over his feet.

'Stone cold!' she announced.

Tom never went anywhere near the house again.

Other than that Norman's recruiting cartoons had little effect, as far as he knew. They were hardly printed and beginning to circulate in large numbers when Germany collapsed and it was all over. Norman was not sorry. He was not particularly proud of his efforts as a war propagandist.

In its issue of 14 November 1918 the *Bulletin* saluted the Armistice with full-page cartoons by both Norman and Low. Norman's showed a muscular figure, Democracy, overturning a throne labelled Autocracy and its ermine-robed occupant, and tumbling them into oblivion; it was printed above the optimistic line, *The End of it for Ever*. Low's bore the title *Haunted* and depicted a terrified Kaiser fleeing across a corpse-strewn battlefield pursued by a ghastly spectre of himself. It was given the star place on page five, while Norman's was relegated to page thirteen. If he felt slighted he did not mention it. Perhaps, like everybody else, he was too comforted by knowing that the war had ended to worry about any bruises to his self-esteem.

# 7

# Behind the Mortal Curtain
# 1918-23

'The war', Norman often said, 'gave me the marching tune I needed'. Reduced to simple terms, what the war gave him was an immutable faith in man's immortality. He rejected once and for all the idea which he had hitherto accepted without question that earthly death extinguished the spirit or soul; now he believed that when the body died and crumbled to dust the ego, sentient, vital and indestructible, continued living on another plane of the universe invisible and intangible to the human senses. It was an all but unbelievable about-face. Some of his friends were as startled as if the head of Soviet Russia had been appointed Archbishop of Canterbury, or *vice versa*. He angrily denied that his creed owed anything to Grandpa Williams's Christianity—what he called 'the Jesus-mongers' were still anathema to him.

Any hint that he was ever drawn to spiritualism roused him to an even fiercer pitch of rage, and time did not alter his almost frenzied insistence on the point. 'I would sooner', he once told Leon Gellert, 'be accused of sodomy'. Gellert and others did not understand his irascibility. His extra-worldly delvings seemed to them to bear every earmark of popular spiritualism, with some minor refinements of his own.

The creator of Sherlock Holmes, Sir Arthur Conan Doyle, visited Australia in 1920 preaching spiritualism and Norman went to some trouble to dodge him. Doyle was eager for a meeting. In a newspaper interview he said:

> It is the artistic world of Norman Lindsay which has impressed me most in Australia. He seems to me a man built on the models of the great sixteenth century Italians—a man who can paint, etch, do sculpture—in short, an artist all through. That was the old Italian tradition, exemplified by Leonardo da Vinci. We find it very seldom these days but it is realized in Norman Lindsay.

Doyle made particular comment on a tendency in Norman's art 'to grow more spiritual', and went on: 'In that direction, I am sure his future lies. What the world needs is spirituality in art, in thought, and in literature. We are sick of the realism of Zola.'* He put out other feelers but these also were ignored. 'I'd have liked to meet him', Norman told a friend, 'but I didn't want any association with his spiritualism'.

Although Norman had been physically far from the battles, the war of 1914-18 had made a terrible impact on his sensitive and imaginative mind. It had smashed his trust in a stable earth and brought him face to face with the stark evidence of the destructive forces underlying the brittle crust of civilization. Jack Lindsay reported an incident involving Bert Stevens which reveals something of the depth of Norman's horror.

> Stevens made some patriotically callous comments about the war and Norman burst out, 'Do you know what you're talking about? The war isn't something over there in Europe. It's here in this room. There's blood everywhere, all round us, on everything, on us. Can't you smell it?' Stevens blinked in dumb dismay.†

Norman was only one of millions of human beings who discovered that their most cherished beliefs had perished in the holocaust. If more articulate than most, he was no different from many others in kind; like them, he could not live in a vacuum, he had to find a new direction. He might have turned to Christianity, Buddhism, Islam or another of the established religious creeds, or to Marxism, Anarchism, Nihilism or some other antireligious philosophy, but none of these systems appealed to him. While he could be dogmatic in asserting his own doctrines and once confided to Syd Ure Smith, 'I can't tolerate a person who doesn't see eye to eye with me', he was an irreconcilable individualist and detested ready-made tenets and cut and dried precepts. For that very reason he was the last man to embrace any creed but one he evolved for himself.

His creed had no name. It did not lend itself to any concise and comprehensible tag. One of his friends dubbed it Normitualism but never used the coined epithet in Norman's presence; he knew that if he so much as whispered it their friendship would be over. Yet, notwithstanding Norman's declared abhorrence of any hobnobbing with ghosts, he was for some years an enthusiastic dabbler in the occult and an ardent experimenter in the pseudo-science of communicating with the psychic world. Later he expressed his scorn of the 'spook addicts' even more vehemently than he voiced it at the time; they were 'moonstruck half-wits' and there was no health in them. He also deplored the efforts of earth-bound people to converse with those on the other plane. Nearly fifty years later he told a radio interviewer:

* *Sydney Morning Herald,* 2 December 1920.
† *The Roaring Twenties* (London, 1960), p. 66.

We can talk to them but they cannot talk to us. We have a different speech problem. They think in different terms. They probably have a different time factor—substances about them are not the same as on earth and so on, so how can they talk to us? No, I think it's stupidity. I dislike it.

Judging by the uncompromising character of those words, he had succeeded in effacing all memory of his own attempts to talk with discarnate spirits which began in the late war years and continued until he became convinced, early in the 1920s, that these psychic explorations were either useless or unwise, and gave them up. Documents in public and private collections attest that he made a series of such attempts, including some highly successful ones by his own account; the authenticity of the evidence is beyond question.

Spiritualism in its crudest forms was inordinately popular in Australia as in some other countries about the time the war ended. Wives who had lost husbands, mothers who had lost sons, and other women who had lost menfolk were looking for any assurance of reunion beyond the grave. Spiritualism seemed to offer it. A fellowship of mediums sprang into being. Many were cynical opportunists with an eye to easy pickings who specialized in presenting so-called *séances* featuring such hocus-pocus as sepulchral voices, illuminated tambourines and trumpets, floating tables, spirit photographs, and cheesecloth 'ectoplasm'. Far more prevalent were sessions in private homes with two or more people working with an ouija board, a planchette or some other device on which a helpful spirit could spell out messages.

David Low, who had been playing at spirit communication for some years, fathered the vogue among Sydney and Melbourne artists. Harry Julius became an adherent and carried it to Springwood. Norman started by saying he would have nothing to do with such a 'drivelling business', but let himself be persuaded to try it and was soon an avid disciple. Rose was his usual partner at the ouija board but it is improbable that she ever thought of it as other than a mildly diverting pastime; she was too sceptical and earthy to delude herself into believing that the messages which the pointer spelt out were the product of anything but a combination of such mortal elements as animal magnetism and the promptings of the subconscious mind. To friends who pressed her on the subject she gave no answer except what one of them called 'a charming Mona Lisa smile'. But Norman, after his first hesitation fairly vibrated with excitement. He talked and acted with the elation of an alchemist who has found the philosopher's stone. For a time he was unable to get enough of it and contrived an ouija board which he could operate single-handed when Rose was busy or uninterested and no other partner was at hand.

He was in an emotionally receptive state when Harry Julius introduced him to these mysteries. Reg had been killed a few months earlier and

Norman recoiled from the thought that he would never see his brother again. The extinction of thousands of young lives before they had fairly begun outraged all his notions of natural justice. And then the ouija board gave him the answer, or what he saw as the answer. Grandpa Williams could have given it to him; indeed, Grandpa Williams had spent his life giving just such an answer to black Fijians and white Australians. It was the plainest answer imaginable to a great mystery: There is no death. Grandpa Williams did not arrive at it by conversing with the spirits—he would have considered the ouija board an instrument of the devil and thrown it on the fire. To him, the immortality of man's soul was an article of faith. He would as soon have questioned the divinity of Christ.

As soon as Norman had begun thinking for himself, he, like Lionel, had rejected Grandpa Williams's belief as insufferable superstition. Each man lived his span, died and found oblivion—any other conception was an invention of priestcraft to control the minds of the credulous masses. Yet now, almost as suddenly as Paul on the road to Damascus, Norman was changed. He never for a moment turned toward Christianity; nor did he accept the idea of one God—he believed there were many gods and none among them all-seeing and all-powerful. But his conviction of the survival of man's spirit was henceforth absolute. His categorical faith influenced all his actions from that time. When Archibald, who had continued to be a close friend and a frequent visitor to Springwood, died suddenly in September 1919, Norman merely said, 'Archie will have a host of friends where he has gone. He wouldn't thank us to mourn him.'

Once the principle was accepted everything was transparently straight-forward: on earth—which Norman equated with 'a sort of hell or testing-place', in Jack Lindsay's phrase*—we develop into what we are, then begin on the other plane where we leave off here, each of us finding his own level among his peers. Norman's Hereafter was not a sphere in which all sorts of spirit folk were haphazardly intermingled but one in which the inhabitants were graded according to the quality of their earthly achievements. If they developed highly here they went correspondingly high there, having carried with them every earthly faculty and gained a whole set of new senses to sharpen their perceptions and strengthen their talents. Norman granted a place in this mystic heaven even to the spirits of the lowliest ones, but saw them as denizens of the nethermost level. There were many other levels and the highest was reserved for the great creative figures in the arts such as Rubens and Dürer, Petronius and Cervantes, Beethoven and Mozart, Shakespeare and Villon. Norman revelled in the satanic humour as well as the splendours of the vision. 'Imagine

* *Meanjin*, March 1970, p. 41.

all the warring religious sects lumped together in one area of space', he would chuckle. 'They make a sufficient loony-bin with their antics on earth. What sort of Bedlam must they be inhabiting elsewhere!'

The detail of the messages which he received on his ouija board is of little importance. He had some long sessions with Shakespeare, Apollo and other immortals, as well as with his father and Reg. None of them seems to have told him anything he did not know or could not have imagined. Sceptics among his friends noted that the sympathies and hostilities expressed by those 'behind the curtain', to use a term Norman approved, always matched his own and that the tricks of speech were often identical with his. None of his unbelieving friends ever doubted his sincerity, or suspected that he was consciously fabricating messages; they saw him as the victim of a delusion involuntarily produced by his subconscious mind.

He was enchanted when Reg gave him news of one of his artistic idols, Turner, whom he called 'the Homer of landscape painting'. According to Reg, Turner was in a fury when they met because the people who supply colours to artists behind the curtain had sent him the wrong shade of yellow.

'What sort of looking man is he?' Norman asked.

'Funny little squeezed-up face, like Whiskers', Reg replied. Whiskers was a small and pugnacious Australian Silky terrier, one of the Springwood pets.

'Well, what else?'

'He's doing some great stuff here.'

'Did he say anything to you?'

'Yes. He said the earth was a rotten place for artists.'

Norman did not hide his occult researches from his intimates. On the contrary, he wanted to open the eyes of his fellows to the wonders he had discovered. Above all, he burned to convert Lionel, a pagan from boyhood, who lived by Einstein's doctrine that men come from nothing and will return to nothing. Lionel listened and grunted. He deplored both the waste of time and the intellectual morbidity involved in what he called 'trafficking with spooks'. Although Norman disavowed any faith other than in a radiant spiritual survival, Lionel could see little difference, 'except for an absence of harps and wings', between his brother's next world and his grandfather's Christian heaven.

He rebelled when Norman demonstrated the ouija board's workings to him as soon as he had unpacked his bag after arriving at Springwood for a fortnight's holiday.

'If you produce that thing again while I'm here,' he said, 'I'll pack up and go straight home'.

Norman was too innately courteous to affront a guest. While protesting that he did not understand such scepticism he kept the ouija
board out of sight for the rest of Lionel's stay and the time passed
agreeably enough.

Soon after Lionel finished his holiday Norman returned to the attack.

'Reg says of you, "Joe is a hard chap to convince about *us*" ', Norman
told him.

'Does he?' Lionel replied. 'Well, I'm afraid he's right.'

Believing that Norman's infatuation with the spirits could do nothing
to strengthen him either as an artist or a man, Lionel hoped it would
soon pass. He placed high value on their friendship and wished nothing
to imperil it, but his patience snapped after he read one long letter ad-
juring him to see the light. He wrote a sarcastic reply and signed it
'Mahomet's Uncle'. That was the first real sign of a crack in their friendship. But the end was not far off.


The years immediately after the war were momentous for Norman,
both personally and artistically. As he moved into his forties—he called
them 'the golden forties'—circumstances were combining to give new
meaning to his life.

Rose wanted children and, smothering his objections, Norman gave
in. He asked Katie for a divorce, quieting his conscience by adding a
lump sum of money to the allowance of five pounds a week he had
made her since the separation. She agreed with some reluctance—and only,
according to one version, after Norman had threatened to stop her allowance—and everything was put in train with a minimum of fuss. The
sluggishness of the divorce courts, however, defeated the steps Norman
and Rose had taken to ensure that their first child should be legitimate.
Norman's marriage with Katie was still undissolved when Rose was
confined. She wished the child to be born at Springwood and Norman
assented, even though Australia was in the grip of the world-wide
Spanish influenza epidemic of 1918 and no nurse could be found. It was
a complicated pregnancy, the baby was stillborn, the doctor was incompetent, and in the days that followed Rose nearly died from septic
poisoning. Her heart stopped twice and each time Norman restored
the beat by massaging the heart region with brandy. It was months
before he was able to rid his ears of the dirge-like howling which
the Springwood dogs set up under the window of Rose's room. He resolved that she should never again be subjected to such a risk, and
when her next pregnancy was well advanced they went to Sydney and
took a furnished house at Strathfield. The divorce decree was made
absolute while they were there, and Jane was born in January 1920,

soon after a clergyman, officiating at the bedside, had joined Norman and Rose in wedlock.

Norman was out of his element at Strathfield and could not work there. He attempted two water-colours but threw them aside in disgust. He was not worried about it. He knew that all would be well as soon as he got back to the mountains; the Springwood air stimulated him as nothing else could. From the time the war ended he had been pouring out pen drawings, etchings and water-colours, many reflecting his new philosophy, and a host of others were taking shape and maturing in his mind. It irritated him to hear his artistic enemies, and even some of his artistic friends, saying he had lost his way. They felt he had turned his back on life and was spending himself in depicting men and women that never were in a land that never was. He retorted that his people and his land were as valid as those Shakespeare created in *The Tempest*. He never pretended that it was not a world of his own. That, he believed, was its justification. He had no intention of being pushed off his chosen road, but its roughness sometimes disheartened him. 'If anyone assumes that going one's own way is the easy way they are very much in error', he once told his sister Mary. 'There's no harder way to go.'

He never wanted to be, nor ever pretended to be, a realistic artist but always insisted that he was a realist. To him, the terms were not only not interchangeable, but were poles apart. He believed the difference was exactly comparable with that between the prose writer, taking his subject-matter from the spectacle of life before his eyes, and the poet, drawing on the recorded experiences of mankind in all countries and all ages including his own, and from it evolving an idiosyncratic vision. Mary once asked him to define reality. He told her:

> The factual procedure of existence, damnable or desirable, passes on into non-existence with every tick of the clock. But from it we extract an emotional experience which becomes embedded in the very substance of our being. Thus we acquire an imagery of life distinct from its factual genesis. This imagery is imperishable. All art is based on it. Therefore the image and not its factual genesis is the true reality.

It was largely this literary, or poetic, element of Norman's mind that made him always welcome among writers and poets but something of an alien among artists.

Whatever his rivals or professional critics might say for or against it, his work made an extraordinary impact on laymen. No artist had ever before stirred Australians in general as he did. Some marvelled and some fulminated; but they took notice. His riggish fauns and frolicking satyrs, bacchanals, bewigged gallants, wantoning nude ladies and all the rest captured the attention of people who had never heard of Rembrandt or Velasquez, never been inside an art gallery, never thought

The Federal Divorce Bill was a topical subject when Norman
drew this cartoon for the *Bulletin*

of a picture except as something to fill a blank space on a wall. They
might not understand what he was driving at but the exuberance, verve
ande gaiety of what he did excited and held them. More than anything
else it was his treatment of sex that drew the public spotlight on to him
and his work and kept it there. To Norman, sex was a wonderful and
joyous thing. 'Sex is not only the basis of life, it is the *reason* for life'*,
he wrote at that time. He was driven by an overmastering purpose to take

* *Creative Effort* (London, 1924), p. 267.

sex out of the darkness in which the puritans hid it and let it be seen for what it was. He never exploited it as an artifice to gain an audience, although his evangelistic fervour sometimes made him guilty of tub-thumping on the sex theme, and he never became resigned to the furies of protest which his work generated. He could not see one reason why sex was a less proper artistic subject than a tree, or a seascape, or a bowl of fruit, and a thousand reasons why it was more important.

He went back to Springwood a week ahead of Rose and Jane, with his son Jack for company. As the hired car bore them through the outskirts of Sydney and toward the mountains, Norman expounded his philosophy of life with the certitude of an oracle. Jack was swept along by the cascade of shining words. Even before they reached Springwood he was a convert.

No two men could have been less like one another, physically or temperamentally, than this reunited father and son. Norman, who reminded Jack of 'a Renaissance sculpture of Julius Caesar',* was volatile, excitable, effervescent, loquacious. Jack, brown-haired, blue-eyed, round-faced, was introspective, unsmiling and taciturn—a young man still far from certain what he believed in but already in arms against bourgeois canons of art, morality and life.

The overtures which had led to this first meeting in eight years had come from Norman. Bertram Stevens had more or less nagged him into making them. Stevens had met Jack when he had come to Sydney to keep his mother company at the time of the divorce proceedings. Nineteen-year-old Jack was showing intellectual promise as an Arts student at the University of Queensland and writing competent verse in his spare time, and Stevens, liking the boy, kept urging Norman to acknowledge his existence. In the end Norman packaged up a dozen of his etchings and posted them to Jack, with a letter suggesting a visit to Springwood. Jack sent a friendly reply, although he experienced a tremor of conscience when he thought of his mother, who had settled back into the routine of life in seedy Brisbane boarding houses, drinking too much and passing the time by telling teacup fortunes. She found some bemused pleasure in watching her boys grow up, and her sister Mary's nearness was comforting, but otherwise her days slouched by in a drab procession.

Yet once the ice was broken between Jack and Norman, their correspondence went apace. Norman had been working on a book, *Creative Effort*,† in which he defined his newly evolved philosophy, with special emphasis on the thesis that the artist is the most important member of

---

* *Life Rarely Tells* (London, 1958), p. 174.

† *Art in Australia* published the first small edition in 1920—120 copies, of which 100 were for sale. An English edition, published in 1924, contained many textual modifications.

the community. He later called it 'a muddled work', a description which few would gainsay, but at the time he was in a simmer of enthusiasm over it and sent Jack a set of proofs. The rationale of *Creative Effort* bewildered and in some ways repelled Jack—among other things he could not agree that the earth existed 'only as a mudflat for the generation of a few geniuses'*—but within an hour or two of meeting Norman all his objections were charmed away.

That first visit to Springwood, when he stayed some weeks, was the beginning of a remarkable father-and-son friendship. Having cast aside all but his innermost misgivings, Jack adopted Norman's theories as his own. A recalcitrant filament of his brain sometimes became agitated and impelled him to question one article or another of the creed, but he succeeded in beating down the temptation. Like Grandpa Williams's Christianity, Norman's special religion demanded that its adherents have faith; it gave no scope for rationalization or doubt, nor for rejection of dogma. Even such a facet of it as the Olympian doctrine was an essential component of the fabric and had to be accepted along with the rest.

This doctrine represented Norman's conviction that the great creative artists down all the ages were products of the same family tree. He believed, with the primitive Greeks, that the gods had come down from Olympus in ancient times and begotten children on the earth people. According to this tenet, the blood of the gods ran in the veins of this race of Olympians and revealed itself in those acts of creativeness which set the great painters, sculptors, poets, musicians and writers apart from, and above, the unblest 'Earth Men'. Norman could not have asked for a more faithful proselyte than Jack, who continued to be for nearly ten years the most unquestioning of all his father's disciples.

Leon Gellert, who had been living in Sydney since 1918 and working as an English master at a high school, was one of the unbelievers, but he did not flaunt his scepticism; his friendship with Norman was as strong as ever and he saw no good reason to jeopardize it. He owed Norman and Rose a big debt for what they had done to find him a job in Sydney, and a bigger one for their help when he had married an Adelaide girl, Kathleen Saunders, at Christmas 1918, and had no money to put down as a deposit on a house for his bride. Apart from his meagre salary, his only asset was a long fantasy poem, *The Isle of San*. Norman was enthralled when he read it in manuscript and at once saw it as a means of raising the wind for Gellert. He did five etchings as illustrations and Rose printed them—600 prints which, marketed in the ordinary way at Norman's ruling price, would have netted the Lindsays some thousands of pounds. *The Isle of San* was issued in a limited edition of 120 copies.

* *Life Rarely Tells* (London, 1958), p. 174.

Not surprisingly, it sold out in a single afternoon and Gellert had the deposit for his house. Some other people did far better. One Sydney bookshop sliced out the etched illustrations and sold them at fifteen guineas each, making a little extra by selling off the denuded copies of the book at two guineas.

So if Norman wished to converse with the spirits Gellert did not mind. He saw it as nothing more than an endearing eccentricity in a man who had shown him unfailing kindness and surpassing generosity.

Although Norman's thinking on human issues was flexible and adventurous, he was never tempted to soften his attitude toward art techniques. He saw the School of Paris and all its works as a product of Europe's moral exhaustion and the neuroses engendered by the slaughter and agony of four years of destructive warfare. His own innovations had all been made within the classical framework, and when Post-Impressionism, Cubism and other experimental art forms came to Sydney after the war he was at first incredulous, then shocked, then angry. It was inconceivable to him that the modernists, whose work he had seen and detested in Europe, had not only kept their influence but greatly extended and strengthened it. In his eyes they debased every established value in art. He still refused to believe that these fooleries would last— people might be gullible but once the novelty wore off they would see through this monumental confidence trick and consign all the perpetrators and their absurd wares to limbo.

He would admit no merit in any modernist. A controversy over the work of the sculptor, Jacob Epstein, swept Europe and America in 1920. The echoes reached Australia and Norman's friend Howard Hinton, a wealthy and public-spirited Sydney patron of the arts, asked his opinion of Epstein. Norman replied by dismissing Epstein as 'a passing phase—the little notoriety which arrests public attention by cutting undignified capers, and is forgotten in a decade'. He was no less scathing in his comments on the other leaders of the *avant-garde*. The 'obscene Gauguin', Van Gogh, Matisse and their kind were, mentally, 'mere savages'. He believed that in twenty years no trace of their work would remain, except perhaps as the evidence of 'an extraordinary craze' which attacked the post-war generation. In an essay in his *Paintings in Oil*, published in 1945, he abated these views a little and, while remaining implacably hostile to all the more daring modern cults, even gave faint praise to Gauguin, Van Gogh and other Post-Impressionists. But nothing he ever said in talk with friends or in personal letters suggested that his thinking on any aspect of modernism had undergone any real or lasting change.

27   *Stop Thief!* an illustration to the *Satyricon* of Petronius

28   One of Norman's ship models

29   Norman working on one of his ship models

While the actions and theories of experimenters in his own special craft angered him most of all, he was also an enemy of modernism in poetry, prose, sculpture, music or any other field of self-expression. He deplored Gertrude Stein's 'baby babblings', and dismissed James Joyce as a charlatan whose work would be kept alive only by 'those academics who enjoy trying to unravel literary puzzles'. The rise of jazz made him nearly homicidal. 'I'd have a gross of gramophone needles driven into the epidermis of every jazz producer with a tack hammer', he told Ruff Tremearne. 'That might discourage them from filling the earth with sounds from Darkest Africa.' Tremearne, no less devoted to the great classical composers than Norman and a music-lover of longer standing, thought the idea admirable.

Norman diagnosed modern art as a symptom of a disease which was infecting all mankind. He hated going to Sydney, or staying there for a moment longer than he must because, to his eyes, the faces of the people in the streets were stamped with apathy and expressed a defeated and spiritless outlook. When *Art in Australia* published examples of work by some of the more celebrated modernist painters he wrote to Syd Ure Smith saying that 'in all those over-coloured and brutal representations' he saw despair, spawned by the exhaustion and disillusion resulting from the war. He kept on saying that modernism would quickly burn itself out and die, and his conviction did not waver as time went on and the movement in Australia grew stronger. In February 1922 he published a long article in *Art in Australia*, under the title 'The Inevitable Future'. This ran to some 12,000 words and in it Norman wrote:

> . . . primitivism as an expression of mind has failed to get even a hearing here. Efforts have been made to introduce it by a few idle busybodies, who think art is merely some 'new idea', some just invented fancy, something to entertain leisure in cultured gabble, but a little derision applied in time withered this noxious growth before it could root.

It is puzzling that he should have so badly misread the signs. Many other Australian artists and art connoisseurs disliked modernism no less fervently but few of them could ignore the evidence that it was tough and durable.

Norman's unqualified assertion that it was finished almost before it had begun was the more surprising since the article in which he declared himself contained some remarkably prescient forecasts of things to come. Although he was writing hardly more than three years after the guns had fallen silent in 1918, he warned that the world was moving toward another, and a more terrible, war 'as surely and relentlessly as the earth itself moves through space and time'. He begged his readers not to be deceived by talk about humanitarianism and the brotherhood of nations, then went on:

L

Today we have only touched on man's capacity for destruction. Tomorrow he will throw battalions across the air, and drive armies under the sea. He will use radio-activity to harness the sun's rays and generate a power that will wipe out cities at a flash. He will cultivate disease bacilli which will depopulate whole countries in a few weeks.

Prophesying that Germany would rise again and overwhelm France, and that commercial enmity between Japan and America would 'involve the whole Pacific in a special hell', he argued that the only way some control might be exercised over man's destructive compulsions was by a restoration of the great creative values in life and art which had been jettisoned in the 1914-18 war. Hence his enthusiasm for what he saw as Australia's rejection of those art values which he considered evil, and the hope this offered for the future. Like much of Norman's philosophical writing, 'The Inevitable Future' revealed an uncanny gift of foretelling distant events coupled with a strabismic view of what was happening under his nose, particularly if that was something in which his emotions were deeply engaged.

It was not only the new wave in the creative arts that repelled him. Most of the spectacular advances achieved by scientists and engineers were, to him, also abominable. He fought Rose's proposal to have a telephone installed at Springwood and for many years would not consent to speak on it. His antipathy to the radio was equally strong. With much reluctance he learned the rudiments of driving a motor car but, after bumping into a telegraph pole and backing into a fence, got out and walked home, leaving the devilish contraption at the roadside. As a means of getting from one place to another he rated the horse and trap high above any motor car; or, for a romantic journey, the hansom cab, which he believed to be 'the most perfect vehicle ever devised for an intimacy of two people'. The only sophisticated mechanical contrivance he ever wholly approved was his player-piano—he could bring himself to overlook its base genealogy since it had revealed to him the glories of Beethoven and Mozart. Left to himself, he would not have abandoned oil lamps for electric light, nor a wood-burning for an electric stove. In general, he held that mechanization, far from simplifying existence, had complicated it by putting man at the mercy of a race of 'arrogant mechanics' who delighted in making tyrannous use of the power which their technical knowledge placed in their hands.

Although Lionel, who had a wide knowledge of chemistry and astronomy, was predictably enthusiastic about the forward march of scientific and engineering technologies, his opinion of the rebel art cults which gained strength between the two wars was as adverse as Norman's. He did not however share his brother's antipathy to the Post-Impressionists, whom he saw as victims of 'a dealer's ruse to affiliate them with the succeeding generation of mountebanks';* it was on Cubism, Dadaism, Purism, Constructionism, Neoplasticism, Vorticism, Expressionism, Surrealism, Synchromism, Numeralism, and the like that he trained his pen and tongue. His was the surest and most articulate Australian voice raised against the modern cult. Norman concurred in practically every word of it and, seeing how well his and Lionel's views agreed, the two might have been expected to join forces to fight the modernists in the 1920s and 1930s. They did not, for in 1922 the seemingly invulnerable friendship which had linked them since boyhood was irreparably broken.

Early in March 1922 Lionel took the night express from Sydney to Melbourne. He was on his way to spend ten days meeting buyers and old friends at a show of his water-colours and to discuss arrangements for a show of his etchings and woodcuts later in the year. The success of both shows was assured. Public recognition had been slow in coming, but Lionel's work was now in strong demand among Australian collectors and had begun to bring him a steady income. After never sparing himself for nearly twenty years to ensure that his wife and their son and daughter should want for nothing, he could at last plan for the time when he would forsake the drudgery of journalistic and commercial art and concentrate all his efforts on the fine work he yearned to do. He had already made up his mind to retire as the Sydney *Evening News* cartoonist in three or four years and go to Europe with his wife for a long stay. He would still be only a year or two past fifty then, and did not doubt that he could find a profitable overseas market for his prints and water-colours. The future looked rosy.

The only dark cloud in Lionel's sky was the unabating stress between him and Norman. Their letters had been growing steadily more astringent over the last year and the cracks in their friendship deeper. Since Lionel did not for one moment regret the sacrifices he had made for the sake of a happy marriage, he did not much mind when Norman twitted him on having turned his back on the Bohemianism of his youth and become a respectable suburbanite, a complacent materialist, and a lost soul. What did exasperate him were Norman's unremitting efforts to persuade him to embrace spiritualism and a belief in man's immortality— 'the glorious resurrection in a Watteau paradise bathed in German mist', as Lionel thought of it with mingled sorrow and stupefaction. He could not begin to understand how a one-time pagan like Norman had become obsessed with this preposterous creed. Their friendship might have been in less danger if Lionel had liked Rose and been able to reach Norman through her, but, while admiring her business skill and thoroughgoing

* Lionel Lindsay, *Addled Art* (Sydney, 1942), p. 3.

professionalism in everything she tackled, he found her hard and believed that her influence on his brother was harmful.

Lionel had been dismayed when he read *Creative Effort*. The book had struck him as being 'the evangel of an inverted Wowser'. He found it pretentious and could think of nobody less fitted than Norman to write it. While Norman was blessed with a wonderful agility of mind and a powerful imagination, his reading had been unorganized if wide; it betrayed the eclecticism of a highly intellectual monkey and, in Lionel's opinion, had supplied none of the background of solid scholarship required for a venture into the metaphysical jungle. Lionel kept on hoping that old Joe would sooner or later recover his sense of proportion and recognize the absurdity of *Creative Effort* and what it stood for. When he did, perhaps they would laugh over it and rebuild the old happy comradeship.

He did not think much about Norman in his first days in Melbourne. There was not time. His show went even better than he had dared to hope and his days were full. A host of old friends dropped in to greet him. He had several cheery meetings with his youngest brother, Daryl, who had married and settled in Melbourne; after coming home from the war Daryl had abandoned a bushman's life and launched himself as a professional artist. Another of Lionel's callers was an acquaintance named John Shirlow, a Melbourne artist and art teacher, who was beginning to make a reputation as an etcher. Shirlow told him that two well-regarded Melbourne men, George Ellery, the Town Clerk, and Bob Croll, a senior officer of the Education Department and a minor writer, were eager to meet him, and suggested lunch. Lionel accepted the invitation. He was always brimming over with ideas clamouring for expression and enjoyed nothing more than an opportunity to air them to a responsive audience. They were five at table, for Ellery's son was also present, and Lionel enjoyed himself. He did not take long to conclude that George Ellery, Croll and young Ellery were intelligent as well as earnest listeners; and although he suspected that much of the talk was far above Shirlow's head he was grateful to their host for at least sitting back in unobtrusive silence.

They ranged over a wide field, with Lionel holding the floor. There was much talk about art and literature. One of the others asked Lionel's opinion of a series of novels which H. G. Wells had written late in the war and just afterwards, expressing a belief in the transcendental. Lionel gave his views at some length. They went on to explore the reasons behind the post-war upsurge of interest in spiritualism; or, rather, Lionel explored them while the others listened. From there it was only a short step to Norman's philosophical somersault and the complex system of ideas he had proclaimed in *Creative Effort*. Exactly what was said will never be known because, naturally, none of those around the lunch table made notes of a discussion which was essentially private and informal. When the party broke up they all thanked Shirlow for bringing them together, voted it a stimulating meeting, and went their separate ways. A few days later Lionel took the express back to Sydney, well pleased with the results of his Melbourne visit.

Two months elapsed before the storm broke. It took the form of a four-page hand-written letter from Norman accusing Lionel of having slandered him in the presence of several witnesses. Norman threatened legal action if necessary to force his brother to keep silent about him in future, and said he wished for nothing further between them but 'an icy avoidance of all contact, and final separation in word, deed and spirit'. Lionel was dazed and unbelieving. The notion that the letter might refer to anything he had said at Shirlow's luncheon party did not occur to him. Indeed, although his exasperation with Norman's ouija board experiments and theories of life everlasting had caused him to make ironical remarks on many occasions, he was not conscious of ever having said anything to anybody, in Melbourne or elsewhere, which might rank as a slander calling for legal action. Then, in a tense interchange of letters, he lighted on the answer: he was supposed to have said in Melbourne that Norman was insane. He was staggered. Norman should have dismissed the tale, but he was in a hypersensitive state; for two or three years trouble-makers had been sending him reports of any and every adverse comment on him and his beliefs made by the over-talkative Lionel, and his resentment had been steadily working toward a point where it had burst into flame.

Having written several impassioned letters to Springwood declaring his innocence of any slanderous talk, Lionel went to work to discover the author of the insanity gossip. It did not take long. Daryl wrote from Melbourne to tell him that Shirlow was putting it around 'and taking your name as having told him'. Lionel wrote to Ellery and Croll asking if either remembered his saying anything which might have been construed as a statement that Norman was mad. Croll replied that it was 'quite untrue' that Lionel had said anything of the kind. 'While we were all critical, some disagreeing with one phase of Norman's work and some another', Croll said, 'we were, as I recall it, unanimous in proclaiming him a great genius'. Ellery's letter, after noting that they had merely discussed 'the metaphysical bias' displayed in *Creative Effort*, added: 'I am quite at a loss to understand what mischievous busybody has been at work distorting a perfectly harmless conversation'. Lionel then wrote to Shirlow in ominously measured terms. Shirlow sent a scared reply. At their meeting in Melbourne, Shirlow's letter said, Lionel had spoken of Norman 'in the most laudatory manner'. Shirlow went on to say that at no time had he himself spoken of Norman 'in the manner you suggest'. He added: 'I did not say he was insane or anything that could bear that meaning . . . So far as I know there is no such rumour here'. It was clear to Lionel now. Shirlow, perhaps stimulated by envy of the Lindsays' success as etchers, had concocted a scandalous yarn based on a conversation beyond his comprehension, then gone about retailing it.

Lionel was cleared but the damage had been done. He and Norman could not unsay the harsh and wounding words they had written. Norman was still too hot with resentment of a fancied wrong to heed an explanation, and Lionel was in no mood to give one. The episode had shocked him to the depths of his being. He knew he could never again think of Norman without suffering a twinge of pain. In the years to come they were to meet a few times, and even to greet one another, shake hands and smile, but never to talk and argue and laugh in the old carefree way. Something had died in each of them and all the wishing could not bring it back to life.

Sickness was aggravating the brittleness of Norman's temper at that time. He was battling against recurrent physical ills and although not the cause of his break with Lionel these probably contributed to the harshness of it. While incapable of self-pity, he relieved his mind by cursing his 'vilely uncomfortable body'. Rose, knowing how close he had been to death after their return from Europe, was worried. It was well that she was a strong woman, because her hands were more than full; as well as Norman and Jane, she now had a second daughter to care for—Helen, always called Honey, who had been born in 1921.

A period of acute nervous discomfort had combined with Norman's bodily ailments to depress his spirits. Bert Stevens had died suddenly in February 1922 and Norman, in keeping with his belief in the spirit's survival, had refused to mourn him. When Rose said, 'Bert will think you a dirty dog for not going to his funeral', he replied, 'I trust and believe Bert is in a place that is beyond such absurd nonsense'. A little later he remembered that a few years before he had written some explosive letters to Stevens, reviling George Robertson. These had originated in his anger over a story somebody had told him that Robertson had said he was exerting a bad influence on Leon Gellert. Norman could not remember everything he had written to Stevens but he knew that, letting his pen run wild, he had tagged Robertson 'a lousy Scotchman', 'a proud Scotch devil', a 'mean beast', and probably worse, and had condemned him to the lowest depths for publishing 'servant girl poets' like Zora Cross and 'music hall poets' like C. J. Dennis. He told himself he had better make sure that Stevens had destroyed the letters. If not, then he must try to get them back. There'd be hell to pay if they fell into Robertson's hands.

He asked Mrs Stevens to sell them to him. She said she was sorry: all her husband's papers were on offer to George Robertson. Norman was in a ferment of anxiety as the days went by. Then at last news reached Springwood that Robertson had bought the papers for £400. Norman was in despair. He had meant every syllable of the epithets he had used of Robertson when he wrote them but they no longer reflected his opinion. His rancour having passed, he had even grown to like the man and would have given anything—a good deal more than £400 if need be—to spare Robertson distress and himself embarrassment. Well, there was only one thing for it. He or Rose must go down to Sydney, see George Robertson and try to make things right. Norman decided that he was too busy to go—he couldn't spare an hour, much less the better part of a day. And, anyway, Rose would be a better emissary, Robertson would listen to her where he'd more than likely throw Norman out into the street. Rose's time was full also but, accustomed to being given the sticky tasks, she sighed and consented, and one day in April went along to Angus and Robertson's big bookshop and publishing office in Castlereagh Street. She climbed the stairs to the first floor more than half-expecting a stormy reception. Robertson greeted her with a smile and the shadows melted after the first few words were exchanged.

'How did you like the things Norman called you in the letters?' Rose asked.

'At first I was surprised', he said. 'I didn't think I loomed so large on his horizon. But I confess I simply had to laugh at some of the names he called me.'

Rose told Robertson that when Norman was 'in one of his moods' he wrote letters until he worked off his spleen. What he said at such times counted for nothing.

'I'd say that his days for intimate letter-writing are over now', Robertson said drily. 'He'll give it up.'

'Not he!' said Rose. She knew Norman too well. 'But I'll take care they don't get posted. I've a box full of his unposted letters now. He works off the high pressure and I put the letters away. He's none the wiser.'

They parted like old friends. Robertson, whose stern exterior hid a generous heart and a good sense of humour, bore no ill will. He had read only a few of Norman's letters, then bundled them up with the rest of Bert Stevens's papers and presented the collection to the Mitchell Library.

Norman could smile once more when Rose gave him an account of the meeting. He wrote to Robertson saying he hoped they could be friends henceforth. With uncharacteristic humility, he apologized for 'the irritable things' which he had scribbled in letters and regretted his lack of restraint in having confided them to 'an ass like Stevens'. Robertson replied telling him not to give it another thought. 'It is extremely unlikely', he said, 'that yours are the only letters extant in which I get a trouncing—but then, on the other hand, there are sure to be others in which I am eulogized, and if Posterity ever takes the trouble to weigh the evidence the verdict will probably be a dashed sight more favourable than I deserve'. Norman and he sometimes had minor differences after that but their friendship, although respectful rather than affectionate, was never again threatened.

The bother over the indiscreet letters, the shock of the rift with Lionel, and the nagging of persistent bodily ills reduced Norman's creative yield but by no means stopped it. Even when he grumbled that he was able to get nothing done his output of etchings, water-colours and pen drawings was still two or three times as great as that of any but the most prolific of his brother artists. It troubled him, however, that he had so much serious work to do and, as he saw it, was doing so little. In this mood he chafed under the demands of the *Bulletin*. Although his cartoons and other drawings did not take up many hours each week, the call to journalistic pick-and-shovelling always seemed to come just when he was at grips with an etching or a painting; and creative momentum, once lost, often took days to recover. It was some consolation that he no longer had to turn out drawings for the *Lone Hand*, which had quietly died early in 1921 after passing from the *Bulletin*'s ownership seven years before. 'Cartoon day' at Springwood was the nightmare. His cartoons were as accomplished and popular ar ever but he was feeling the strain and, about the time that the crisis in his conflict with Lionel loomed, he asked the *Bulletin* for a few months off. Macleod, now in his seventies but no less active and forceful, and Samuel H. Prior, who had succeeded Edmond as editor in 1915, knew the *Bulletin* needed Norman's work, but they could not deny him a break. He put aside the journalistic shackles with a feeling of relief and, free to give his creative energies full play, plunged into the work he wanted to do.

Macleod and Prior guessed it was only a matter of time before the *Bulletin* would lose him altogether. They were ready to pay high to keep him but they knew that money might not be enough. His temporary withdrawal gave them a good chance to look for a possible successor and they tried several different guest cartoonists. Only one really pleased them. This was a young man named Percy Leason, who had come to Sydney from Victoria to work for Smith and Julius as a staff artist. Leason did not have Norman's dramatic power or Low's cutting edge but he had an engaging style, an eye for character and a gift of comedy. Many of the major political cartoons in the second half of 1922 were his and he continued to make frequent appearances when Norman returned as cartoonist-in-chief.

Norman did not go back to his *Bulletin* work with any zest. He wanted the time it ate up, not only for the work on which he put a lasting value but also to propagate his personal philosophy, for his evangelistic zeal was as strong as ever. Seeing the danger signals, Macleod and Prior kept a tight hold on Leason. It was a prudent act. Only six months of 1923 had passed when Norman decided to finish with journalism. He had been at it for over a quarter of a century and it had paid him well, but now the years were flashing by and time was precious. Why, in another year or so he would be half-way through 'the golden forties', yet here he was pottering about with drawings which were forgotten a week after they were printed.

Macleod and Prior said his retirement was unthinkable. He was a kind of national institution, they told him—he had a patriotic duty to go on using his skill to make Australians think and laugh. Norman replied that he had made his decision and would not unmake it. They pressed him to stay on the staff doing only one drawing a week: the chief cartoon. Surely that would leave him ample time for his serious work? He listened with, for him, astonishing patience while they marshalled all their arguments, then said no. He was done with journalism and no inducements they could dangle before him made him waver. They might as well have tried to shift Ayers Rock.

So in the end they shrugged and gave up—the *Bulletin* would just have to make do with young Leason. As for Norman, his heart had never been lighter. Now he could please himself.

# 8

# *On the Crest of the Wild Wave*
# *1923-29*

The angriest storm his work had yet provoked broke without warning. He heard the first rumblings in the middle of 1923 while he was still pressing the *Bulletin* to free him from journalistic servitude. These quickly grew in strength and violence until the uproar dwarfed the clamour roused by any of his earlier pictures. It was his first full-scale experience of what he afterwards called the 'witch-burning furies of the mass mind', and it appalled him.

The occasion of it was the selection of pictures to be shown in a representative exhibition of Australian art in London. Lord Northcliffe, the father of modern journalism and the most powerful British newspaper publisher of his time, had suggested the exhibition, while visiting Australia some two years before in the course of a world tour. Ure Smith, who had succeeded seventy-year-old Julian Ashton as president of the Society of Artists, saw the possibilities. He and Ashton sounded a number of leading artists and influential laymen, and found most of them enthusiastic. Norman had given the idea his approval when Ure Smith first put it to him; the essential thing, he had said, was to get together a show which would convince 'the dull English' that Australia was a nation with an ideal of civilization. Then, after a few weeks, he had changed his mind and told Ure Smith he believed that such an exhibition would leave the English public unmoved, that the English critics would dismiss it as an expression of mere provincialism, and that its only positive result would be to depress and unsettle Australian artists and connoisseurs when they read what London said of it. He had not made his objections publicly known and had agreed to let a group of his own works be included, albeit with some misgivings—he expected his best pictures to be damned as licentious and probably attacked in the

English newspapers. He was convinced too that English eyes would fail to discern the harsh beauties of Hans Heysen, the subtleties of Elioth Gruner, and the peculiarly Australian merits in the work of many other artists.

Norman was one of the few influential doubters and the exhibition was made ready. Works by about a hundred artists were chosen. Heysen, Gruner, Arthur Streeton, Fred McCubbin, Hugh Ramsay, E. Phillips Fox, George Lambert, W. B. McInnes, Florence Rodway, Ambrose Patterson and most of the other significant Australian artists of the period were included. In June 1923 the collection was put on public show in Sydney and thunder began to roll. On 16 June the *Sydney Morning Herald* printed a leading article praising the idea of advertising Australia and Australian art through a London exhibition. In the last paragraph the editorialist bent a severe and grandmotherly frown on Norman, although without naming him:

> The selectors have seen fit to include a number of works—namely, black and white—which are frankly indecent, and which should never have been shown at all, much less chosen to represent Australian art . . . The brilliancy of the genius which produced them is not, cannot be, denied, nor can the cleverness and the mastery of line be questioned. Indeed, it is because of these very qualities that they are criticised. There is no prudery in this protest, although we shall, of course, be charged with it; but merely the desire to speak of what we believe to be 'mean things' with indignation. We recognise the desire of every citizen to choose for himself within a most elastic limit what books or pictures he pleases. But we do not recognise the right—and must protest against its claim—of anyone to thrust upon this exhibition, in the high and sacred name of art, a set of pictures whose subject and execution suit better the pages of the *Satyricon*.

The topic erupted in the correspondence columns. Some letterwriters congratulated the editor on his stand 'in the interests of decency and morality' and against this 'slur upon our art'. Others urged the government to stop Norman's pictures from being shown in England with the Australian exhibition. The Women's Section of the Australian Protestant Truth Society declared that Norman's pictures were 'an insult to the moral and artistic outlook of Australians'. A meeting of the Women's Reform League gave a certain Miss Hebblewhite a rapt hearing when she assailed Norman's work:

> One wonders fearfully what will be the status of the future citizen when art such as this is lauded to the skies, art which brings to the surface the animal primitive passions, lewdness, sex revelation, and nudity, against which even artists have raised their hands in protest and disgust. The human figure is God-given—it is divine. We are all aware of that fact, but when there is an obsession on the part of great artists to portray that figure in all positions suggestive of bestiality and nudity, the pure-minded citizen is filled with nausea.

A deputation waited on Mr Albert Bruntnell, the New South Wales Minister for Public Instruction. The chief speaker, Mr D. R. Hall, said he valued Australia's reputation too highly to allow it to appear in England that the man who produced such pictures as Norman Lindsay's was a representative Australian artist. It would appear in London, said Mr Hall, as though Australia had a large percentage of degenerates who were afflicted with sex mania; otherwise such pictures could not find a market. Many artists were able to portray nude figures without giving offence to any but prudes, but this was not so of Norman Lindsay. In the galleries of England, France, Belgium and Holland one saw no pictures so outrageous as those included in this collection. Having listened, the Minister replied that he would not decide whether Norman's pictures were objectionable. If they were either indecent or immoral, he said, it was for the police to take action. The deputation left, disgruntled but helpless.

The opening of the exhibition, at Burlington House in Piccadilly, the home of the Royal Academy, was fixed for 11 October. Elioth Gruner, who had gone to London representing the Society of Artists, was finding difficulty in publicizing it because the 'godfather' of the project, Lord Northcliffe, had died the year before. The pictures arrived by sea in September, and events at once solved Gruner's problem. The British Customs authorities decided to inspect Norman's pictures before letting them be shown. London dailies splashed the news and the Australian exhibition became a lively issue. According to one account, the action was inspired by the anti-Lindsay coterie in Australia; according to another, by a Sydney newspaper looking for a sensational story. The Customs people asked the Royal Academy to adjudicate, and after some days the pictures were released. By then the exhibition was the talk of London art circles. So was Norman. 'Whatever else may be said—and much has been said—of his pictures, no one could honestly allege that they are at all indecent', Gruner told a newspaper interviewer. 'We are all proud of him, and none of us in the artistic world shares the prejudices of the purists.'

A large crowd blocked the approaches to Burlington House when the doors opened on 11 October. Modishly gowned women and immaculately dressed men jammed the rooms within a few minutes and the doors had to be closed. Hundreds of people were shut outside. Most of them waited on through the afternoon, and three or four were let in every now and then as people inside left. Norman's nudes were the magnet. As one reporter noted, 'Nearly every one squeezed through the crowd to see them first'. One royal personage, on seeing the drawings, 'stood back, ejaculated "Gad, what wenches!" and strode briskly forward. The second, after her equerry had tried to bar the way and refused to accompany her into the wicked room, made a thorough survey and then remarked with truly royal innocence, "But why has he put stockings on some of them?" '*

The show was a popular success but opinions of its artistic worth were mixed. Most of the critics praised Lambert, Ramsay, Streeton, Heysen, Gruner and a few others, and nearly all were dazzled by Norman's technical wizardry but disturbed by what he did with it. *The Times* said:

> The poetry of his conception is marred by a crudity of detail, and a wonderful imagination is blended with an almost repugnant reality. It is unfortunate that his great genius is so often directed to the apotheosis of the unpleasant.

The *Morning Post* said:

> Lindsay is one of the most brilliant of living pen draughtsmen. In one or two of his somewhat foolish fantasies there are passages of great technical beauty, but his mind seems to be perplexed with memories of inspired Gibson Girls and dreams associated with Bavarian sausages, sauerkraut and beer. Lindsay has other moods, influenced perhaps by the airy heights and vast distances of his native land. He then creates works which are things of beauty and a joy for ever.

One of the major figures of the British art world, Sir William Orpen, R.A., told a *Daily Express* reporter on the opening day:

> The exhibition is good. The work shows great promise for a young nation. But please ignore the black spot—Lindsay. His work is bad. It shows no sign of art, no technique—nothing. Ignore it.

In a considered criticism for the Sydney *Sun* and the London *Sunday Express* Orpen wrote of Norman:

> I understand in Australia there has been much talk as to whether his work is indecent or not. Why any one ever took any interest in it is beyond my comprehension. His works shown here are certainly vulgar but not in the least indecent. They are extremely badly drawn; they show no sense of design and a total lack of imagination. What a joy it is to pass from these stupid blunders and find cheek by jowl George Lambert's boy's head—full of young life and showing the true joy of the artist in putting it on paper with great feeling!

Norman would have cared less if the critic had been almost anyone else—he believed that Orpen and John Singer Sargent were the two outstanding European painters of their time. He was sufficiently moved to give the Sydney *Sun* a statement directed at critics 'incapable of conceiving art from any other aspect than the usual studio gabble on aesthetics, when they do not descend to the depth of Mrs Grundyism worthy of the immortal Podsnap himself'. He also wrote a two-page reply for *Art in Australia*, in which he said that Orpen's attack might fall 'under the heading of bad manners, but hardly under that of serious criticism'.

---

* Attributed to Gruner in Jack Lindsay, *The Roaring Twenties* (London, 1960), p. 121n.

Whether Norman's pictures were good or bad, it was to see them, a *Daily Graphic* columnist wrote, that crowds were still queueing up outside Burlington House every afternoon when the show had been open a fortnight, 'just as if they were outside a theatre'. Some people, he reported, had to wait for an hour; and when closing time came it sometimes took an hour to empty the room in which the Lindsay drawings hung.

If many of these people were there for other than purely aesthetic reasons the result was still a powerful advertisement for Australia and Australian art.

The London hubbub made Norman irresistible to Australian weavers of legends. Some component of his personality had always inspired them and now the myths surrounding his name grew bigger and gaudier. His friends knew the truth: it would have been all but impossible to find a more abstemious and less concupiscent man in his personal habits. The public did not know it and did not want to; for most Australians he was a Bacchanalian profligate and nothing could alter it. He did not let it bother him. To hell with the gossips! They could talk themselves hoarse! This was the price a man must expect to pay if he treated the mob with disdain. He never pretended that the miracle of sex did not fascinate him as an artist. He could see beauty in it, but to his eyes the amorous writhings of the human animal were the stuff of comedy first and foremost. The most startling drawings and paintings that he ever publicly exhibited were almost prim alongside the specimens of gay and uninhibited erotica which he did for his own and his close friends' amusement. Many of these have been lost, but some are extant in private collections; now and then one turns up under a dealer's counter.

At least he could afford to go his own way without asking leave of anyone. Buyers were waiting to snap up every drawing, etching or painting he did. Few Australians of the day who lived by their own exertions and not on wealth inherited from astute or lucky forbears had a larger income. No other Australian artist earned more, and only Streeton, Lambert, Longstaff and one or two others commanded anything like so rich and ready a market. Norman had Rose to thank for much of his affluence. She revelled in matching her wits with dealers and beating them. He was glad to leave all the business management to her; he knew he would be lost in that trackless and shifty world. Her critical faculty was equally precious to him. When he knew he had gone wrong in a picture but could not tell where, he always turned to Rose. Having studied it she would perhaps say, 'That figure is breaking the movement' or 'That bit of colour is out of key', and she was always right. Knowing her dislike of fulsomeness, he never expected anything but the most laconic praise from her. If she looked at a picture and said 'Yes, it's all right', he knew he could rest content. But his success was founded on his own qualities above all else. The strength of the public demand for his pictures was an acknowledgement of his creative power and technical mastery, helped by the bouts of irate shouting which his work was forever inciting. He detested his notoriety, but accepted it as the inescapable penalty of his refusal to bow to the Wowsers. And it was cheering to know that although the wave he was riding was a wild one at least he was on its crest.

At Springwood he and Rose lived in elegant style, with a cook-general, a housemaid, a nurse for the girls, a gardener, and usually a bush-worker or two. 'I'm uneasy away from gum trees and the good earth', he told his friend, Sir Baldwin Spencer. 'I find the silence of nature an immense stimulus to work.' These were not careless words. When the walls of his studio became overbearing and he needed a change of surroundings, he took a pick, shovel and mattock and put in an afternoon cutting a foot-track or helping to dig a bathing dam. If he let himself be coaxed, bullied or otherwise cajoled into going to Sydney he grumbled all the time until he was back in the mountains. While his sister Mary was on a visit to Springwood, Rose arranged that the three of them should spend a few days in Sydney, combining business and pleasure. They took three single rooms at the Hotel Australia. The first night Norman behaved impeccably; he even made no demur about dressing in evening clothes and escorting Rose and Mary to the theatre.

Rose stormed into Mary's room next morning.

'He's gone', she said.

He had risen early and slipped away, leaving a note to say he was catching an early train to Springwood. A series of business and social engagements had been made and Rose, with Mary in attendance, had to keep them and explain Norman's absence as best she could.

His antipathy to Sydney in some measure reflected his disappointment with the drift of the art movement there. Although taking no active part in running the Society of Artists, he deplored the growing influence of the modern group in its affairs and wrote some reproachful letters to Ure Smith on the subject. Ure Smith's deification of the elegant, witty and dashing George Lambert, who had taken Sydney's art and social worlds by storm when he returned from Europe in 1921, particularly hurt Norman. He admired nothing about Lambert the artist except his technical ability and detested Lambert the man for his swaggering arrogance, which Norman saw as a disagreeable mask for an insecure and timorous ego. He felt that Ure Smith had discarded him for Lambert and was guilty of an act of betrayal.

His self-chosen isolation was by no means altogether healthy. It was

The Wowser's Wife and—

good for technical concentration but not always for his peace of mind. He chewed over any adverse comment on his work or philosophy which came to his ears, inflating casual remarks into tirades of denigration and imagining that supposed friends as well as known enemies were continually talking treason against him. But solitariness gave him a nimbus of his own, and most notables from overseas or other Australian states who visited Sydney wished to meet 'the mad artist' who lived in the Blue Mountains producing works which roused both songs of praise and hymns of hate. Many did meet him, but with only a few exceptions they had to go to him. They rarely interrupted his work; he would come out of his studio for lunch, but nearly always excuse himself as soon as the meal was over and get back to work, leaving the burden of the entertaining to Rose.

An occasional visitor of compelling personality made him break his rule. Dame Nellie Melba was one. She was in Sydney helping to manage the 1924 Melba-Williamson grand opera season and singing many of the great soprano roles. She owned many pictures by Australian artists including some of Norman's, and wanted to judge for herself if the defamatory tales which Australians spread about him had any more substance than the ones they spread about her. Early in her career she had been branded a drunkard by the unscrupulous journalist John Norton, in articles in the Sydney-based scandal sheet *Truth*. The story stuck and many Australians continued to believe it, even after

Melba demonstrated its falsity by holding her place among the world's greatest opera and concert singers when she was in her sixties.

Melba, elegant in a brown suit cut to hide the thickening of her ageing figure, motored up to Springwood for lunch. She was accompanied by Beverley Nichols who, although unknown then, was to make a big name as a writer within a few years. This suave and handsome young Englishman had taken Melba's fancy when, as a Fleet Street reporter, he had been sent to interview her in London. Soon after arriving in Australia for the 1924 opera season she had cabled him to travel out and join her. They were constantly together, with Nichols acting as a private secretary and taking notes of her recollections for *Melodies and Memories*, the autobiography he was 'ghosting' for her. Australia did not impress Beverley Nichols much, but Norman Lindsay did. In his book *Twenty-five*, he gave a chapter to the Springwood visit under the title 'Showing How a Genius Worshipped Devils in the Mountains'. One thing he discovered was that Norman, whatever the truth of the stories that he was a libertine, was no toper. As Nichols described it:

> We went back into the house and drank. I watched him. He talked of the wine as though he were a Bacchanalian. One had the impression that he was only five minutes off a bout of drunkenness. Yet, he sipped only a mouthful, and even that was taken with pursed lips, as an old lady takes her tea.*

* Beverley Nichols, *Twenty-five* (London, 1926), p. 220.

M

The Wowser

Norman disliked Beverley Nichols but liked Melba. Before lunch was half over he knew she was one of the most satanically alive, vital and self-engrossed human beings he had ever met. He no longer wondered how she had reached not only the supreme heights of the grand opera world but had stayed there after her youth was gone. It was plain to him that she had triumphed by her ruthless pugnacity no less than by her magical singing powers. He had no fault to find with her on that account. He believed that nobody lacking Melba's combative spirit could ever have won such recognition in the theatre; or, for that matter, could have achieved complete self-expression in her own art.

Her earthy bluntness charmed him. He did not doubt that she had a multitude of human faults but, listening to her talk, he knew there was not a shred of humbug in her. The lunch table conversation inevitably turned to the national propensity for defaming any Australian who rose above the ruck. Melba was caustic about it. Slander had just been busy with her. She had cancelled several opera appearances through illness and the gossips were saying she was drinking again.

'Oh, the horrible people of this country!' she burst out. 'Why do I get this treatment here? Everywhere else I am respected. Here I am insulted.'

'Ignore it', Norman advised her, speaking with the wisdom of experience. 'It's the greatest compliment this country could pay you. At least when you are on the stage you have the satisfaction of knowing that you dominate them and they are your subject creatures.'

That day he did not follow his established custom of saying a few graceful but firm words of farewell immediately after lunch and escaping to his studio—he was enjoying himself too much. Sitting on with Melba, Rose and Nichols long after the meal was over, he launched into a panegyric on Beethoven the composer and Beethoven the man. Melba listened while Norman gave her in detail an analysis of Beethoven's greatest works. Most of the theories which he threw off like chains of fiery light had never before crossed her alert but matter-of-fact mind. She was enthralled.

'Can you believe it, Beverley?' she said. 'He knows more about Beethoven than I do.'

When it was time for her to leave she and Norman parted with regret on each side. In a few hours they had formed an impregnable friendship.

'Looking back now, I wish I'd made writing my profession', Norman once told his friend John Tierney, more widely known as Brian James, the novelist and short story writer. 'The formless rubbish the modernists turn out makes me gag at having the degraded label of artist tagged on to me. One can have some sense of dignity as a writer but none as an artist.' He said it only about ten years before he died, at a time when he was in despair over the longevity of modernism, and Tierney thought it was no more than one of Norman's dyspeptic exaggerations. It possibly was; yet throughout his life most of his intimate friends were poets and prose writers, and for forty years he exerted probably more sway than any other man of the time over the growth and direction of Australian letters.

Although he had earlier helped McCrae, Gellert and a few other writers, it was in the mid-1920s that he reached his full stature as a literary pathfinder. His sons had a big part in making it possible; without them he would hardly have met so many of the young Australians who began struggling to express themselves in words between the two world wars. That would have been a dire loss to several young writers who later made a mark, and also to Norman. He gloried in being a kind of soothsayer, guiding and spurring and reassuring the young and talented, and if that instinct had been denied an outlet something inside him would have withered. As it was, Norman's capacity to imbue an unfledged poet or novelist or essayist with faith in himself never faded. It was nearly as strong in his eighties as in his forties; and, lacking it, Australian literature would have had fewer flights of fine poetic imagery and memorable prose passages.

Jack was the first of the Lindsay boys to break away from Brisbane and seek the intellectual stimulus offered by Sydney and by nearness to Norman. He was a brilliant student but after graduating B.A. he left the University of Queensland under a cloud. A page of erotic poems which he contributed to the undergraduate magazine *Galmahra* was the reason. The editor of *Galmahra*, P. R. Stephensen, was called before the Students Council to answer a charge of having published 'obscene' verses, and although the trouble blew over, the episode helped Jack to make up his mind to quit Brisbane early in 1921. Sydney was the obvious place to go. He did not know how he would live there, but he was determined to pursue his poetic star and also to link his destiny with his father's; Norman's personality and philosophy still hypnotized him and the spell was to last for nearly a decade.

Percy Lindsay, who had moved from Melbourne to Sydney in 1917, put Jack up while he was finding his feet. Although married and the father of a schoolboy son, Percy was as cheerfully irresponsible as ever. He earned a modest livelihood by doing journalistic drawings and illustrating books, and eked out his income from these sources by sometimes selling one of his oil paintings of a landscape or a Harbourside scene for a few pounds; nobody guessed that many of these pictures would one day be collectors' pieces and fetch thirty and forty times the prices Percy put on them. He did not chafe under the thought that he was living in obscurity while his younger brothers, Lionel and Norman, strutted in the limelight. On the contrary, he preferred his own shady corner, for he asked no more of life than beer and friends and time to enjoy them.

Jack was beginning to get the feel of Sydney at the end of a month or so when Ray arrived. Ray, who had been working as a reporter on a Brisbane newspaper and hating it, bundled up his few possessions one day and caught the express to Sydney. He wanted to be a painter and he was not going to fritter his youth away in Brisbane writing paragraphs about street accidents and municipal council meetings. Jack and he moved into a derelict five-shillings-a-week attic room with a glassless window. It was up five flights of stairs at the top of an ageing Woolloomooloo building which looked fit to collapse the next time a high wind charged across the Harbour. There was no furniture worth mentioning and they drew their water from a cold tap on the landing below but they felt like monarchs who had come into their kingdom. Now each of them could work out his salvation or go to hell in his own way. Katie managed to hang on in Brisbane for three or four months; then she too headed for Sydney with Phil and took rooms in a Darlinghurst boarding house. The separation from Jack and Ray had been too much for her, even though the move meant cutting short fifteen-year-old Phil's education.

It was only a matter of time before Norman became acquainted with Ray and Phil as well as Jack. All through their childhood they had known him as a distant god living on a mountain and they naturally found their way to him. The reality was utterly different from anything they had imagined. Phil recorded in his autobiography that he felt 'quite awkward and old' in the presence of his father who, never still, 'smoked incessantly at cigarettes, rolled like a child in his chair, bellowing with laughter, kicking his legs up, and bouncing like an excited dog round the studio'. The Lindsay boys did not abandon their mother or show her any less affection, but she knew the pull of Springwood was strong; Norman had so much to offer and she could not have made a contest of it even if her nature would have let her. She was a little hurt by her sons' enthusiasm for their father but made no attempt to discourage the association. In a letter written when Katie died many years later Phil told Norman that 'she never said a word to your discredit, and, whatever the rights or wrongs of such marital breaks, few are the women who can refuse to try to defend themselves. It was always with a tender amusement with which she mentioned you, half-laughing.'

Although Springwood was two hours or so from Sydney, it became a mecca for Jack, Ray and Phil and their friends. Rose made them welcome, and Norman was surprisingly tolerant even when their unannounced appearances on the doorstep deranged his well-laid working plans. He was pleased to hear the house ringing with youthful voices raised in affirmation, dissent, exultation, reprehension and great argument. These young men, with their flexible and questing minds and their boundless faith in the promise of tomorrow, gave him hope. The passing years had sapped his confidence in Hugh McCrae as a cultural force. McCrae could still write enchanting verse but he was too hedonistic ever to drive himself to it. Soon after the war he had published two new books of lyrics, *Colombine* and *Idyllia*, but only under the prodding of the energetic Norman, who had illustrated both. McCrae had moved back to Sydney from Melbourne after the war and often spent a few days at Springwood, but Norman, while enjoying his company as much as ever, was privately appalled by his indolence. Leon Gellert had also been a disappointment. At one time Norman had offered to give him two or three acres at Springwood on which to build a house, with the idea that they should collaborate on a great series of works. Gellert had adroitly backed away; his liking and admiration for Norman were unchanged but he had no wish to live in another man's shadow. He had plugged on at school-teaching and freelance writing until 1922, and then joined Ure Smith as co-editor of *Art in Australia*, in succession to Bert Stevens. His job gave him little time to think about poetry, and Norman saw him as a man who had bartered a heaven-sent talent for a weekly pay cheque.

Norman forgot his disillusionment with McCrae and Gellert as the friendship with Jack, Ray and Phil ripened. They never showed him any filial deference and he would have been petrified if they had. They called him 'Norman' from the beginning and he treated them like an understanding older brother rather than a father. The boys were far apart from one another physically and temperamentally, but this only made them more interesting. Jack was in deadly earnest about poetry, art, music, philosophy and everything else, but Ray, tall and darkly handsome, about nothing but painting, and Phil, small, fair and coltish, about nothing but writing. Other than that both Ray and Phil were wild youngsters to whom laughter, girls and mischief were the chief reasons for living. And drink. They did not mind whether they drank beer, cheap wine, whisky, gin or anything else so long as it stirred their minds and loosened their tongues. Like Norman, Jack was nearly a total abstainer, but Ray and Phil each had an insatiable thirst and an iron stomach. So did many of their friends. When the fancy seized them, they and their drinking cronies and assorted girls would pile into a car borrowed or hired in Sydney and go hurtling into the Blue Mountains to make an unheralded night swoop on Springwood. Norman and Rose managed to be patient, but it was often hard. Most of the invaders were empty-headed young rollickers with no interest in anything but boozy junketing. There was no escape from their bibulous inanities until, one by one, they flopped to the floor in drunken sleep, leaving Norman exhausted, fuming and depressed, as dawn peered in through the windows at seven or eight recumbent forms.

But there was a credit side which compensated for these periodical ordeals. Some of the less boisterous minority whom Ray and Phil, as well as Jack, brought to Springwood had uncommon qualities of mind and personality. Several journalists were among them, notably Godfrey Blunden and Brian Penton, each of whom was to become a novelist of some distinction, and Kenneth Slessor, who had already shown flashes of the talent which was to mature in a few years and gain him a place of honour among Australia's major poets. John Kirtley, a quiet young man who worked for a Sydney stockbroker but was more interested in experimenting with fine printing on his own small hand-press, was another. There were four or five more, some of whom achieved little in the end or fizzled out altogether for want of talent or staying power, or both. With the exception of Ray none of the group were pictorial artists, and this blank gave Norman no sense of loss. Will Dyson in youth, and Julian Ashton and Elioth Gruner later, were the only three major figures of the Australian art world with whom he ever established deep and easy personal links. He admired the work of Streeton, Heysen, Longstaff and a few other of his Australian contemporaries, but there it ended; talk with any of them, he found, dried up once it turned away from the technique of art. And although Ure Smith ranked as a friend for many years Norman counted him as a publisher and journalist rather than as an artist.

He went wrong about some of the writers and other young men who clustered about him in the 1920s. That was inevitable. He always tended to over-estimate the talent of anybody he liked, not to mention the readiness of the individual to sacrifice himself—and others—in the struggle for self-fulfilment. One of his worst miscalculations concerned a pianist and composer named Adolf Beutler. Both Jack, who took Beutler to Springwood, and Norman saw him as a potential genius. For a time Norman was lyrical about his 'fine soul' and 'the noble quality of his music' and gave him unstinting encouragement and practical help but dropped him in the end after deciding that greatness was not in him. In later years Norman remembered him as 'about the greatest pest that ever infested my isolation at Springwood'. He could never forgive men like Beutler who funked their destiny. The fears and doubts which oppressed lesser people did not exist for Norman. His faith in himself and his own mission was absolute; he not only hoped he could move mountains but knew he could.

He fired many of his disciples with faith in his conviction that Australia was destined to become the cradle of a new renaissance. Jack and Slessor, and Frank Johnson, a young Sydney bookseller who wanted to become a publisher, were among them .They talked of launching a literary quarterly, and Norman promised to draw a set of black and white decorations for each issue and write short stories and literary essays; he also gave them a name for it: *Vision*. The first issue appeared on 1 May 1923, and although the tone was brashly adolescent—'We would vindicate the youthfulness of Australia, not by being modern, but by being alive', ran an editorial declaration—*Vision* had some brilliant moments in its short life. There was no money to pay contributors. Jack, Norman, Slessor, Hugh McCrae, Dorothea Mackellar, Robert D. FitzGerald, Phil Lindsay and the others whose writings filled its pages worked for love. Some had a variety of pen-names. Norman was James Flack and Charles Partridge as well as himself.

. .*Vision* lasted only four issues, but it was a rallying point. Norman was overjoyed to find there were so many young men still uncorrupted by bourgeois opportunism and not caring which side their bread was buttered. While keeping up an unbroken flow of etchings, pen drawings and water-colours, he found time to throw his weight into the efforts they were making in other directions also. He illustrated Jack's first book, *Fauns and Ladies*, a collection of lyrics, which Kirtley printed on his hand-press. He also illustrated Slessor's first book of verse, *Thief of the Moon*, which Kirtley printed a few months later. These two limited editions were fine examples of the bookman's craft. To Norman, they seemed to symbolize Australia's waking sense of beauty.

One of Norman's pet theories was that attack was essential to all creative self-expression. He believed it tested the artist's endurance and forced on him a deeper understanding of the concept of life he was striving to define. He spoke with some authority, because attackers never ignored him for long. Between the wars in particular no other Australian was so volleyed and thundered at on high and edifying moral grounds.

The mere sound of his name roused leering curiosity in many minds, and Arthur Streeton, the landscape painter, felt he could exploit this for his own gain when he came home to settle in Australia after living in England for fifteen years. He held a show in Sydney at the end of November 1923, while tongues were still wagging over the fuss roused by Norman's drawings in the London exhibition. Streeton's reputation was such that he did not need to resort to sensationalism, but, according to Norman, he could not resist the temptation to push his show. The story, as Norman told it was this: He put up a small booth in a corner of the gallery in which he was exhibiting, and placarded it 'For Men Only'. Inside he hung one of Norman's pen drawings. This depicted two lovers with doves hovering over them. Only a lecherous mind could have thought it suggestive, but word spread that you could see one of Norman Lindsay's spicy pictures at the exhibition.

Norman knew nothing about the episode until a friend advised him to go and see the exhibition 'in your own interests'. Puzzled, he sent Rose. When she told him the story he felt sick rather than angry. He had known Streeton since the 'Charterisville' days and had never found any reason to dislike him. He also respected Streeton, one of the founders of the Heidelberg School, as an accomplished painter who, especially in his early years, had done some masterly landscapes. Indeed the drawing now on show had been a present from Norman to Streeton some years before. Norman could not bring himself to tackle Streeton. Why waste reproaches on that commonplace mind? Nothing would penetrate the skin of a man so crudely insensitive. Norman simply made a pact with himself never again to acknowledge Streeton's existence, and he never did.

The discovery that artists of standing and integrity were capable of looking at his work with the eyes of a spinster Sunday school teacher was harder to bear. It was forced on him when Adelaide organized an Artists Week in July 1924. The major event was a national exhibition. Most leading Australian artists agreed to show pictures. Norman was one; he sent off eleven etchings, pen drawings and water-colours and thought no more about it. Some weeks passed and then newspapers all over Australia printed the news that three of his etchings—*The Funeral March of Don Juan*, *The Apex of Life*, and *The Festival*—had been banned. In London the story was published, with footnotes recalling the flurry that Norman's drawings had caused at Burlington House nine months before. The Royal South Australian Society of Arts, in whose rooms the exhibition was to be held, had imposed the ban. The society's hanging and selection committee ruled that 'the subjects dealt with were such that it would not be in the public interest to let the pictures be shown'. The next day the *Advertiser* published a leading article endorsing the society's stand and reproving Norman. 'He handles with consummate skill', the editorialist wrote, 'subjects that are disagreeable to most people because of their animal suggestiveness'. Norman met the crisis by withdrawing all his pictures from the exhibition, and arranging for a one-man show of his pen drawings, etchings and water-colours to be held at Preece's Adelaide gallery in Artists Week.

Percy Grainger, the Australian-born composer and pianist, chanced to arrive in Adelaide on a professional visit just then. To an *Advertiser* reporter Grainger, having described Norman as 'one of the greatest living artists . . . the equal of Titian or Velasquez', said:

When Australia was first colonised few of her colonists came from the comfortable middle classes; they came from the top and the bottom of the social scale for the most part. That is why I think in Mr Lindsay's work, as in my own, the raucous voice of the slums insists on making its claimant appeal. Mr Lindsay has a great power of expression, and he feels the irresistible force of the rivers of life which are running high in this young country. I can see nothing degenerate in his work. His later pictures in particular, in their infinite delicacy of execution, reveal him as a master craftsman and an apostle of beauty. He has a tremendous influence on Australian art from which he is seeking to strip the false trammels and conventions, and it is a great and welcome influence.

On 29 July Norman's pictures—ten water-colours, six pen drawings and some twenty etchings—were all hanging in Preece's gallery, ready for the opening next day. Sir Tom Bridges, the Governor of South Australia, went there in the morning for a private view. The same afternoon he declared open the Artists Week exhibition before a large audience of Adelaide's social, artistic and political élite. After extolling 'the beautiful works on the walls' at length, he ended his speech by saying that he had been privileged that morning to see what might be called an annex of the exhibition, in Preece's gallery. He was anxious that they should all see it. There was work there of rare imagination and perfect technique.

A British regular officer who had retired from the Army to become the Governor of South Australia in 1922, Bridges was an intelligent man of independent and flexible mind. His personal popularity was immense even among citizens who normally sniffed at vice-regal utterances, and Preece's small gallery was packed out when Syd Ure Smith opened Norman's show next day; Lionel Lindsay was with him—they had come from Sydney to represent New South Wales at Artists Week. The newspaper critics were dazzled. The *News* said Norman's works were 'an astounding revelation of the heights to which genius may attain'. The *Register* described them as 'those of a creative genius'. Even the disapproving *Advertiser* remarked on their 'exquisite freshness' and 'perfection of line'.

Day after day a queue stretched down the stairs and out into the street. Opinion on the morality of Norman's pictures was still divided, however. On Saturday 2 August the *Register* published an article on its main news page by Professor Coleman Phillipson, a teacher of Italian at the Elder Conservatorium in the University of Adelaide. Professor Phillipson denied Norman's right 'on any grounds, social, ethical, or aesthetic, to prostitute his gifts by descending for his subjects to the garbage of the gutter, the gross debaucheries of the degenerate, and the repulsive aberrations of the perverted', and appealed to him 'to turn his attention to nobler subjects and things of good report, subjects more worthy of his great skill and power, so that by creating truly beautiful works, he may give us a little gladness and delight during our brief hour in this troubled pilgrimage'.

The Adelaide affair depressed Norman for months. He concluded that Australians did not know whether to regard him as 'an artist or a

monstrosity'. He even talked of selling up and settling in Europe, hoping
that there he might work in peace and perhaps in time forget Australian puritanism. In March 1925 he went so far as to let the Leicester
Galleries, in London, mount an exhibition of his etchings and water-
colours. The advance publicity was good. The newspapers reminded
Londoners that this was the Australian whose pictures had raised a
storm in 1923 and asked what shocks 'the Rubens of the Blue Mountains' had in store this time.

Most of the newspapers were friendly until the *Sunday Express* printed
a 'splash story' about the exhibition a week after the opening. The writer,
Phillip Page, was obviously working under the direction of the editor,
James Douglas, who had become a Fleet Street star by his verbal
scourgings of anybody and everybody suspected of impure deeds, words
or thoughts. After warming up in a paragraph or two, Mr Page wrote:

> The old 'Yellow Book' which shocked people in the early nineties with some
> of the least daring efforts of that strange genius Aubrey Beardsley would
> have felt its mustard covers turning pink with shame were they to shelter a
> single etching, a single watercolour of the man whose prurient productions
> London is flocking to see . . .
> Norman Lindsay . . . has the doubtful distinction of displaying the most
> lascivious pictures that have ever been hung on the walls of a London gallery.
> They are clever, yes, though not remarkably so; but they are utterly foul.
> A nude drawing may be as chaste as Diana or as evil as Messallina. Lindsay's
> nudes are of the type an elderly roué keeps locked in a secret panel in his
> smoking-room to show after dinner, with shame-faced pride, to a few port-
> laden cronies. Young men buy something like them on their first trip abroad.
> If anything were to be seen on the stage one-tenth as scabrous, the hulla-
> baloo 'would stretch from here to Mesopotamy'. Yet the snowy-headed roll
> merrily in to stand three-deep before the scarcely mentionable.

Many of them rolled in also to buy and the exhibition yielded nearly
£1,200. But the moral thunderings of the *Sunday Express* went by no
means unheeded. Some other newspapers and periodicals took them up;
and, inside the Leicester Galleries, the outlook on life reflected by the
pictures on show was vigorously denounced as well as vigorously acclaimed in well-bred accents.

In Springwood Norman's hopes crashed. The news made him realize
that England's mind had not broadened since he was there and that her
smut-hounds were no less priggish, censorious and bluenosed than Australia's. If he had ever been serious about settling in Europe—which is
doubtful—the idea perished then.


When Will Dyson came home to Australia in 1925 Norman was ready
to let bygones be bygones. Rose agreed and they invited Will to stay at

Springwood. They found him changed, not so much physically as in spirit.

His beloved Ruby had died in 1919, in the Spanish influenza epidemic, and he was lonely and resentful. His work and his little daughter's company gave him only partial solace. The taste of success had turned sour on his tongue although his professional name was still high. Indeed he had come out of the war with a growing reputation as a serious artist, which his later work affirmed and enlarged. As an Australian official artist on the Western Front he had done some superb front-line studies (and been twice wounded); and, while his postwar topical cartoons in the *Daily Herald* lacked some of the characteristic Dyson bite, they were, technically, as accomplished as of old. But he was out of tune with London and with himself, and when he received a munificent offer to go to Australia and join Melbourne *Punch* he accepted it.

The Melbourne *Herald* organization had bought the long-established *Punch* and, having restaffed it regardless of cost, was trying to turn it into a high-grade sophisticated weekly. Will had been home only a month or two when he knew he had made a mistake. His satire was too penetrating and his wit too stinging for Melbourne, or at any rate for his employers. He found himself required to dissipate his talents in turning out safe and innocuous comic drawings which revealed little of the real Dyson. The intellectual standards of a community ruled, as he said, 'by bumbles and linen-drapers' filled him with contempt but, unable to muster the energy to break his five-year contract and go back to Europe, he stayed on and settled into a chronic state of cynical disillusion.

He was in a black mood when he went to Springwood. Norman and Rose did their best to blandish him out of it and once or twice they saw flashes of the Will Dyson they had known. These never lasted more than a few moments; then the sullenness flowed back and submerged them. Norman's ardours seemed only to aggravate Will's discontent. He was edgy and sarcastic, and it was hard to find any topic which did not lead on to a peevish wrangle. The only subject he seemed able to discuss with animation was the new-born economic doctrine of Social Credit. He believed it offered a remedy for all the world's economic ills and a blueprint for a foolproof egalitarian society; to talk of its principles and theories made his challenging eyes flash as in the days when he had seen conventional socialism as the hope of mankind. Norman was not impressed. He told Will that he considered Social Credit just one more recipe for an earthly Utopia which could never be. Will retorted that he must be either blind or callous to the plight of the masses, and after a few ill-humoured exchanges they let it drop.

According to Norman (and his account was no doubt basically true although it possibly held a strong element of dramatization), the visit was doomed from the start. It wobbled towards an end when Will, after looking at a group of Norman's recent pen drawings and etchings, grunted that they were nothing but 'metaphysical cartoons'.

'All right', Norman said, using his set formula for answering anybody who attacked his work in what he felt were meaningless and destructive terms, 'you may be quite right about them, but you'll notice that the damn' things are hanging there and not taking any notice of you'.

'Oh, to hell with you!' Will said, and flung out of the studio.

After giving him time to cool down Norman went out into the garden and joined him, but Will was still sunk in black thoughts. He launched into a tirade against the myth that life was worth living—the whole thing was a hoax, a brazen swindle.

'And the simple solution of it is staring us in the face', he gloomed. 'Suicide.'

'If the solution were as simple as that', Norman replied, 'there wouldn't be any problem at all in the whole bloody business'.

'Oh, to hell with you!' Will said again.

He packed his bag and went back to Melbourne after saying a stiff farewell. Norman and Rose were glad to see him go. They had looked forward to his coming, but he had been a tense and trying guest; they supposed he had found them equally trying. They knew that the gulf which had opened in London and grown with the years was too wide to be bridged now.

A week or so later Will made another trip from Melbourne and presented himself at Springwood, mumbling that it was a lot of nonsense for two grown men to act like this. Norman said that of course it was, and they did their best to laugh the quarrel off and then to avoid touchy subjects while Will stayed. There were no outward shadows when he took his leave that time but Norman knew they would never recapture their old friendship. Will doubtless knew it too.

Norman did not grieve. He held the conviction that the collapse in later years of what passes for a friendship in youth is evidence that a basic antagonism has always been at the core of it. He never saw the smallest danger that his friendship with Ruff Tremearne or Hugh McCrae or Elioth Gruner would fail; he could meet any of the three after a break of a few weeks or a few years and feel not the slightest strangeness. He was aware that his own frailties of character, especially his almost pathological sensitivity to adverse comments on his work or philosophy, often strained his friends' patience. Soon after Will Dyson's unhappy visits to Springwood, Norman revealed his thoughts in a letter to Tremearne:

> When I think of you, I think of one untouched by all the disruptions and angers that have fallen between all my old friendships, and for which, I suspect, I am as much to blame as they . . . It is a great test, I think, for love to survive

through youth to middle age, and still retain that freshness which makes two little boys find all interest and all importance in each other's being.

Norman was a little mystified by the strength of his liking for Gruner. As a rule he recoiled from any man in whom he sensed a homosexual taint, yet never from Gruner. The reason was that Gruner had not only a fine mind but also a nobility of spirit rare in human beings.

He had stayed in Europe, studying and painting, for more than a year after trimming off the loose ends left by the Australian exhibition in London. On his return to Australia he went to stay at Springwood every now and then, and once or twice Norman and Rose visited him at his small and immaculately kept house in Sydney to listen to gramophone music; like Norman, he was a devotee of Wagner. Norman had never before been sure that Gruner had capitulated to his homosexual impulses but he was soon unable to doubt it. Although at first Gruner showed an interest in one woman or another he drifted more and more into associations with young men whose psychological peculiarities were unmistakable. They made Norman shudder, but his liking for Gruner the man as well as his opinion of Gruner the artist's ability and integrity never wavered.

Norman rarely asked for criticism of his work except from Rose but sometimes when a specific aspect of a picture was worrying him he tried to persuade Gruner to give an opinion on it. He never succeeded if a drawing or an etching was in question; being a colourist, the reticent Gruner evidently felt unsure of his judgement of black and white. He once offered an estimate of Norman's paintings, however. After studying several in silence he said, 'You always go wrong in colour somewhere'. The usually hypersenistive Norman did not resent it but the finding, which Gruner did not elaborate, haunted him. Perhaps, in the secret recesses of his mind, he endorsed it.

Their friendship was one of the precious things of Norman's middle years. His delight in Gruner's painting was equally precious to him. He saw Gruner as 'the greatest master of atmospheric values and of the painting of pure light that the world has ever known'. And, if this was an example of Norman's inability to harbour an admiration without magnifying it, the opinion was at least one that he held for the rest of his life.


People who relied on their eyes and did not know Norman imagined him to be physically delicate. Others, like his brother Daryl, who said that inside Norman was 'a dynamo geared to top pitch that never ran down',* knew better. His skinny body and spindly limbs had the tough-

* *The Leafy Tree* (Melbourne, 1965), p. 59.

ness of steel wire and in his time he came through illnesses which would have put a professional strong-man in the graveyard.

Rose in a burst of annoyance once told him, 'Next time I marry I'll marry a bloody butcher, not a genius who looks like a half-starved jockey'. Cyril Dillon, an artist friend from Melbourne who was visiting Springwood and heard Rose unburden herself, thought the description perfect. But Norman's vitality was out of all proportion to his bulk. Even the fittest and brawniest of his friends could not nearly match it, yet many of them saw him as a candidate for an early death. Arthur Adams, a Sydney journalist and writer, published a poem before the 1914-18 war in which he likened Norman to a candle flame flickering in the wind. Adams was only a little older than Norman, but the flickering candle flame outlasted him by more than thirty years. Norman, who was proud of his own durability, liked telling the story.

Although his output of work was enormous in the 1920s he had more bouts of illness then than in any other decade of his life. He insisted that this was nature's way of compelling him to relax. He could not bring himself, even in his forties, to take holidays as other men did; only jangling stomach nerves or congested lungs would stop him, and after such an enforced spell he always plunged into work again, refreshed in mind and body. In one year he was laid up for some days every month but as soon as he could get up and dress he would stumble back to his studio, damning the doctors and vowing he knew more about his body than they did. He had one term in hospital until, beginning to feel better, he rebelled and bullied Rose into taking him home. At another time his weight fell to about ninety pounds. He was too weak to object when a doctor ordered a special diet of meat juices, egg flips, fish, chicken and other easily assimilated foods. For some months Rose cooked every mouthful he ate or drank, and steadily the flesh thickened on his bones and his strength came back.

His Daemon drove him without pause. It was more relentless than ever. He gave the impression of a man afraid that he would die while he had done little of real value. Everybody around him was aware of his insatiable lust for work. One morning he paused for a few words with Mick, a local man who often came in to do odd jobs in the grounds. Norman liked Mick who, being meditative and slightly sardonic, was oppressed by the enigma of life and always seeking an answer to it. Gnawing at the riddle that day, Mick asked, 'What's it all about anyway? All a man gets out of it is three meals a day and a bed, and a bit of a loaf on Sundays reading *Truth* or having a yack over the fence with some bloke who happens to be passing'. He broke off and looked at Norman, then went on, 'Now, you're what I'd call a happy man'. Astonished, Norman asked, 'What makes you say that,

Mick?' 'Well,' said Mick, 'I notice that the minute your breakfast is over you make a dead break for the studio, and you sit there working all day. A man must like his job who sticks to it the way you do, and I reckon a man who likes his job can be called a happy man.' Norman had to agree that it was about as close to happiness as any human being could hope to come.

Money was no problem and it never crossed his mind. To the disappointment of some of his admirers he had drifted away from the pen in the mid-1920s, but his etchings and water-colours sold as fast as they came from his hands. Yet while giving so much of himself to the task of putting his concept of life into pictures he never repelled any of the young would-be intellectuals who came to him at Springwood seeking encouragement. To proselytize them was a part of the grand design. All his actions made it plain that he meant every word when he told a friend, 'I am fanatic enough to believe that my thought is something the world needs'.

His eldest son's devotion to the philosophy enunciated in *Creative Effort* gave no sign of wavering and Norman saw him as an invaluable disciple. Jack had one altogether admirable quality in Norman's view; he was a worker rather than a talker. He did a verse translation of Aristophanes' *Lysistrata*, which he and Kirtley felt would make an effective de luxe edition. They told Norman, who had formed a high opinion of Kirtley's work, and he agreed to draw a series of fine-line illustrations for it. Jack and Kirtley worked on *Lysistrata* together and put it out in a limited edition of sixty copies. No better example of quality publishing had ever originated in Australia, and even by world standards it was a splendid book. It was also the first book to bear the imprint of the Fanfrolico Press. The name—suggested by Norman who had written, for his own amusement, a series of short stories set in a fabulous country ruled by the Duke of Fanfrolico—was to gain the respect of collectors of de luxe editions in Europe and America over the next five years.

The response to *Lysistrata* turned Kirtley's eyes to wider horizons. He suggested to Jack that they should take the Fanfrolico Press to London. They went to Springwood and saw Norman. He was torn. On the one hand he disliked the thought of Jack and the gifted Kirtley deserting Australia just when they were making an impact; they were needed, and Jack in particular, Norman believed, to speed the birth of the new renaissance. On the other hand, Norman wanted to spread his ideas as far and as wide as possible, and if Jack and Kirtley could find a foothold in London the Fanfrolico Press would become a platform of international influence, which it could never be while based in Sydney.

Norman's support was indispensable. Jack and Kirtley intended making books illustrated by him the backbone of their early publishing programme and they would not be able to pay him, so everything hung on his willingness to give them his work for nothing. They talked and he listened, and then he told them he would keep them going for three or four years anyway. They could have the book rights of pretty well all the illustrations he had done, the *Satyricon*, *Lysistrata* and McCrae's *Satyrs and Sunlight* among them. He also promised to illustrate other books for them. And then there were some of his own writings which he would illustrate and give them to publish—he had one or two book-length items, he said, which ought to suit the Fanfrolico Press down to the ground. He felt a glow of excitement. He knew that the planting of Fanfrolico in English soil would add to his work but he believed it would open up a vast new field to him. No man imbued with the passion of the evangelist could resist it, and when Jack and Kirtley boarded their London-bound ship at Sydney early in 1926 they had his blessing. He even paid Jack's fare and bought him a new suit.

It was not just a wild dream of youth. They launched the Fanfrolico Press in London with a limited edition of *Lysistrata*; the collectors liked it. A few months later they published a translation of the *Satyricon* by Jack, with the 1910 illustrations; the collectors liked that too. Jack and Kirtley were running hand-to-mouth but neither had ever imagined they could make a fortune by quality publishing. They were doing what they wanted to do and paying their way, and nothing else mattered. They put out a book of Kenneth Slessor's verse, *Earth-Visitors*, illustrated by Norman, and a verse-drama by Jack, *Marino Faliero*. Jack was not daunted when Kirtley grew homesick after eighteen months and went back to Australia. Jack's old university friend, P. R. Stephensen, joined him as manager. Inky Stephensen, the Queensland Rhodes Scholar for 1924, had just come down from Oxford after taking honours in Modern Greats. He was an energetic young man of large but erratic intellectual ability, and together he and Jack kept the Fanfrolico Press galloping onward. Norman, on the other side of the world, could see that at least he had not backed a failure. While it was impossible to tell where all this effort would lead in the end, the Fanfrolico imprint was becoming known, and in America as well as in England.

But Norman sometimes had misgivings on another score. Some of the young group around him became a little restive as news of Jack's success and his acceptance by London literary people continued to trickle back, and two or three talked of going off to Europe. Norman discouraged them. He knew his own roots were buried so deep in Australian soil that he could never do work of true value in any other environment and he never doubted that this was true of every creative person. Believing that all expatriates became hybrid creatures, he was fearful of seeing talented young Australians who were their country's best cultural hope drift off into nothingness. Still, he could do only so much, and he was not too surprised when Brian Penton invited himself to Springwood for a weekend in 1928 and reported that he had booked his passage and would be in London before the end of the year.

The dwarfish Penton, with his upstanding shock of dark wiry hair, bright and derisive eyes, and waspish tongue, was a man to be reckoned with in any company. Although only twenty-four, he had made a reputation with a trenchant and often devastating political column in the *Sydney Morning Herald*. He also found an outlet for his undersized man's malice by ridiculing absent friends in cruel and lacerating phrases, but Norman, while disliking this trait, managed to overlook it. Penton, who was working on a novel, seemed to be a young man whose literary skills Australia needed, so when they parted Norman wished him well abroad, only urging him not to stay away for good. Penton said he wouldn't—he merely wanted to taste the air of Europe before settling down in Australia.

Then another would-be deserter presented himself at Springwood: Phil. He had been living the life of an out-at-elbows Bohemian in Sydney, drinking too much, eating too little, scraping together a few shillings now and then by casual journalism, and scribbling away at novels that were never published. He often went to the tiny King's Cross flat which his mother was now renting, but did not live there; he could always find a bed with Ray or with some other friend and he liked being free. Phil had long dreamed of getting to London. The very names were magical: Piccadilly, The Strand, Limehouse, Belgravia, Chelsea Reach, Trafalgar Square, Wapping, all the rest. He also missed Jack and longed to be with him. Then Penton went. A few months later he wrote to Phil saying he had joined Jack as manager of the Fanfrolico Press: after a series of personality clashes with Jack, Stephensen had left to found his own publishing house, the Mandrake Press.

Phil mooched about Sydney, despondent and brooding. Jack was making a name in London. And in Sydney Ray was being mentioned as one of the coming painters—only a few months before he had scored a resounding success with a one-man exhibition and netted enough money to marry and rent a good flat. How much longer, Phil asked himself, must he be the odd man out while his brothers prospered? There was no hope for a young writer stuck in Australia. Life was leaving him behind, all because he could not find a lousy thirty-eight pounds for the one-class ship fare to London. Norman was his only hope, but he knew Norman's views on expatriate writers. And, although Norman often slipped him something when he was flat broke, thirty-eight pounds was real money— he couldn't bring himself to ask his father for such a sum. Then, astonishingly, he was riding out of Sydney on the train to Springwood.

N

It was a raw July night, Ray was with him and they were both drunk. Ray's counsel had decided him. 'You'll rot here', Ray had said. 'Better to die over there'—meaning London.

They cornered Norman in the studio and talked hard. He heard them with a sinking heart, crestfallen to know that Phil wanted to follow Jack and Penton at the very time that Australia needed its own creative writers to shape the national consciousness. 'It's unfair for creative Australians to go running off overseas', he said. Ignoring, in his anxiety to dissuade Phil, the existence of a small but determined group of authentically Australian novelists, he went on: 'England has innumerable excellent writers. Australia has none.'

'Whose fault is that?' Phil demanded. 'Australia drives its writers abroad. There's not even one real publishing house in this country.'

They argued for a long time and in the end Norman shrugged and gave in. Very well, he said, he'd pay Phil's fare. And he just hoped to heaven he was doing the right thing! To Phil, the clanging train that carried him and Ray back to Sydney was a winged chariot.

At Springwood Norman flung himself into work and tried to forget that another of the young men whom he had built his hopes on was running away from Australia. He had no inkling that the next significant deserter was to be himself.

# 9

# *The Phase of the Hunchback*
# *1929-34*

Soon after turning fifty Norman knew that something was amiss with him. It was not a physical illness. His body was behaving well, even his treacherous stomach and lungs had given him no trouble for months, yet he could not lull himself into believing that all was as it should be. His capacity to create had—overnight, it seemed to him—fallen into a bottomless trance. He would go to his studio and sit for hours with a pencil and a blank sheet of paper in front of him, waiting for images to form in his mind; nothing would come, or at any rate nothing new. Sometimes he would get an idea for a picture and draught it out, then look at it and say 'I've done this before' and throw it away. He had never been short of ideas, his mind had always been crowded with them, but now it was blank.

He tried to assure himself that this was a symptom of some minor psychological ailment which would soon pass, like a cold in the head or a touch of rheumatism. He shut himself in his studio day after day and wrestled to wake his conceptual faculty from its coma. It was no good. The weeks of futile striving became months and at last he had to admit to himself that he was rubbing his nerves raw to no purpose. That was a bitter hour. He remembered having heard that this kind of thing—a form of mental and nervous debility, possibly brought on by despondency resulting from self-doubt and often associated with a period of partial or total sexual as well as intellectual impotence—was liable to attack creative artists in their late forties and early fifties, but he had never imagined that it could attack him. It was damnably unfair! The one thing above all others that had given his life meaning had been taken away; thus deprived, he could no longer propitiate his Daemon. He felt lost and hopeless. He called it 'the Phase of the Hunchback'. This was a personal adaptation of an idea expounded in *A Vision,* an abstruse work of metaphysical philosophy which the Irish poet, W. B. Yeats, had published privately in 1926. Jack had sent Norman a copy of *A Vision* and he had found it enthralling but puzzling. Now he believed he understood the significance of Yeats's Hunchback. 'I could not escape the shadow of the Hunchback', he said years later. 'I was alone with myself. For me, it was the black of the moon.' He was unable to bring himself to tell even Rose. He felt that her feminine practicality would reject the explanation as absurd. He preferred to let her suppose he had grown tired of working and taken to loafing. That he fooled her into swallowing anything of the kind for long is to be doubted.

It was mystifying because in everything else his mind was as agile and his hand as sure as ever. He could toss off straightforward illustrations and journalistic drawings in the old effortless way, shape a garden statue without faltering, fabricate an intricate ship model with all his customary concentration and dexterity; he could even invent a range of characters for whatever novel or short story he happened to be writing as a pastime and steer them through a pattern of hilarious or dramatic situations— usually hilarious, because he believed humour to be 'a supreme expression of the indomitable human spirit'. It was only when he tried to find inspiration for the work which was his reason for living that the light refused to shine.

Once having faced the crisis, he was able to think about it with some detachment. He concluded that he had overworked himself to a point at which he had used up all the material he had gathered in his fifty years of life; until he renewed the supply, that part of his mind which he had always called on to meet his needs must take a holiday. He supposed that recovery might not come for years; or perhaps ever. Whether valid or not, that was his own diagnosis and it brought him no cheer. Meanwhile, he had to escape from himself. Anything was better, he decided, than drivelling about in what he had come to think of as his blank black limbo of a studio and finding that every composition he started to sketch out was only a stale variant of something he had already done.

So he took to dancing. Rose suggested it. Norman, who had all his life derided dancing as an asinine recreation suitable only for mentally retarded people, made a token objection but surrendered quickly enough. Jane and Helen's governess, a girl named Sylvia Massey, was an accomplished dancer, and in a week or two she had Norman fox-trotting and waltzing like a ballroom veteran. Rose had long been in the habit of getting up parties to join in the local town dances in Springwood, and now Norman, tricked out in the stiff shirt, black tie and dinner jacket which he had always tried to dodge, went along also. He liked to dance all night until the band played its closing number at two or three in the morning. The exercise gave him a physical glow, even if it did nothing to set the creative juices flowing again.

Only two or three of his intimates suspected that he spent some years living in the shadow of the Hunchback, uncertain if he would ever pull clear of it. To most of his friends and acquaintances he appeared unchanged, except that they now saw him in Sydney more often than at any time since he had gone to live in the mountains. Having earned a reputation for avoiding invitations to dinners, supper parties and other social affairs on any flimsy excuse, he suddenly became a frequent diner-out, especially with the circle which revolved about Syd Ure Smith. He was as active and vocal as a cricket on these occasions. Gay and voluble, full of tumbling and infectious laughter, delighting in pouring out his own theories and listening to other men's, he seemed to be without a care.

The break in the stream of his work never became obvious. Rose had always kept a firm hand on the number of pictures she released for sale, feeding them out with a prudent eye on the absorptive capacity of the market. The fecundity of Norman's output had been such that his sales had provided the handsome income which he and Rose needed while leaving in reserve an abundance of works worth many thousands of pounds. Now that the source had dried up, Rose was still able to go on supplying the demand by drawing on this stockpile. She could go on doing it for some years if need be. Of course, if Norman's creative faculty were dead and not merely sleeping . . . Well, they would cross that bridge when they came to it.

He tried not to think about his state of conceptual paralysis but it was never far from his mind. He could shut his mind to it for a while but when he was alone the Hunchback would come out of the shadows and lean on his shoulder, leering and gloating. Years later Norman told Ruff Tremearne that his early fifties had been 'the worst of all hells'. He said, 'I wouldn't go through them again for a promise of paradise filled with lovely girls'. From one who held, as an article of faith, that 'no man is worth a damn unless the spectacle of femininity has an eternal interest for him', those were strong words.

The law of compensation seems to have chosen the very time that Norman was in those depths to launch him on an international novelist's career. The news reached him in a letter from Brian Penton reporting that Faber and Faber, one of the leading London houses, were delighted with Norman's novel *Redheap* and intended putting it out in April 1930 as one of their Spring books. Norman had written the first version of *Redheap* nearly fifteen years before as a way of keeping his mind off the war. He had never given more than a passing thought to publishing it but a few of his friends had read it in manuscript. Penton was among them, and on his farewell visit to Springwood before sailing for Europe he had persuaded Norman to let him take *Redheap* with him.

Norman felt a tingle of exhilaration. He knew that writing would never give him the satisfaction he found in drawing and painting but it provided some kind of outlet for his need to express himself. He wondered how London, where he was already known—and in some quarters notorious—as an artist, would respond to him as a novelist. Although a few months earlier Fanfrolico had put out a handsome edition of a so-called novel by Norman, *Madam Life's Lovers*, this was really a philosophical essay thinly disguised as fiction; it had attracted some notice from collectors of limited editions but none from readers of conventional novels. And while tens of thousands of Australians had read and chuckled over *A Curate in Bohemia*, that little farce about long-ago Melbourne was not known abroad. So, for every practical purpose, he would make his first appearance as a novelist outside his native land with *Redheap*. He was glad about that. *Redheap*, which he called 'a bucolic comedy', was the most substantial novel he had attempted. It had strong elements of satire and owed a clear debt to both Dickens and Sinclair Lewis. It owed a debt also to a diary which Lionel had kept in his Creswick adolescence and lent to Norman many years before, not dreaming that anything in it would ever be printed even in the guise of fiction. Nobody acquainted with Creswick could fail to recognize Redheap as a pseudonym for Norman's home town. All the characters were composites of Creswick people whom he had known in his youth, often with strong touches of comic exaggeration. Norman did not imagine that *Redheap* was faultless, but he felt it was a competent, and an entertaining, study of the sham, hypocrisy and smugness common to life in all Australian small country towns in the 1890s.

Disapproving moralists pursed thin lips when word passed that a novel by Norman was about to appear in print. They knew what to expect from this fellow Lindsay who had so often outraged their sensibilities with his pictures—it was not to be doubted that his novel would be equally nasty! Their worst fears were soon confirmed. Australian press representatives in London were waiting on Faber and Faber's doorstep to pounce on review copies of *Redheap*. The Melbourne *Herald* led the field with a story under provocative headlines: 'Norman Lindsay Writes a Novel. Will Police Permit Its Sale in Australia? Reviewer Has His Doubts'. The writer gave the opinion that *Redheap* might be banned in Australia by the police 'even should it escape the prohibition of the Commonwealth Customs authorities'. He described it as a 'full-length novel in which sex receives the most attention' and declared it to be 'not a nice book to leave on the family bookshelf for all to read who like'. Four days later the *Sydney Morning Herald* told readers that *Redheap* was an outspoken story of small town jealousies and bitterness—too outspoken for most tastes, for the sordid things of life, however true, form but poor material for entertaining reading . . . Generally the book is to be regarded as a story of unpleasant people and unpleasant episodes. Mr Lindsay has apparently no intention of making them anything else.

Other Australian newspapers were passing similar judgements, and *Redheap*'s fitness or otherwise to be read by Australians was a burning public question. The *Sydney Morning Herald* made it the subject of a leading article in which the writer noted that this was 'not the first time Mr Lindsay has disparaged his country'. The article was headed 'Literary Matricide'.

The spate of newspaper talk spread alarm and despondency in Creswick. On the evidence of the details mentioned in published reviews of *Redheap* a number of dignified townsfolk deduced that Norman had used them as models for characters having playful sexual appetites and other regrettable habits. Worse, they guessed that other Creswickians would have no trouble in identifying them. 'Lisnacrieve' felt the waves of agitation, and Mary Lindsay was conscious of dark looks directed at her back by certain citizens of each sex whenever she was out doing the household shopping. Mrs Lindsay, who was in her eighty-second year but still brisk and lively of mind, was troubled. Remembering that Norman, on his visits home, had encouraged her to gossip about local events and local people, she was fearful that much of what she had told him would be seen to have found its way into *Redheap*.

A story persists that Mrs Lindsay wrote to the Department of Customs saying that *Redheap* was a libel on the people of Creswick and should be barred from entering Australia. Whether or not this is true, the Customs authorities did not lack encouragement to act. A few days after the first review appeared in the Melbourne *Herald* a Victorian legislator, Mr Horace Richardson, made a speech in the State Parliament appealing to the Federal Government to ban *Redheap*; Mr Richardson had been a leading member of the Baptist Church for many years and was a former president of the Victorian Baptist Union. The member of the Federal Parliament for Bendigo, Mr Richard V. Keane, took up the cry in the House of Representatives. A Labour government was in office and Mr Keane, a Labour and trades union stalwart, urged that *Redheap* should be proscribed because it contained 'serious reflections on the morality of a certain community in Victoria'. Some weeks elapsed while a copy of the book was hurried out from England and read by the Acting Minister for Customs (Mr F. M. Forde), the Commonwealth Solicitor-General (Sir Robert Garran), and three officers of the Department of Customs. On 21 May Mr Forde announced the decision to the House of Representatives: *Redheap* was prohibited from entering Australia on the ground that it contained passages which were indecent or obscene. Sixteen thousand copies were in a ship nearing Sydney. They had been sent to meet orders from booksellers throughout Australia. Customs officers boarded the ship in Sydney and sealed the consignment, which had to be shipped back to England.

*Smith's Weekly,* a gaily irreverent crusading Sydney newspaper with an Australia-wide circulation, invited Norman to write an article about the ban. He gave them a full-page spread which he illustrated with a series of drawings depicting a bemused Mr Forde clutching a copy of *Redheap* and twisting himself into a variety of contorted attitudes in his struggles to understand what he was reading. Having warmed up by pouring a little prefatory scorn on Forde, Garran and 'the Babbits of the Customs Office', Norman went on:

> Silly devils! They can no more censor *Redheap* than they can censor the atmosphere. All they can do is make temporary nuisances of themselves, and cause Australian booksellers to lose a little present profit. A fine spectacle they present, making a noise like an egg, censoring a book that has already sold out its first edition in England! And a fatuous position they put Australia in, refusing to let its people know anything about a conception of life which is being read by thousands of people outside Australia.
>
> Do they really think they can keep this country as an ignominious little mental slum, isolated from the world of serious intellectual values? Do they think that an ostrich policy of sticking their own silly heads in the sand is going to save them from exposure elsewhere? Doesn't it occur to them that a pose of importance on their own local dunghill will hardly compensate them for the annoyance of being laughed at abroad? . . .

Turning to the effort by officialdom to 'coerce opinion on matters of culture and sociology', Norman said:

> This is pure Medievalism. It is the Star Chamber, the Inquisition.
>
> And, moreover, it is going to have a most disastrous effect, once Australian consciousness is aroused to the seriousness of the problem it involves.
>
> That is obvious to all who think. I leave it to those Federal authorities who can think to think seriously about it.
>
> As for you, Mr Forde, pass—for the present. But, oh, what a perfect ass you are!

So Australians had to break the law to read *Redheap* in their own country, although they and other people could read it without let or hindrance almost anywhere else. It continued selling well in England; and when it was published in America later in 1930, under the title *Every Mother's Son,* it scored an immediate critical and popular success. A few copies of the British and American edition were smuggled into Australia and, disguised by brown-paper jackets, went from hand to hand and were read dog-eared. One or two found their way to Creswick.

A suspicion that the Australian ban was imposed, not for the stated reason, but to shield living people who figured as characters in the novel, endures to this day. It is true that the Irish Free State, whose book censorship policy was even more repressive than Australia's, saw *Redheap* as indecent and bolted the door against it. Three other publications were added to the Free State's long literary blacklist at the same time: Aldous Huxley's *Antic Hay*, George Ryley Scott's *Sex and Its Mysteries*, and the London *Sporting Times*. Norman howled with glee when he heard he had been interdicted in such widely assorted company.

The sour atmosphere generated by the *Redheap* fuss did not help to sweeten Norman's break with Jack. Small differences between them had grown into large ones, and in the end their friendship had gone to pieces. Feeling he was being exploited, Norman had lost patience and written to say he would have no more dealings with Fanfrolico. Jack was not conciliatory; he believed his father had snatched at an excuse to free himself from an arrangement which had become irksome. Jack did not deny that he had taken Norman's drawings and paid nothing for them, but he believed the ledger was in balance; as he saw it, Fanfrolico's chief reason for existence was to promote Norman's philosophy and it had done that handsomely.*

There was another less obvious factor in the collapse of the association: Jack's faith in Norman's Olympian dreams and occult theories had steadily diminished to vanishing point. Coming to see his father's ideas as nothing more than a collection of myths, he no longer glowed with the zeal of the torch-bearer. Norman must have sensed this spirit of disaffection and did not mourn when the Fanfrolico Press died in 1930. Jack had worked hard to keep it going but in vain, largely because the world-wide economic depression had wrecked the market for de luxe editions. Putting Norman out of his mind, he went off to hide in a backwater of rural England and embark on a poverty-stricken bid to make a career as a biographer, historian and novelist.

Norman's disenchantment with Jack and his resentment against the assailants of *Redheap* were losing their sharp edge when *Art in Australia* published a Norman Lindsay Number in December 1930. The whole issue, seventy-six pages, was devoted to him and his work. Eight of his water-colours and thirty-five of his black and whites were reproduced.

* Jack insists that Norman never wrote a letter breaking off relations, or that if he did it must have gone into Rose's bag of unposted letters. 'Norman never at any time objected to our activities on the Press', Jack wrote to the author. 'In fact we only used drawings he did for us before we left Australia, or had agreed about—for example, the illustrations to McCrae—except for *The Antichrist*, where we used a few of his already published drawings, and for *Women in Parliament*, which he illustrated at our request as a companion book with *Lysistrata*. He also did some half dozen very slight drawings for Lascelles Abercrombie's *Phoenix*, which were never used. I had been to some extent withdrawing from his positions but the break came only when, in 1930, I wrote demanding that he should not cut my mother's allowance. Norman's idea that he wrote a letter of protest a year or more earlier is one of his typical self-justifying dramatisations produced long after the event.'

An editorial article, which acclaimed him as 'pre-eminently Australia's provocative genius', went on:

> He has always been outside the main stream of Australian art, wholly uncon-
> cerned with naturalism, and one of the few artists in this country who have
> followed traditional methods of composition . . .
> Norman Lindsay's work has fallen into three categories—pen-drawings,
> etching and watercolour. His essays in oils have been sporadic only and it is
> not a medium he cares for greatly. As an original illustrator with the pen he
> developed a technique which, for fluency and amazing versatility, had ad-
> mittedly few rivals in the world.

He valued those words. His creative faculty had not revived and, not knowing if it ever would, he drew comfort from being assured, in a magazine edited by two men of the calibre of Ure Smith and Gellert, that he had done something of lasting value. Besides, such a salute was a token of goodwill from Ure Smith after the shadows which had darkened their friendship.

Thousands of copies were snapped up as soon as the issue came off the press. After that sales held steady around a hundred copies a week. Although Australia was in the trough of the depression and the magazine cost three and sixpence, the demand continued and by June 1931 some 5,000 copies had been sold. Then the police arrived. They—or perhaps somebody behind the political scenes—decided that some of Norman's pictures in *Art in Australia* were obscene. A squad of policemen raided the *Art in Australia* offices and seized blocks, stereotypes and unsold copies. A sergeant leading the raiders made his feelings clear when he growled, 'I've read what this man has had to say about the police force'. He evidently meant the following remarks by Norman reported in a nine-page interview with Kenneth Slessor published in the Norman Lindsay Number: '. . . Australian officialdom is still the pure product of the convict system. A policeman's baton to settle all questions . . . There is something extremely disgusting in having one's work pawed over by policemen.' The policemen were now pawing Norman's work in earnest.

News of the raid was headlined in the dailies and, without awaiting the formality of a court decision, Mr Walter H. Childs, the Commissioner of Police, described the Norman Lindsay Number of *Art in Australia* to reporters as a 'filthy book'. Mr Childs, who had risen from constable's rank to the police chief's chair in a career spanning nearly forty years, did not say how many, or which, of the pictures were 'filthy', but *Self Portrait*, possibly Norman's finest etching, was undoubtedly among them. This depicts Norman himself, face tormented and wrists shackled, crouched like a prisoner in a dark cell and surrounded by a whirling mass of nudes, satyrs, demons, threatening fists, a skull, and a grotesque dwarf armed with a wooden sword. Its statement of the artist's travail in an environment teeming with forces hostile to free expression acquired a compelling topicality as the law moved into action.

On 10 June Ure Smith and Gellert appeared in the Sydney Central Summons court to answer charges of 'having caused to be issued an obscene publication'. After brief formalities, the hearing was adjourned for a month. A few days later Norman and Rose went to Sydney to discuss the prosecution with Ure Smith and Gellert and to offer their help in fighting it. They were walking along a street when they noticed a *Smith's Weekly* poster outside a news stand. WILL NORMAN LINDSAY BE ARRESTED? It asked. The words left an ineffaceable scar on Norman's mind. Even thirty years later he could not recall them without shuddering.

The poster was based on the main story of the week which reported that Norman might be dragged before a police court 'to stand before a magistrate . . . in the company of petty debtors, dirty restaurant-keepers, fruit-barrowmen, and other minor offenders. Queer company to offer a genius whose name is known throughout the world'. The story was unsigned but the writer was Kenneth Slessor. Slessor, who had joined *Smith's Weekly* in 1927 and was later to become editor, went on:

> That such a great Australian as Lindsay, acknowledged master both in prose and line, should be in danger of the petty humiliation of police court proceedings is a culminating insult. All his life Norman Lindsay has fought with courage and inspiration against the arbitrary restrictions of departmental bureaucrats, but never before have these minor officials dared to hint at such a public vengeance.

The affair had become a *cause célèbre*. No art question had ever before stirred up such a ferment of argument and speculation in New South Wales. It was a vexed issue in other states also. Every Australian metropolitan newspaper treated it as hot news.

One evening a barrister named Herb Moffitt* was drinking in a Sydney bar with a group of newspapermen. A talented black and white artist in his spare time who often contributed comic sketches to the *Bulletin* and sometimes to *Smith's Weekly*, he had been a friend of Norman for many years. One of the party was Adam McCay, a capable journalist when sober and a brilliant writer of light verse. McCay, born and educated in Victoria, had been a crony of Lionel in their youth and a frequent visitor to Creswick, and there he had fallen under surreptitious observation by the adolescent Norman who had later used him as a comic character in several novels, including *Redheap*. After serving his journalistic apprenticeship in Melbourne, McCay had gone to Sydney and was literary editor of *Smith's Weekly* when the *Art in Australia* crisis blew up.

---

* Later Judge Moffitt, Judge of the New South Wales Workers' Compensation Commission. He was not related to Norman's Melbourne friend, Ernest Moffitt.

When Moffitt joined the drinkers that evening McCay, a compulsive but entertaining talker, was spreading himself on the likely outcome of the prosecution and the possible consequences to Norman. Suddenly he interrupted his discourse to hoot with laughter.

'What's up, Dum?' one of his audience asked.

McCay said he had just had an inspiration. It would yield a wonderful news story. They'd go to the Commissioner of Police and urge him to have Norman's place at Springwood raided in search of sexy drawings. The police were bound to find some 'rorty stuff', which they could take away and use as evidence in a case against Norman.

Moffitt swallowed his drink, mumbled that he had to be home early, and hurried out of the bar to a telephone. He was almost stuttering with agitation when he rang Springwood and told Norman what McCay proposed. Norman thanked him, then went and flopped into his chair, weary and disgusted. He almost wished Moffitt had left him in ignorance. If the police came they could hardly fail to find what they wanted—at that time any work of his would have been automatically adjudged indecent. He had four or five bad days, waiting for a police posse armed with a search warrant to kick in the door. They did not arrive. Norman never found out if McCay had thought better of the stunt or if the Commissioner of Police had jibbed at it.

The adjourned case against *Art in Australia* came on at the Central Summons Court on 8 July. The proceedings were an anticlimax. The police prosecutor said he had no evidence to offer and the summons was dismissed. The court ordered that all copies of the magazine and the other material seized by the police should be returned. The outcome was no surprise to Ure Smith and Gellert. They had some influential friends who had pulled a wide variety of political strings to help them, and the police had been told to drop the case.

The affair ended there for everybody else but not for Norman; for him, it was a kind of Pandora's Box. In the mass mind he became a sensationalist who drew and painted sexy pictures with the object of shocking the public into taking notice of him. He raged against the injustice of this judgement but to no purpose; time lessened but never wholly dispelled it. Six years after the police file was closed John Holroyd, who was managing the mail-order department of Robertson and Mullens, a large Melbourne bookseller, opened a letter from a Chinese merchant in Rabaul, New Britain, ordering 'one of Norman Lindsay's delightful pictures of nude ladies'. The Chinese said he wished to hang it on his bedroom wall, so that he would see it in the morning and have 'delicious thoughts'. Holroyd found a copy of the Norman Lindsay number of *Art in Australia* and posted off a reproduction of a suitable painting. The Chinese merchant sent a cheque and a note expressing his gratitude.

Norman did not hide his relief when the *Art in Australia* prosecution was dropped but, coming on top of the *Redheap* ban, it was too much to be patiently borne. He said to Rose, 'To hell with this bloody country! Let's get out of it and breathe some clean air for a while.' Rose did not object. She thought a change of scene might help their marriage to throw off the middle-aged blight which had settled on it. They booked for America in the *Aorangi* on 23 July. For Rose it was a wrench to leave Jane and Honey at Springwood, even though she knew they were in safe hands, but for Norman it was a moment of deliverance. He could not—for the moment—even bear to think about his self-imposed mission of building a national culture. A few hours before the ship put to sea he wrote an embittered letter to Howard Hinton, who was visiting Europe, saying that his disgust had reached saturation point. Australia, he added, did not 'deserve to have a culture'. He told reporters in a last-minute interview that he did not know if he would ever see Australia again. 'I shall come back if it pleases me and I shall stay away if it pleases me', he said. As the *Aorangi* cleared Sydney Heads he sent a wireless message to the Sydney *Daily Telegraph*: 'Goodbye best country in the world, if it was not for the Wowsers'. Then he went out on deck and watched the land fall away. As always when the sea was about him, he had a sense of peace.

New York seemed gigantic. The skyscrapers dwarfed Sydney's tallest buildings, the speed was bewildering, the noise roared and rumbled all day and night like the tumult of a monstrous surf. This was a new world to Norman and Rose and they took some time to lose their feeling of strangeness.

Norman was elated to discover that his name meant more to Americans than he had ever dared to hope. The success of *Every Mother's Son* was the chief reason. Some quality in the tale of an Australian country town had caught the fancy of American readers and the novel had sold in thousands. A few people knew his pen drawings, etchings and water-colours, and collectors of limited editions knew his illustrations for Fanfrolico books, but most of those whom he met were astonished to learn that he was not a writer who dabbled in art but an artist who dabbled in writing. He did not grieve about that when he found that, by and large, only modern art counted with New Yorkers and all other values were in the discard. He grew accustomed to going into private homes as a guest and meeting people who could talk well on books, the theatre, and life in general but whose interest in visual art ended with the latest eccentricities. Their ability to see all kinds of aesthetic subtleties in what he called the 'modernistic imbecilities' decorating their walls baffled him, and he did not want them passing judgement on his work.

One night he dined, for a change, in an apartment where he found no reason to quarrel with the host's pictorial taste. One of his own etchings was hanging between a Rembrandt and a Zorn. That restored some of his sagging faith but did not encourage him to proclaim himself an artist. Anyway newspaper interviewers showed no interest in Norman Lindsay the artist. They wanted to hear about his books, not his pictures. He told them he was working on a novel, and one reporter asked if he expected the theme to bring the Australian Customs authorities down on his neck. 'I consciously do nothing to merit censorship', he replied, 'but it would be impossible for me to write a textbook on arithmetic without having the censor ban it'.

He and Rose had brought a large collection of his pen drawings, water-colours and etchings with them, thinking they might hold an exhibition. They saw that the time was not opportune; the depression lay even heavier on America than on Australia and every New York art dealer's rooms were crammed with pictures which nobody could afford to buy. It would have been madness to throw Norman's pictures away at the miserable prices then ruling. And there was no need. Depression or no, magazines were still being produced and novels published, and Norman was in demand. The *Cosmopolitan* magazine paid him $1,000 to illustrate a short story and pressed him to sign a three-year contract. He said he'd think about it but had no intention of going back to the journalistic art grind, even at the *Cosmopolitan*'s astronomic fees. He was busy enough keeping pace with the calls on him as a writer. High-paying magazines were printing his articles and publishers wanted his books. The first people to see the novel he had finished in New York were Farrar and Rinehart. They accepted it,* and paid him an advance of $1,000, and asked if he had anything else. He nearly said no, then remembered *The Cautious Amorist*, written some twenty years earlier. He had come on the typescript when he and Rose were packing for America. 'What shall I do with this?' he asked. 'Throw it in for luck', she said. Now, in New York, he delved into his trunk and dragged it out. Farrar and Rinehart seized on it and paid him another advance of $1,000. He was elated to know that he could live well in New York simply as a writer if need be, even when times were hard.

One day he called to discuss some publishing details with Stanley Rinehart.

'Are you related to Philip Lindsay?' Rinehart asked.

'Philip?' said Norman. 'He's my son. Why?'

'We're buying his novel.'

'What novel?'

* This novel was published as *Mr Gresham and Olympus* in America and as *Miracles by Arrangement* in England.

'It's called *Panama Is Burning*. A grand yarn full of pirates and light ladies and bloody deeds. It's bound to be a huge success.'

'Well, I'm damned!' said Norman. So Phil too was fascinated with pirates! Norman approved of that. Pirates had never lost their magic for him and never would. 'I'll do the dust-jacket, Stanley', he volunteered. 'I think I know what's needed.'

'Delighted', said Rinehart. 'I was hoping you'd say that.'

Since Phil had gone to London Norman had heard almost nothing of him. Phil had chosen to lie low because, being guiltily conscious that he had left Australia against Norman's wishes, he could not bring himself to admit how badly things were going with him. After teetering on the edge of starvation for a long time, he had added to his troubles by marrying and becoming the father of a baby daughter. *Panama Is Burning* was the turn of the tide. It launched him as one of the most popular and accomplished historical novelists of his time. When it was eagerly accepted for publication in both England and America nothing pleased Phil more than the thought that at last he had a success which he could report to his father—all his life he hungered for the approval of the god in the Blue Mountains.

Soon after Norman delivered the dust-jacket Rinehart, on a business trip to London, met Phil and told him that his father was in America and why he had gone there. Although excited and astonished, Phil could not hide a sardonic grin. It was comforting to know that even Norman, the dedicated apostle of cultural patriotism, had been compelled to flee Australia to escape the stifling priggishness and intellectual inertia.

New York was friendly and stimulating but Norman was never really at ease there. Away from his native earth he felt hardly less alien than an Arnhem Land Aboriginal set down in the middle of Sydney. He could not come to terms with the pace of New York social life. A year or two of it would have killed him. Although—or perhaps because—Prohibition was still in force, Norman found himself becoming a 'reluctant boozer', in his own words. He was forever forcing himself to swallow drinks before, with and after meals, on rounds of visits to speakeasies, and as a guest in private homes where the parties went on until two or three in the morning. No pussyfoot, he believed that liquor was an essential lubricant of civilized living and once said, in a characteristically sweeping judgement, 'There would have been no Russian Revolution if the people had not been debarred the safety-valve of liquor'. But, for himself, he did not want or need drink. Even a mild surfeit of wine or spirits caused him agonies of indigestion, leaving him jaded, sluggish and heavy-headed next day. He marvelled that many of his New York friends were able, like his sons Ray and Phil, to wake after a debauch lasting till the small hours and go about their business with seemingly clear heads.

He liked many Americans, however, and found them almost embarrassingly hospitable. Sinclair Lewis, Ogden Nash, Fannie Hurst, Hervey Allen, Christopher Morley, Edna Ferber, Hendrik Willem Van Loon and other writers treated him as one of themselves. To his lasting regret he did not meet H. L. Mencken, the American literary celebrity of the day whom he admired above all others. He could have arranged it easily enough but recoiled from the notion of thrusting himself on Mencken without some valid reason. Remembering how many visitors to Springwood had gone there purely to gape at him, he resolved that he would not inflict himself on a man whom he ranked, then and always, as one of the few Olympians of his generation.

And all the time he was tormented by thoughts of Australia. The outlook of Australians at large sickened him but he could not master his yearning for the country itself; his eyes ached for the warm tones and the clear strong light, his body for the dry heat. He knew that Australia was the only land in which he could ever be content; to try to break free of it was for him, he told himself, in a phrase borrowed from one of his literary gods, Rabelais, simply 'pissing against the wind'. But what good reason could he find for going home? Now that his creative faculty had failed him, what could he do in Australia to justify himself?

He found the answer on a cold and blustery December day when he opened a letter from his friend, Godfrey Blunden. Writing from Sydney, Blunden mentioned that government currency manipulations and taxes had forced up the price of imported books by more than thirty-five per cent.* It was only a casual remark but Norman seized on it. This, he reasoned, could open the way for Australia to launch a native book publishing industry on a daring and adventurous scale, thus creating conditions in which a vigorous school of creative writers would thrive and grow. Australian book publishing had been almost wholly a sideline of firms like Angus and Robertson, whose chief business was bookselling, or occasionally of a printer with literary inclinations. These people all tended to follow a play-safe policy, so that Australian writers of any originality had to go cap in hand to overseas publishers with their manuscripts, more often than not to meet a rebuff. This, Norman believed, was no longer good enough. A progressive publishing industry was indispensable if a national literature were to evolve, and there'd never be a better time to found one. He did not go out of his way to admit that the plan had another merit also; this was that it would give him a perfect

---

* This was made up by a conjunction of the twenty-five per cent exchange rate, which Australia adopted when it devalued the national currency in December 1931, with a so-called primage duty of ten per cent and sales tax of two and a half per cent, which had been imposed on books and many other commodities in 1930 as a revenue-raising measure in the depression. In 1932 the government exempted books from primage duty and sales tax on the ground that these placed  'a heavy impost on students, schools and universities'. The exchange rate, of course, continued to apply.

motive for going home. For who was better fitted than he to advise and guide, and rally support for, an infant publishing industry?

He went to Farrar and Rinehart and urged them to set up a publishing house in Australia. They said it couldn't be done; American and British publishers, they explained, had a long-standing agreement which made Australia a British preserve. Norman bustled about New York and put his suggestion to the principals of several other large publishing houses. These all echoed Farrar and Rinehart: Australia was British publishing territory and their hands were tied. Norman was incensed. These people seemed to think they could treat Australia like some primitive dependency inhabited by savages armed with bows and arrows! Whatever his own view of the intellectual backwardness of the Australian masses and of the attacks on freedom of expression by Australian bureaucrats, this evidence of cultural colonialism was intolerable. After a day or two he simmered down. Since the Americans were immovable, he would take his proposal to England. He never doubted that he could persuade some big London publishing house to hoist its flag in Australia. He'd only need to put the case and one of them would jump at the idea.

He and Rose crossed the Atlantic in January. Their ship, the *Baltic*, had to butt her way through a winter gale which hewed the ocean into racing mountains of grey water. Norman landed at Liverpool feeling that he had been in the grip of a gigantic mangle. To make matters worse, he had a cold and boarded the train for London complaining that he felt as if he was trying to think with his head under a feather bolster. Drizzling rain was falling on London when he and Rose arrived. He wondered if it had been going on ever since they had left twenty-odd years before. He shuddered and, as soon as they booked in at a hotel, sneezed his way into bed and stayed there for a week.

Word that he was in London soon reached the Fleet Street news editors. Remembering the stir his pictures had caused in London, and the Australian upheaval over *Redheap*, they sent reporters to see him. He was glad to talk for publication; he wanted the London publishers to know why he had come. The newspapers responded well. The *Daily Express* called him 'the man with a bomb in his brush' and played up the interview under a double-column heading, with a photograph. Several other London dailies were equally kind.

Norman's spirits rose as callers came to the hotel wanting to see him. Brian and Olga Penton were among the first. Since the collapse of the Fanfrolico Press Penton had made a living as a Fleet Street reporter and was working hard at a novel in his spare time. Phil presented himself with his wife Jeanne, a beautiful girl with shoulder-length chestnut hair and shy blue eyes. He and Norman, jabbering in excited

o

unison, talked about everything from books and art to the miseries of the London winter and the shortcomings of English heating systems. Jack, rusticating far from London for economy reasons, did not show up. His writing occasionally brought in a few pounds but it was hard to keep going. At this time he was renting a tiny cottage in a Cornish village and subsisting on a diet of practically nothing but wild blackberries. He fought down his longing to go to London and see Norman. 'I knew if I did', he wrote later, 'I should succumb to his charm, I should begin to whittle down and modify my new convictions, I should end by returning, even if in a less intense form, to my discipleship'.*

Will Dyson was another who did not call. He had gone back to London and rejoined the *Daily Herald* in 1930, at the end of his five unhappy years in Melbourne, and now he was seriously ill. Pushing aside the memory of their last doleful meeting at Springwood, Norman and Rose went to the hospital to see him. The visit depressed them. Will's eyes had lost their old-time truculence, and much of the pungency had gone from his talk and much of the edge from his personality. He seemed tired, like a man who has run a long and exhausting race and wonders if the effort has been worth while. His body was not yet ready to die (indeed, he lived until 1938, when death came to him as he sat in his chair), but his spirit was flat. This malaise was subtly reflected in his work. He had not regained his old place as the pre-eminent London cartoonist; David Low, now with the *Evening Standard*, had supplanted him. The *Daily Herald* missed him, however, and the editor, desperate to find an acceptable substitute until Will was well again, invited Norman to take over as 'guest cartoonist'. The proposed fee was large but Norman said no. He wanted only to do what he had come to do, then make for home with all speed. 'I've been pickled too long in a dry climate to stand this damp, dark one', he told Phil.

It was not the climate alone that bothered him. He made a round of the big publishing houses but nobody was interested in opening a branch in Australia. One or two said they would think about it and bowed him out; others dismissed the idea out of hand and made it clear that he was wasting his breath and trying their patience. Even Norman's own publishers, Faber and Faber, were not impressed, although as the author of *Redheap* he commanded some respect there. A director received him when he went along to the Faber offices in Russell Square, and, having heard the proposal, puffed out his cheeks and shook his head. No, he said. The idea had merit but it was far ahead of its time. Perhaps in ten or twenty years . . . Now, if Mr Lindsay would forgive him, he really must be off—he was overdue in conference. Norman grew to detest the word 'conference'; he met it everywhere. He also came to detest the dingy

* Jack Lindsay, *Fanfrolico and After* (London, 1962), p. 220.

ante-rooms, in which he was always kept waiting before being admitted to the Presence, and the dingy spinsters presiding over them.

He writhed under his inability to persuade anybody to accept his conviction that, given some assurance of publication, a splendid school of Australian novelists would spring into being. He was convinced that a number of talented but yet unpublished Australian writers such as Blunden and Penton, and an Adelaide man named Leslie Meller, could do work equal to the best that Britain or America was producing. He knew Meller, a South Australian public servant, and a war veteran who had been severely wounded in the Gallipoli campaign, only through correspondence. This had grown up around the typescript of a novel, *Quartette*, which Meller had sent him some years before, asking for an opinion on it. Notwithstanding faults in the style and construction, Norman had seen it as the product of a rare and sensitive mind, and Meller had rewritten it three times under his guidance. The final draft happened to reach him in London and left him in no doubt that Meller was a novelist of uncommon subtlety and power. He sent *Quartette* to Faber and Faber, albeit with little hope that they would recognize its merits. He was unjust to them. They accepted it in a few days on the recommendation of one of their chief readers, whose enthusiasm matched Norman's. 'This boy has genius', the reader said in an excited note. Even this response did not persuade Norman that Australian writers could look to English publishers with any confidence. His experiences as he peddled his plan around London confirmed a belief he had formed on his prewar visit: it was impossible for an Englishman to like or understand an Australian, or, indeed, for an Australian to like or understand an Englishman.

Brooding thus, he suddenly saw the light. If Australia wanted a publishing house of its own, then Australians would have to find the money and back it themselves. Well, that much might be managed, but wherever would they recruit a man with the technical knowledge required to organize and direct so specialized a business? A ready-made solution was at hand. Norman and Rose had made friends in London with Inky Stephensen, Jack's old Fanfrolico associate. Norman liked the tall, fair mettlesome and talkative young Queenslander; he also applauded Stephensen for having spurned Marxism, after conducting a noisy flirtation with it which had brought him into disfavour at Oxford. The Mandrake Press had foundered in the early months of the depression and Stephensen, at a loose end, effervesced with excitement when Norman talked of Australia's need to publish its own books. He stood up and strode about the room, waving his arms and tossing out thoughts on how it could be done, why it must be done, what it would cost. When Norman asked him if he would be interested in going out to Sydney and running a modern publishing house, he said he'd jump at the chance. He agreed that Norman should go home and look into the prospects of finding financial backing. Once that was arranged, he said, he'd need a month or two to wind up his affairs in England. Then he and his wife Winifred would head for Sydney and as soon as they got there he'd go to work. By heavens, they'd make things hum!

There was nothing else to keep Norman in London. March came in cold and gusty and the *Mongolia* was listed to sail for Australia in a fortnight. Rose booked their passages, and in April they saw Australia for the first time in nine months. The shipboard reporters went to Norman and he told them about the publishing plans which he and Stephensen had evolved. They aimed, he said, to publish twenty-five Australian novels a year—stories of life in Australian cities, not stories of 'bushwhackers and bushrangers'—as well as 'selected English and American novels'. He foresaw a new era for national literature. 'Australian writers', he said, 'haven't a chance under present conditions'.

When the *Mongolia* put in to Adelaide he had his first meeting with Leslie Meller, a slight, dark man, quiet, diffident, and deeply serious over the mystery and craft of letters. Meller's shyness quickly melted and he outlined the theme and characters of a new novel he was working on, *A Leaf of Laurel*. Norman told him he must push ahead with it—*Quartette* would put him on the literary map but he must keep himself there. If Faber and Faber didn't want *A Leaf of Laurel*—'And they'll be damn' fools, Leslie, if they don't grab it! Damn' fools!'—Australia's own publishing house would be a going concern by the time it was ready and would leap at the chance to publish it. He took the liberty of offering Meller a piece of personal advice. 'Don't underestimate yourself', he urged. 'You'll meet plenty of discouragement and need all your resources to keep on working as a novelist. Try to remember that too much modesty can be even more destructive than conceit.' Like many another writer, Meller went away burning with the creative enthusiasm which Norman had an uncanny power of generating in nearly everybody who excited his confidence in them.

At Sydney Norman and Rose hurried from the ship to Springwood and found little change there, excepting only that Jane and Honey had grown taller and more self-contained. Autumn leaves were crisp underfoot and the cool April air was soft. Norman went to the studio and pottered about for two or three days trying to find a theme for a picture. At last he threw down his pencil and pushed away his paper in disgust. The Hunchback still had him in its grasp.

Businessmen were enigmatic beings to Norman. He was nearly as uneasy among them as a landsman adrift in an open boat on the high seas, but although he shrank from the thought of going out in search of money to finance a publishing house there was nobody else to do it. This was one business project he could not shuffle off on to Rose. She was busy enough bringing up her daughters, managing Springwood, and seeing to routine business without giving precious time and energy to a frail and visionary project. The astute Rose saw the potential hazards of the undertaking, while Norman saw only the potential splendours. He believed it would succeed because it deserved to succeed. All his life, as he knew himself, he was 'the dupe of an illusion that the desirable was attainable', and this was just one more example.

He wrote buoyant letters to Inky Stephensen in London, but as he delved into the problem he began to realize that he had shouldered a forbidding task. The depression had hardly begun to ease and, while everybody applauded his scheme as a contribution to national self-sufficiency and aesthetic progress, nobody had any money to risk in a company formed to publish books. Syd Ure Smith could offer nothing but advice; he had his hands full keeping *Art in Australia* and his other business interests off the rocks. Hugh D. McIntosh would have backed Norman except for one disability: the stormy economic winds and his wilful extravagance had wrecked his newspaper and theatre empire and he was about to be declared bankrupt, with liabilities amounting to nearly £300,000.

Norman had no money to put up—he had never accumulated money. As long as he had a few pounds for the needs of the moment he was content to let Rose hold the purse strings; she had done it for twenty-five years, and only she knew whether they were wealthy, comfortably off, or broke. One day she went to him and told him, in her blunt way, that their money was nearly all gone. The market for pictures had fallen dead as the depression had taken hold, and it gave little sign of reviving. Their travels had been expensive, and all the time the cost of running Springwood had gone on. Norman, said Rose, would have to find some way of earning money or they would be on the bread-line. What was he going to do about it? There was only one solution: journalism. He did not relish the thought but at least he had no worries about doing the work. His technical skill was all it had ever been. That was something the Hunchback had left untouched when it had sneaked up behind him and stolen away his conceptual faculty.

He went along to the *Bulletin* office and saw Sam Prior. As chairman and managing director since 1927, Prior had less time to devote to editorial detail, but the character of the *Bulletin* was still his paramount concern. Never having stopped mourning Norman's retirement or abandoned hope that some day a miracle would restore him to the *Bulletin*, Prior gave him a cordial welcome. The reigning staff cartoonists,

Ted Scorfield and C. H. Percival, were hard-working but pedestrian, and the *Bulletin*'s black and white comments on world and national issues were no longer discussed, laughed over, sometimes praised and sometimes damned as they had been in the days of Phil May, Hop, Low and Norman Lindsay. Prior, who had made a private vow that he would move heaven and earth to bring Norman back, could hardly believe that the man himself was suggesting it. Admirers of Low, Dyson and other stars would never persuade Prior that Norman had any rival as a black and white artist—he was the one man who could, simply by the power of his pen, triple the weight of the *Bulletin*'s influence in public affairs.

'When can you start?' Prior asked.

It was the self-same question that Archibald had asked at their first meeting thirty years before.

'As soon as you want me', Norman said.

Norman did not know that the tall and self-possessed Prior was doomed. Prior did. He had been fighting failing health for some years and wanted to leave the *Bulletin* in the best possible shape when he died. To him, as to most of the men down the years who took a salient part in shaping its policy, the *Bulletin* was not merely a weekly newspaper but a kind of religion. He lost no time. The first paragraph on the Personal Items page on 10 August 1932 ran: 'Thousands of readers will welcome the announcement that Norman Lindsay, the world's greatest black-and-white artist, has rejoined the staff of the *Bulletin*, and his cartoons and other drawings will be regular features of the paper from next week onwards'.

Norman's first cartoon, on 17 August, was a comment on the economic depression. A topical adaptation of his famous drawing on the outbreak of war in 1914, it carried the title 'The Devil Strikes His Gong and the War God Listens'. It showed a devilish figure, black and menacing, beating a gong labelled Want, Misery, Stagnation and Depression, while the war god, wearing his horned helmet, crouched in the shadows, watching. It dispelled any fears that Norman's brain, eye and hand had lost their journalistic cunning.

He had not forgotten book publishing but the prospects were bleak. On an impulse, he went to Sam Prior about it.

'H'm', said the canny Prior. 'How do you know Australians want to read novels about Australia? You believe they would be willing to pay for them?'

'I'm sure of it', Norman replied. 'Damn it all, they've no real choice at present. They can like what the English publishers send out here or they can lump it.'

Norman talked hard. Australia, he said, had the authors and the

One of Norman's later cartoons from the *Bulletin* of 1933

readers; the only thing lacking was a modern publishing house to fuse the two.

As he swept on in a rush of words some of his enthusiasm entered into Prior. For many years the *Bulletin* had been a more or less spasmodic dabbler in book publishing, and one novel bearing its imprint— *Such Is Life: Being Certain Extracts from the Diary of Tom Collins* (1903)\*—was well on its way to become an Australian classic. Prior was probably swayed as much by an ambition to create a regular book publishing offshoot as by any immediate profit motive. He was sixty-three and, knowing he had only a little time left, saw his chance to build a personal monument. He also wanted to keep Norman from taking his book problem to some other Sydney newspaper group, and perhaps falling into their hands and being lost to the *Bulletin* as a cartoonist. He talked it over with his son, Ken, also a director, who had been business manager of the *Bulletin* since 1919. The upshot was that they and their co-directors agreed to find most of the money to start the Australian Book Publishing Company Limited.

Toward the end of September Inky Stephensen, full of bouncing confidence and high expectations, arrived from England to manage it. He said the company would need modern printing and binding machines; an order was rushed to Europe. He also said it must have a name that people would recognize and remember. Norman suggested the Endeavour Press, and everybody said it was an inspiration. Norman rather thought so too. For him, Captain Cook and the *Endeavour* symbolized daring, fortitude and courage, and with Stephensen at the helm the Endeavour Press would bear the name honourably and well. Norman did not doubt it.

Stephensen swept about Sydney exuding mental and physical vim. Norman was impressed, and so were the Priors. Stephensen had vision, imagination, thrust. And charm; nobody was proof against his gay, unstudied and rather boyish charm. And energy; his suite of rooms on the third floor of the *Bulletin* office hummed with activity. He and his wife were at Springwood nearly every weekend while he and Norman charted a course for the Endeavour Press. He estimated it could pay its way if the sale of each book averaged 6,000 copies. Neither he nor Norman thought this figure extravagant; nor did either question that, magically, a new school of young Australian writers would burgeon and supply the Endeavour Press with more good books than it could handle.

The public birth notice took the form of an article in the editorial page of the *Bulletin* on 2 November 1932; this outlined an ambitious programme. Norman's cartoon that week was a salute to the venture. It depicted koalas, a kangaroo, an emu, a goanna, possum, wombat, platy-

\* Tom Collins was the pen-name of Joseph Furphy (1843-1912).

pus and other bushland creatures, all dressed as men or women and each with a parcel of manuscript tucked under an arm, crowding toward the open door of the new publishing house.

The cartoon was an almost frighteningly accurate prophecy. Manuscripts came in like an avalanche. Norman had volunteered to be the firm's reader. Now he quailed as he pondered the hillock of packages. Well, no matter! If volume meant anything, there would be no lack of stuff to publish for years to come. He dug into the hillock and began reading. His spirits sank. Here and there a writer showed some glimmer of literary sensibility but most of them were hopeless. Nearly every manuscript was dog-eared, battered and grubby after going the rounds of English publishing houses; many still bore the labels of London literary agents. Once or twice he came on a novel which had possibilities but needed wholesale recasting; then, hoping that the effort would achieve something, he spent hours writing an exhaustive analysis for the author's guidance.

'Found a masterpiece yet?' Stephensen asked him one day.

'Nothing we could even print', Norman confessed.

'Don't worry. It will come', Stephensen said, and rushed off to a business appointment.

Preparations to begin publishing early in 1933 were in hand but the deadline loomed nearer with no book worth printing in sight. One day Norman was in the *Bulletin* library, gloomily searching through bound volumes of the *Lone Hand* for something that might make a book. A story of his own caught his eye. It was one of his autobiographical tales of small boys in the town he called Redheap. He read it and found himself chuckling. He flipped over the pages until he turned up another. It was no less entertaining. By George, if only there were enough of these yarns they might make a reasonable book! He knew the tally, in the *Lone Hand* and the *Bulletin*, must run into double figures. He burrowed into the files and kept at it until he had listed seventeen of his small-boy tales. They would need a little rewriting to weave them into a novel, but the characters and situations would stand up. This was the genesis of *Saturdee*, which is widely recognized as the most successful of all Norman's books for adults, a classic of its kind, and unique in Australian literature.

Stephensen liked the idea of launching the Endeavour Press with it; any book bearing Norman's name was assured of a healthy sale. The Priors shuffled at first—the trouble over *Redheap* and *Art in Australia* was still vivid in their minds—but they concurred once they were satisfied that *Saturdee* would not invite a conflict with the law. The Endeavour Press published *Saturdee* at the end of February 1933* and there were

* The flyleaf of the first edition bears the line 'First Published January 1933' but the book was not ready until a month later.

no censorship upheavals. It went out to face the world wearing a brilliant yellow dust-jacket designed by Norman, the critics praised it, and Australians bought it. A Red Page reviewer, John Dalley, a novelist of some repute as well as an accomplished journalist, called it 'a comic masterpiece' and said, 'Mark Twain himself never recaptured the idioms of his childhood as completely, and no one has penetrated so far into certain murky recesses of the small boy's soul'. A few addicts of the illusion that all children are sweetly innocent until the world corrupts them frowned on *Saturdee*, but nobody else found moral fault with it. Even those Creswick citizens who had denounced *Redheap* liked *Saturdee*; they amused themselves by identifying the characters with their real-life models—Norman himself, Ruff Tremearne, Lionel, and an assortment of other small boys, small girls, hobbledehoys, and adults who had graced Creswick in the author's youth.

It was a good beginning but the Endeavour Press did not thrive. There was no single reason for its slow but steady decline after a promising start. The most decisive factors appear to have been Stephensen's incapacity and faulty judgement, the timidity of the *Bulletin* management, and Norman's exaggerated notions of the number of high-grade Australian writers waiting to rush forward with manuscripts. And of course the times. Most Australians were pressed for money to buy food, clothing and shelter in the straitened 1930s, and few had much to spend on books. Stephensen committed himself to publish two books a month. This was a gross over-estimation of the Australian appetite for indigenous books and—at that time—of the Australian capacity to write them. In its two and a half years the Press published some twenty in all. *Saturdee*, Brian Penton's *Landtakers*, G. B. Lancaster's *Pageant*, 'Banjo' Paterson's *The Animals Noah Forgot*, and one or two more earned a profit. Most of the others just paid their way or lost money.

The Priors grew glummer as the debit balance rose. Norman and Stephensen were both directors but the real power lay with Sam Prior, as chairman, and Ken Prior, who was also on the board. Sam Prior died on 6 June, and Ken Prior succeeded his father as *Bulletin* chairman and managing director, and also as chairman of the Endeavour Press board. He had lost all faith in the mercurial Stephensen and a series of disputes between them quickly created a situation which could have only one outcome. The board met on 18 September and sacked Stephensen. Pleading illness, Norman did not attend that meeting. Perhaps he could not bring himself to take a hand in toppling his erstwhile favourite. Stephensen stalked out vowing to form a publishing company of his own. Norman was well pleased to see him go. He blamed himself for having taken Stephensen at face value—for having failed, in his own words, 'to detect the megalomaniac under the mask of a brisk man of affairs'.

He was still convinced that, efficiently managed, the Endeavour Press could succeed. Ken Prior, although less sanguine, was willing, now that Stephensen had gone, to give the Press a chance to make good or dig its own grave. He asked, rather pointedly, when all those talented Australian writers, whose early appearance Norman had foretold, might be expected to present themselves bearing manuscripts which could be turned into best-sellers or even into reasonably saleable books. Norman could not think of a ready answer, but nobody could say he was not trying his level best! From the start he had done all the reading; sometimes he would refer a manuscript to Cecil Mann, the Red Page editor, for a second opinion, but otherwise he worked single-handed. For a while he shuttled between Springwood and Sydney two or three times a week by train. Then he took a room at the Wentworth Hotel and spent most of each week in Sydney; often he went back to Springwood only for weekends. He always had a manuscript in his hand or beside his bed. More than 300 manuscripts had arrived in the first rush, and although the flood had slackened it had not stopped, so there was always a backlog of reading to be done. From first to last he found among the unsolicited manuscripts by unknown writers only one workmanlike novel—*The Doughman*, by Robert Tate—and not one book of verse worth printer's ink.

When Ruff Tremearne was on a visit from Melbourne Norman showed him a stack of manuscripts and groaned, 'There isn't a page in the lot worth reading. They make me think of Sam Johnson—what is good in the damn things is not original, and what is original is not good.'

Ken Prior's lurking fears of Norman's literary advice quickened when news broke in May 1934 that Australia had banned *The Cautious Amorist*. Tens of thousands of Americans had read that farcical tale of island castaways without being corrupted. Then a London publisher put out a British edition and shipped a consignment to Australia. The Customs Department swooped on it. Some thousands of copies were returned to London. Norman hardly bothered to discuss the ban even with friends; he was becoming used to the ways of Australian censors. He was only thankful that somebody other than the Endeavour Press had published *The Cautious Amorist* and was suffering the Australian backlash. Not that it made any difference. He was beginning to see that the Endeavour Press was misbegotten. The root of the trouble was that Australia had no school of writers turning out publishable books; that would take years to evolve. The Press was ahead of its time. There were not nearly enough competent authors to keep it going.

Norman knew the end was near as Christmas 1934 approached. Ken Prior decided to give the Press a few more months to market its unsold books but there was to be no more publishing. Norman wished he had never fathered the project. While achieving little it had cost him an enormous amount of time which he might have put to better use. Or perhaps he was wrong. He could at least thank the Endeavour Press for giving him a means of pushing the Hunchback to one side if never of keeping it there for long.

The future had a grey look. He did not relish the prospect of beating a retreat from Sydney and settling in at Springwood again. He shuddered at the thought of sitting in his studio and driving himself to draw or paint pictures which, to him, were not worth doing—pictures he would lavish all his skill on and then scrap because they said nothing he wanted to say or nothing he had not said before. He had turned out a few water-colours and two or three oils since coming home from London but none of these seemed to him to rise above the merely decorative; for all their technical merit, they reflected only the surface of his mind. He had another reason also for wishing to escape from Springwood. The psychological discords of middle age had upset the balance of his life with Rose and there was no consolation in knowing that much of the fault lay with himself. The bond which had linked them ever since they had come together as lovers was frayed and close to breaking point. They had always struck sparks from each other but their differences had been short-lived; now they could sometimes find release only in a protracted and bitter quarrel, and he detested living in a state of tension and making Rose live in it.

He decided to move to Sydney, leaving Springwood to her and the girls. He had no idea if the separation would be temporary or permanent; he only knew that he must break away and think out his personal problems, and if possible find his lost creative ability again. He told Rose he was taking a lease of a studio flat at 12 Bridge Street, a large old building just around the corner from the *Bulletin* office; it would, he said, save him the tiresome weekly train journey to and from Sydney. She could always find him there, and he would visit Springwood every now and then; and of course there'd be letters. Rose nodded and kept her thoughts to herself. Perhaps she too felt that a period of marital decompression would be no bad thing.

# 10

# No. 12 Bridge Street
# 1934-45

In Norman's last twelve or thirteen years he often had a dream which never varied. It came first in his late seventies soon after he gave up the lease of the studio flat at 12 Bridge Street in the 1950s and settled down for the rest of his days at Springwood, and then recurred every few months. The events of the dream unfolded in logical sequence. They were as clear as anything he ever experienced in waking.

In the dream he was in Sydney, intending to catch a late afternoon train to Springwood. Having a little time to kill, he dropped in at his favourite secondhand bookshop run by Stan Nicholls in Crane Place, near Circular Quay, and browsed among the books. Dipping into the thumbed pages of classics he had not opened for decades and savouring again passages he had always loved, he lost count of time and suddenly realized he must hurry to catch his train. Half way to the station he groped in his pocket and found he had no money for the rail fare. He made haste back to Stan Nicholls's shop to beg a loan. Finding it locked and shuttered, he went to a near-by tobacconist's where he was known, but it was closed also. Night had fallen and he wandered the streets, wondering how to get a meal and a bed. He thought of going to a hotel and explaining his predicament, but shrank from the fear of a refusal. Then he remembered 12 Bridge Street and all his anxiety fled. He went there at a run and, with a singing heart, gave a succession of long and loud rings on the bell beside the street door. Nobody answered. He rang again, but the building stayed black and silent. Desperate, he hammered with his fists on the heavy door, then stepped back and stared up at the rows of unlighted windows, praying that somebody would look out and come down to let him in. Standing in the dark and empty street, he shouted and shouted, trying to rouse one of the tenants.

The dream always ended there and he would wake with a sense of emptiness and frustration. He did not know what some Freudian analyst would have made of it but he knew what it meant to him; he believed it was the expression of his subconscious longing to go back to the place in which he had been more content perhaps than anywhere else in his adult life—above all, the place in which he had defeated the Hunchback.

When he moved into 12 Bridge Street he was despondent about his chances of ever again drawing or painting anything of value to himself. The Hunchback held him in bonds lighter than air but stronger than steel. He knew it was all in his mind, a figment of his neuroses, but this did nothing to dispel it; the very intangibility of the fetters made them the harder to break. His income from the *Bulletin* met all his living costs, but he could find no satisfaction in merely earning money to clothe himself, his wife and his daughters, to provide them with shelter, and to feed them. If that was all life held then it was a nullity; there was no purpose in the struggle, no meaning in the journey—animal survival might be well enough for the mass of mankind but it was of no use to him who had known the torment and the ecstasy of creation until the Hunchback laid hands on him.

There had to be some way out of the psychological morass. He racked his brains thinking about it, all to no purpose. Well, he told himself, he must find something to do if only as a time-filling occupation. He decided to tackle oil painting. He had never done more than play about with the medium but now he settled down to make a methodical and calculated attack on it by hard study from the living model. He went to work with the humility of a student, not trying to paint pictures which expressed his concept of life but training all his skills on the basic technical problems. It was nearly six years since he had worked by a regular daily pattern. He likened himself to an old soldier, highly trained and strictly disciplined in his prime, who returns to the army after a lapse of years in which he has let his drill go to pot, but he knew the analogy was crude and incomplete; the old soldier's clumsiness was purely physical and could be put right in a few weeks of intensive re-schooling, whereas disuse had corroded Norman's sensory mechanism while leaving his physical deftness unimpaired. The thing he had to do was rebuild the intricate network which linked eye, brain and hand. It might be impossible; at the very least it would take years. He gave himself over to it with all his prodigious powers of concentration.

Finding models was easy. As soon as word spread that he had moved in to 12 Bridge Street nearly every model in Sydney came toiling up the stairs wanting to pose for him. For one thing, he paid above the ruling rate. For a second, any model who posed for Norman Lindsay acquired a special seal. For a third, he had a knack of making his models like him.

This liking was indispensable; he could not work from a model with whom he could not establish a sympathetic bridge; it was like painting a dummy. He sometimes used a male model but his overmastering interest, both as an artist and a man, in the female body and the female mind meant that eleven in every twelve of his models were girls or women. He had long before perfected a technique for getting the best out of them. He deliberately stimulated their self-esteem by flattering them, sometimes subtly, sometimes laying it on thick to suit the individual temperament. It influenced the colouring in their cheeks, the brightness of their eyes, the assurance with which they took a pose. It never failed him.

The flat was on the second floor. It had a studio with a good painting light, a bedroom, a bathroom, and simple cooking facilities. A woman came in every morning to sweep, dust, make the bed, and cook breakfast while Norman shaved and bathed. All the arrangements suited him to perfection. And there, while labouring at the craft of oil painting, he found the strength to overthrow the Hunchback. He did not know it was happening. The months went by and, little by little, he began to master the technique of oils but his creative powers were still dormant; or, for all he knew, stone dead. Then, for no logical reason, his lost creativeness came back. In his own words, he found 'the old mechanism of form imagery working as well as, if not better than, ever before'. His own theory—that the merciless ritual of hard work which he set himself effected the cure by acting on his mental being and nervous system until the sleeping cells woke—is unsatisfying but as good as any other. There is less doubt about the superficial circumstances of his recovery. Years later he recalled:

After a couple of years of hard study I had acquired a competent control over the medium of oils and then, quite suddenly, my conceptual faculty was restored. I made no conscious effort. It was like a bright light coming on in my mind. I began turning out compositions, large and small, and they began to sell. It was unbelievable at first. I wondered every night if I'd wake next morning to find myself creatively impotent again, but a day came when I knew there was nothing more to fear. I was once more in command of my artistic destiny.

What part if any late love played in restoring Norman's nervous balance and his mastery over himself is conjectural. If he had an affair of the heart at that time he never spoke of it. This proves nothing; he was as reticent in such matters as men like Hugh McCrae were cheerfully unguarded. Some of his close friends supposed that the views he often expounded on the value of a new love in stimulating the creative powers of an ageing man reflected personal experience. He was fond of citing Charles Dickens in support of his theory; Dickens, he insisted, could not

have given the world *Great Expectations* and *Our Mutual Friend* unless
he had renewed himself in middle age by leaving the mother of his ten
children and taking a young actress, Ellen Ternan, as his mistress.

The intimate details of Norman's personal life in the 1930s hardly
matter. The essential thing is that, for some reason or combination of
reasons which can only be guessed at, he conquered the Hunchback and
became a whole man again, surging with creative power. Nothing remained of the black and sterile years through which he had passed except the memory. And even that soon faded. He had no wish to go back
and live at Springwood but the emotional dislocations which had played
a big part in driving him to Sydney began to mend. He and Rose were
able to meet again in an atmosphere of amiability instead of stiff restraint.
She looked at his oils and liked them. She was no freer with praise than
she had ever been but, knowing that one approving word from her was
worth fifty from almost anybody else, he felt a glow of elation.

Rose said she would manage the selling side. She did it with all her
customary skill in practical affairs. It ultimately evolved into a comfortable family arrangement. Honey married a man named Bruce Glad, and
Rose, having set them up, in 1939, in a commercial art gallery in George
Street, was able to feed Norman's pictures to the market without depending on outside dealers. It suited Norman to leave the huckstering to
Rose. It meant he could go on painting with an easy mind.

Life at Bridge Street moved now like a smooth-flowing river. It was a
state not of happiness in any simple sense—he was too complicated a
man to be capable of anything but momentary happiness, which he once
defined as 'a child's dream of flowers and butterflies and sunshine'—but
of absorption in the incessant and agonized struggle of the spirit to
conquer the inertia of the flesh. Although he believed with Browning,
one of the poets he most admired, that 'a man's reach should exceed his
grasp', he once said, 'There is neither pleasure nor happiness in the
damned effort to achieve it. The best one can say of it is that it becomes
an obsession which takes hold of the mind and ousts all lesser interests.
I suppose that's something.' To him, it was nearly everything.

The Bridge Street building had no lift and he numbered that among
its special blessings. Anybody wishing to reach his door had to climb
forty-four stairs, and the prospect daunted many would-be intruders
wanting to kill time at the expense of his work. Any bores who braved the
stairs rarely got farther than the landing. When somebody knocked he
would open the door a few inches and, unless the caller happened to be
a friend, exclaim, 'Sorry, I can't let you in—I've got a model sitting', and
cut short any objection by slamming and bolting the door. An unwanted
caller sometimes roused him almost to violence. He had just started work

30   Springwood

31   One of the Springwood sculptures

32   Norman with one of his models and her family. In a note to the author Norman commented:

> The girl in the photo is the one whose externals I took for Bradly Mudgett's little model Cora, in *Age of Consent*. The pen drawings in the novel I took directly from her, and those, you will note, are reproduced in her eldest daughter, the three delightful youngsters being of her begetting.

on a large oil painting one morning when somebody knocked. He hurtled across the studio and flung the door wide, grasping his brush like a dagger. 'To hell!' he bellowed and banged the door shut. His model, James Robb, collapsed with laughter. Norman fell into a chair and did not recover his shattered calm for half an hour. That was the only time that Robb, whose lean and mobile face glowers, laughs, leers or threatens from a score of Norman's paintings, ever saw him in a rage. Norman later solved the problem of keeping all but a sprinkling of unwanted callers outside by inventing a cabbalistic knock for those friends who never violated his working routine and were always welcome when they came. After that he simply ignored the knocking of the uninitiated.

His routine rarely varied. Waking early, he breakfasted, then put in an hour or two on whatever novel he happened to be writing before setting his palette for the day's painting. On every week-day but Thursday, which was kept free for the *Bulletin* cartoon, the model took his or her pose at ten o'clock and Norman painted until four o'clock, with an hour's break for a simple lunch. He and the model shared it, and sometimes a friend came in to join them. Both artist and model were ready to call it a day at four. He had always found oil painters as a class duller company than most men and been puzzled to account for it; now he understood. It was a matter of sheer weariness. Even when rising sixty Norman, as spare and hardy as a wind-beaten stringybark, had more physical endurance than most men of forty, but a day's oil painting left him spent. When he stopped and cleaned his palette he wanted to do nothing so much as fall into a chair and relax, while his taut mind uncoiled and his fatigued body rested. If one or more of his intimates dropped in for a yarn he was glad to see them; talk with anybody he liked revived him.

His mental world embraced the whole earth and sometimes reached well beyond it, but his physical world rarely extended more than a few hundred yards from Bridge Street. He cooked most of his own meals and bought everything he needed in a shopping centre around the corner in Pitt Street; if inclined to eat out, he could always count on a good dinner at Aarons's Hotel, near by. Two or three times a week he picked up an armful of novels and magazines at Swain's bookshop and library. Reading was still nearly as necessary to him as breathing, but when he was tired from oil painting the classics were often too much for him. Turning to the kind of literary ephemera he had always spurned, he astonished himself by becoming an admirer and a connoisseur of the mystery-detection novel. He liked Dorothy Sayers, Philip MacDonald, H. C. Bailey, G. K. Chesterton (for his Father Brown stories, not for his 'serious' novels, which Norman thought pretentious rubbish), Margery Allingham, Anthony Berkeley, and three or four of their peers. He also became a devotee of the American magazine, *True Detective*, which published

P

detailed stories of actual crimes, written by journalists who had reported them in the line of daily newspaper duty.

An occasional visitor flinched at sight of a copy of the magazine lying about the studio. Norman, who was devoid of intellectual or social snobbery, never apologized for it.

'Going highbrow, I see, Norman!' one caller remarked sarcastically, as he contemptuously flipped through the pages of *True Detective*.

'You talk like a bloody fool', snapped Norman. 'You've never read the magazine so you're not qualified to pass an opinion. As a matter of fact every story is a valuable study of criminal psychology, and if you don't find the subject interesting I'm sorry for you.'

He liked studying the portraits of criminals in *True Detective*. Every human face and what could be read from it enthralled him. He would study photographs of killers, embezzlers, judges, prelates, cowards, heroes, poets, politicians, doctors, soldiers, and any and every other kind of human being, carefully scrutinizing each set of features through a magnifying glass in search of the physical key to the individual personality. Although he did not always accept or reject people on the evidence of what he saw in their faces, his understanding of the logic of physiognomy was uncanny. His friend John Frith, art editor and caricaturist of the *Bulletin*, had one enlightening experience of it.

Among Frith's specialities was the modelling of caricatures of public men in plasticine. These three-dimensional variants of the orthodox caricature were cast in plaster and then in metal, and photographed for reproduction. They were not only a popular *Bulletin* feature but also a source of extra income to Frith because one of the subjects often bought the metal copy to sit on an office desk, a boardroom table, or a study mantel shelf. Frith had just finished a model of the head of the Australian industrialist Laurence Hartnett, at that time managing director of General Motors-Holden Limited, when Norman walked into his room in the *Bulletin* office one afternoon.

He spent five seconds studying the model and then said, 'That's dreadful!'

'Do you know him?' asked Frith.

'No', said Norman. 'I've never seen him. But you set out to flatter him. It sticks out a mile.'

Frith had to admit it. Hartnett, whose strong and aggressive features were a caricaturist's joy, had told him, 'If I like it I'll buy it, and have a series of casts made. I'll send one to each of our branches.' Tempted by the notion of having examples of his work on show throughout the General Motors-Holden empire and anxious to produce something Hartnett would like, Frith had done a bloodless likeness instead of a caricature. He put his fist through the plasticine head and spent the rest of the day modelling a new one. He took it over to Bridge Street next afternoon and unveiled it.

'Marvellous!' Norman chirrupped. 'Bloody marvellous! Now I can really see him.'

Frith never again tried to flatter anyone who sat for him.

Bridge Street was more like an exclusive club than anything else. Kenneth Slessor, slight and sandy-haired, and almost incoherently shy except with close friends, was a foundation member. So was the reserved and introspective Godfrey Blunden, whose first novel, *No More Reality*, came out in 1935; Norman greatly admired it. Brian Penton was also an early member but his visits became progressively less frequent and he eventually dropped out altogether. He lost face with Norman when, having published a sequel to *Landtakers* in 1936, he turned his back on creative writing and set himself with ruthless determination to become a newspaper editor. Having so often heard him wittily ridiculing daily newspaper editors and all they stood for, Norman concluded that Penton had elected to join them because he was either a humbug or a coward; and, whichever cap fitted, not worth knowing.

Hugh McCrae would have been welcome at Bridge Street but he almost never went there; he had practically stopped writing poetry, and perhaps even his graceless hedonism was not proof against Norman's undisguised disapproval of creative people who let their talents rust. Norman held that art demanded 'an eternal exercise of the will' and that any man who neglected to use his talent for a long time could not pick it up again at his own convenience. He lost patience with those who broke this law— brief candles that gleamed for a while, then went out. One of his bitterest disappointments was over Leslie Meller, who became disheartened and let systematic writing slide after publishing his second novel, *A Leaf of Laurel*, in 1933. Norman never ceased believing that Meller had been born to make a unique contribution to Australian literature, and could not quite forgive him for abandoning the struggle.

To Norman, young men or young women who might achieve something and were determined to try were always better company than older ones who had achieved something and then given up. In this spirit he played the literary godfather to Kenneth Mackenzie, a Western Australian in his early twenties who had gone to live in Sydney about the time Norman broke away from Springwood. He was enraptured with Mackenzie's gifts and helped him to find publishers for his first novel, *The Young Desire It*, and his first book of poetry, *Our Earth*; he also ensured the success of *Our Earth* by illustrating it. Mackenzie justified Norman's hopes. The two books of verse and four novels* standing to

_____
* His novels were published under the name of Seaforth Mackenzie.

his credit when he was drowned in 1955 all bore the stamp of an original and sensitive mind. He would probably have built a major literary reputation but for his early death.

Douglas Stewart, who was to become Norman's closest friend for the last thirty years of his life, entered the Bridge Street circle a little later. Stewart, a small, dark man, was quietly spoken and sparing of words but calmly tenacious and intellectually forceful. He was twenty-five when he arrived in Sydney from his native New Zealand in 1938, and, having joined the *Bulletin*, soon became editor of the Red Page and started developing his extraordinary talent as a poet. Norman began meeting him at conferences in the *Bulletin* office when key members of the staff gathered to discuss the cartoon for the coming week; being only a few steps from the office, Norman often went to these conferences instead of waiting for the editor to send the cartoon idea to him. They were noisy gatherings and Stewart was so reserved that Norman hardly noticed him until one day somebody mentioned Aldous Huxley.

'Huxley invented a religion and then converted himself to it', Stewart said.

'That's good! Who said it?' chuckled Norman, supposing it was an aphorism coined by some eminent literary wit.

'I did', Stewart said.

That was the start of their friendship, and Stewart was presently a full member at Bridge Street. He was often bidden to lunch with Norman and the model of the day, and of these visits he wrote:

> Actually even a writer soon gets to share the professional, undisturbed outlook of the painter, and I don't remember much more than the slightest sense of the unusual in sitting by the coal fire eating sandwiches for lunch with a naked and (sometimes) beautiful girl. The one who does linger in my memory with something of wistfulness, something of regret, was an extremely strict and shy young lady who dived behind a screen when I came in and left floating on the air the impression of an exquisite white bottom, like a swan.*

Time had not weakened the pull of the intellectual magnetism which had always drawn poets and writers to Norman. If anything it was stronger than ever. Those who had names yet to make knew that he would listen to them, advise them, and help them find publishers; those who were established knew that he would give them strength when they flagged on the journey across one of the arid stretches which from time to time bar the way of every creative soul.

A small group of young painters also looked to him. The ablest was a girl named Margaret Coen, whom Norman had known since her student days. She was beginning to make a reputation as a water-colourist and, while helping her with advice, he was fearful of playing the teacher, to

* *Bulletin*, 1 March 1961.

her or to anybody else. He believed that good artists made bad teachers. 'They impose their own methods on students and so turn them into imitators of the teacher', he said. 'The good teacher is one who expounds the principles of craftsmanship and leaves the student to find his own individual expression in it.' The little artists' group often spent Sunday in the open air, painting the figure in landscape. Johnny Maund, a solicitor who did some good work as a water-colourist and was also a collector and connoisseur of painting, would pack them and a model into his car and drive out into the bush or to one of the beaches. Norman found these outings refreshing interludes in his battle with oils.

He tried to prod Ray into working harder at painting. The results were disappointing. Ray's enthusiasm had weakened after the success of his 1928 show, and having gone to Bridge Street a few times and worked from the model alongside Norman he ran out of energy; the discipline seemed to irk and dispirit him. He liked sitting about and yarning with his father, who found him a fluent and pungent talker, with a sound understanding of values in all the arts and a racy sense of humour. As a painter he had talent but lacked fixity of purpose, and Norman wondered if he had strayed into the wrong calling. In Norman's opinion, Ray had a better mind than either Jack or Phil and would more than likely have excelled either of his brothers had he made writing his life's work.

Although so few painters turned to Norman he never denied help to any who did come. John Frith was with him once when a painter burst in and said he was in despair about a technical facet of water-colour— struggle with it as he would he could get nowhere. Norman spent more than an hour showing him where he was going wrong and making sure he would not go wrong again, then sent him on his way rejoicing.

Frith was astonished. 'It's extraordinary', he said. 'It's taken you forty years to learn how to do that, yet here you give it away to somebody you hardly know simply because he comes along and asks you.'

'But don't you see', Norman replied, 'if I can teach him to do what I can do then I've got to make myself just so much better to keep ahead of him!'

Frith doubted that many successful artists would have seen it like that.

Yet, as always, the writers who hung on Norman's words heavily out-numbered the artists, and his studio flat became an informal meeting place for writers—mostly young writers but some older ones also—who needed the faith in themselves that he could give them. Although he always repudiated any suggestion that he was what he called 'a literary bloke', he could hardly deny the growth of his reputation as a writer, or reject the aura it gave him. By the late 1930s he had published eight novels and made a deep study of the novelist's craft, particularly by read-ing and analysing the works of Joseph Conrad. He was continuously experimenting on his own account; indeed, it was Bridge Street that yielded perhaps his most skilfully constructed novel, *The Cousin From Fiji*. He always specially liked *The Cousin from Fiji* because, be believed, the gay story of Ballarat in the 1890s was an unerring reflection of his tranquil state of mind when he wrote it.

The puzzle remains: Why should Australian writers, as Douglas Stewart asked, have accepted a painter as their cultural leader? Stewart wrote:

> Writers undoubtedly come to him . . . not only because of the understanding he can bring to their work but because of the tremendous enthusiasm with which he receives it—if it is good. Bring him but twenty lines—but eight lines—of good poetry and he receives it as lesser men would receive first prize in a lottery. The writer who brings him a single short story with 'the real thing' in it is likely to leave his studio committed to writing a novel, re-assured that he has the power and rather disconcertingly convinced that he has the duty to do it.*

Those words shed a little light on the enigma. Nobody is ever likely to give the whole answer.

Blood was not necessarily thicker than water for Norman, and his links with 'Lisnacrieve' slackened in the 1930s. His mother's death in 1932 was a factor. He had never been as close to her as most of the others—for the reason, Lionel said, that he saw her as the gaoler of his delicate childhood, 'and the sick are always revengeful'. Even so, one of his substantial links with Creswick snapped when she died. A breach with his brother Daryl, who was well placed in Melbourne to keep close touch with 'Lisnacrieve', did not help to mend it. Why they fell out is not clear. Daryl said the reason was 'a difference of opinion on family matters', while Norman ascribed it to his resentment of an outburst of destructive criticism of his work by Daryl. At any rate, from that time the two never spoke nor exchanged letters. Readiness to forget and forgive was not one of Norman's more conspicuous virtues, and his rancour was deep and lasting. His comments on his brother's appointment in 1941 as director of the National Gallery of Victoria were scornful; and when in 1956, Daryl was knighted for his services to art Norman, who believed that any title was an 'absurd prefix', grunted, 'Well, the fellow has got his deserts'.

Mary continued to be Norman's main channel of communication with 'Lisnacrieve'. Their friendship never waned, and even when they did not meet for years they went on writing voluminous letters to one another; these embraced every conceivable topic, from music, books, and the importance of the nude, to Creswick identities, the idiocy of doctors, and the excellence of cats. As a result they never grew apart, and their minds met as readily in maturity as they had in childhood. Mary dodged personal involvement in Norman's intra-family quarrels and kept the

* *The Flesh and the Spirit* (Sydney, 1948), pp. 276-7.

peace between herself and Lionel and Daryl, but she was always closest to Norman; she seemed to understand his need of an enduring nexus with 'Lisnacrieve' and Creswick. She was hardly less close to the complex Bert, long settled in London and a confirmed expatriate who, after living more than half his adult life abroad, went home in the late 1930s to spend his last years at 'Lisnacrieve'. Something in both Norman and Bert doubtless stirred the spinster Mary's frustrated maternal instinct.

No shadow ever fell between Norman and Percy. Percy made thousands of friends in his lifetime and none of them ever quarrelled with him; nobody could quarrel with Percy. He rambled through the world doing enough bread-and-butter drawing to bring in sufficient money for his undemanding needs, and painting whatever appealed to him. Every day was a joy and every path bordered with flowers. The intensity of feeling that brought Norman and Lionel, and then Norman and Daryl, into conflict was beyond his comprehension. Each of them was an awfully decent chap, which was Percy's designation for everybody, so why did they have to scrap among themselves like Kilkenny cats?

Percy liked spending an hour or two at Bridge Street every once in a while and Norman liked him to go there. Percy brought many good things with him, and none better than his gift of laughter. Norman held that what he called 'Rabelaisian belly-quaking laughter' had died in the First World War and been replaced by a tight and pallid substitute, sardonic and mocking. Only he, Percy, McCrae, Ruff Tremearne (who nearly always went to Bridge Street for a week or two of his yearly holidays from his job as the Melbourne *Herald*'s music critic) and a few others of their age ever laughed with backthrown heads and open throats; his younger friends saw the funny side of life but acknowledged it with a smile, or at most a sparing chuckle. Norman always felt a little shifty when he went off into unrestrained guffaws in the presence of Stewart, Blunden, Mackenzie and others of their generation. He suspected them of thinking his cheerful uproar just a shade vulgar.

The mystifying thing about Percy, in Norman's eyes, was that, although never scrupling to put pleasure before work, he did not know the meaning of bad conscience. Norman sometimes questioned if, for all they were children of the same parents, they really belonged to the same species.

'You never let up, do you, Joe?' Percy said as he browsed around the studio one afternoon, peering at the evidences of Norman's huge and insatiable appetite for work. 'You're a queer chap!'

'Damn it all', Norman barked, 'you're the queer one, Joe. I marvel that you can look yourself in the eye when you shave every morning.'

'It's dead easy once you form the habit', replied Percy, who had formed the habit before he could walk, and shouted with laughter at the sight of Norman's face.

Percy regretted the estrangement between Norman and Lionel but did not think of trying to reconcile them; he knew it was impossible, and anyway he was no do-gooder. The original causes of the separation had been aggravated by later events. Among these was Lionel's dislike of *Redheap*, especially the lampooning of his adolescent self in the character of Robert Piper. He had written to Norman in protest; the letter, Norman admitted, was 'justly embittered'. After resigning as cartoonist of the *Evening News* in 1926, Lionel had visited Europe and built a considerable London market for his etchings and woodcuts. He believed, rightly or wrongly, that this success, and his acceptance by leading British artists and collectors of the day, had inflamed Norman's jealousy. In Lionel's own words, 'I have never been forgiven my London success'. Whether or not this was just to Norman, it was Lionel's conviction and one of the insuperable obstacles to a lasting peace with his brother.

Several men of greater intelligence but perhaps lesser human wisdom than Percy each believed himself capable of healing the long-standing rift, only to discover their error when they made the attempt. In the 1920s the two had now and then responded to the good offices of such friends by exchanging amicable messages but these had led nowhere, and when Norman went to Bridge Street he and Lionel were as far apart as ever. Robert Menzies was one who thought it a pity. Menzies, at that time Federal Attorney-General and later to become Prime Minister, was a friend of both Lindsays. He preferred Lionel's company and met him more often, but sometimes called at Bridge Street and was always warmly received there. Norman admired his taste in literature and his skill as a raconteur, and patently delighted in his conversation, so Menzies had some ground for supposing that he might succeed in reuniting the brothers.

Moved by an altruistic ambition to raise the status of artists in Australia, he was working to rally support for the formation of an Australian Academy of Art (which was founded in 1937 only to expire within ten years). Norman was among a minority of successful artists who would have none of it; he said it would turn artists into 'funking tradesmen', fearful of doing anything to offend the public or the Academy, and that, as it was, Australia was not producing enough passable art to feed the periodical exhibitions of the existing societies. Taking this opposition to his pet scheme in good part, Menzies used the openings which discussion of the project afforded to manoeuvre Lionel and Norman into two meetings, each time at dinner. As he described it: 'On each occasion they got on splendidly, sounding so like each other that I could hardly distinguish between them. Subsequently each of them said to me, to my fascinated delight, that the other "was a good chap, but talked too much!" '* But

* Foreword to Daryl Lindsay, *The Leafy Tree* (Melbourne, 1965), p. ix.

his hopes of seeing brotherly love reborn were dashed. Both times Lionel and Norman parted in seeming harmony but went on going their separate ways.

Syd Ure Smith tried hard too. He and Norman were still friends, although they never quite recovered the intimacy which their differences over modern art and George Lambert had tarnished. Another cause of irritation had also come up. Norman, ignoring the economic problems which beset high-grade magazines in the depression, blamed Ure Smith for letting the *Sydney Morning Herald* publishing group take over *Art in Australia* and the *Home* in 1934; Ure Smith and Gellert stayed as editor and co-editor but Norman felt they were no longer permitted to make any but emasculated editorial judgements—they had sold themselves to a 'damned newsrag'. On his side, Ure Smith often found Norman maddeningly exasperating but, being a man of ample patience and uncommon diplomacy, he managed to save the friendship from going to pieces in a bitter quarrel. He was fond of Norman. He was also fond of Lionel, and hoped for a long time that the disaccord between the brothers could be charmed away. In the end he knew they were irreconcilable. Any mediator was wasting their time and his own.

The patriotic emotions which had seethed in Norman in August 1914 did not stir in September 1939. He could not call them up twice in a lifetime. The passions roused by martial music and marching men were for younger blood, not for his.

Although he had foreseen for years that war was inevitable, his *Bulletin* cartoons in the last months, and even in the last weeks before Nazi Germany atacked Poland did little to suggest that Australia would be drawn into the conflict. They did not, however, express his personal viewpoint but the policy of the *Bulletin*, which was ardently preaching that Britain and the Empire should refuse to become entangled in any European war. He had not modified his stand that, as a cartoonist, policy was no concern of his. He knew that Dyson, Low and some other black and white men were adamant that the cartoonist had a sacred duty to draw nothing which conflicted with his own opinions. Norman could not see it like that; he believed that an artist who accepted a newspaper salary was in duty bound to accept editorial direction also. The chief architects of *Bulletin* policy just before and during the Second World War were the editor, Jack Webb, and two of his senior associates, David Adams and Malcolm Ellis, and if Norman sometimes disagreed with them he never disputed their authority.

Whatever his personal thoughts, his cartoons on the European turmoil of the late 1930s were, technically, of a high order, but they gained in force and fire once war broke out and the *Bulletin* dropped its isolationist cry. All Norman's friends were familiar with his detestation of 'the obnoxious blood-lusting Hun', and now that he was free to take the gloves off, his weekly drawings were as savagely anti-German as anything he had done in 1914-18. He poured into them all his scorn of the Nazi leaders, and all his loathing of the Germans as a nation. It was consoling to be able to let his head go after running on a tight rein, but he ever afterwards recalled those first months of the war—the 'phoney war' period—as a haunted time of uneasy waiting. The atmosphere was oppressive and artificial. The only event to make a lasting mark on his memory was purely personal: the death of Elioth Gruner.

Norman had seen little of Gruner for some years. He liked the man no less than ever but could not tolerate some of his homosexual associates. One—in Norman's words, 'a specimen of the worst type of he-she parasite'—seemed to be always at Gruner's elbow like an odious shadow, alienating him from his friends and putting him into conflict with himself. Gruner had become more withdrawn and introspective as he grew older. Seeking escape from the torment of his thoughts, he turned to drink; it only deepened his melancholy. He painted less, and although his best work was still delicate and bewitching in its lyric beauty he largely abandoned morning light, in which he had always delighted, and took to painting late afternoon subjects. Norman had no doubt that these studies, emphasizing the long shadows of a dying day, betrayed the innermost secrets of Gruner's mind and revealed him as a doomed man. It was one of Norman's convictions, based on his own experience, that, while any creative man might delude himself and those about him into accepting his conscious states of mind as valid, his work would expose what was going on behind the pretence. The paintings of Gruner's last years were, Norman held, striking evidence of the truth of the theory.

The spectacle of a man wishing himself into the grave was not unique in Norman's experience. He had seen another friend, Rayner Hoff, do it in the last uneasy years of peace. Hoff, a young Englishman, had settled in Sydney soon after the First World War and made a name as a fine sculptor. Norman admired his technical skill and creative gifts, his resolute mind, and his capacity for clear thinking on life as well as art. Then the puritan element, disliking the quality of sex vitality in Hoff's nudes, singled him out for attack. He wilted. Having smashed up his marriage, he died in his early forties after injuring a kidney while surfing. Norman considered that Hoff's death was self-inflicted no less than if he had put a pistol to his head or swallowed poison. 'It's absurd to suppose', he said, 'that chance has anything to do with such an ignominious death as being dumped in the surf. That only happens to a man who is already morally dead.' He was convinced that Gruner too was morally dead in his last years. One of Norman's friends, Doctor Francis Crosslé, an Irishman of discerning literary and artistic tastes, tried to save Gruner from himself. Crosslé twice snatched him from the edge of death after destructive drinking bouts and, having weaned him off liquor, steered him back to work. When Gruner relapsed for a third time Crosslé said to Norman, 'I can't do it again. He wants to die. Let him!'

Gruner died in the early hours of an October morning of 1939. If Norman's philosophy had warranted his mourning any man's death he would have mourned Gruner's. As it was, he merely shrugged when he heard the news. It was no surprise. And why grieve for one who had gone to a place among the Olympians?

When the German armies broke through Holland and Belgium and overwhelmed France, Norman did not see it as a prelude to Germany's total victory, and become a prey to panic. For a highly strung man, he had a level head. He was also endowed with what Phil Lindsay called a 'peculiar belief in Destiny's rewards', and this enabled him to reject any fear that the disaster in Europe could extend to Australia. Being convinced that the intellectual upsurge, for which he had hoped and worked so long, was at last under way, he had unquestioning faith that nothing would be allowed to impede it. An impregnable trust in the wisdom and incorruptibility of the gods was a central pillar of his creed—Hitler and his hosts might subjugate the whole of Europe but, damn it all, they'd never lay their hands on a country in which a new renaissance was about to flower!

Hundreds of thousands of Australians did not share Norman's optimism. Many, believing that Britain was about to surrender and Australia to fall under German rule, turned their eyes across the Pacific and saw North America as the only secure place. Rose was swayed by these prophets of doom. She proposed that she and Norman, with Jane, and Honey and Bruce Glad, and a six-year-old girl named Lu Scholes, should go to America. Lu was the child of a friend of the Lindsays, William Scholes, a Sydney manufacturer. His wife had made it impossible for him or the child to go on living with her. Rose, who was always gentle and compassionate with children, had taken the little girl to live at Springwood and accepted the responsibility of bringing her up. Norman refused to consider America. So did Jane; she had been living away from Springwood for some time, working for a spell at share-farming, absorbing local colour, and making observations of character which she later put into a novel.* Their opposition did not deter Rose. She packed up a collection of Norman's best pictures, which she had been assembling at Springwood ever since 1912, and set off for the United States with the Glads and Lu Scholes, intending to stay in America until the war ended.

Norman did not regret his decision to stay behind.

* *Kurrajong* (Sydney, 1945).

'But can't you see?' a pessimistic acquaintance asked him. 'After those cartoons of yours you are the first man the Germans will shoot when they invade Australia.'

There was some ground for this belief. Norman's cartoons always depicted Hitler as a hag-ridden nincompoop, Goering as a podgy lout, Goebbels as a vicious little cur, and their lesser henchmen with like contempt; Mussolini made occasional appearances as Hitler's oafish and blustering toady.

'If the Germans ever got here', Norman replied, 'I'd ask nothing better than to be shot. But since they won't get here, or win the war either, there's no point in this drivelling discussion.'

He had work to do and wanted to get on with it. His creative powers were at the flood, and when he finished one big oil ideas for two or three more were always jostling one another inside him. Although *Reverie, Don Juan, Imperia* and a few other comparable gallery pieces were already done before the 1940 sequence of war crises exploded, as many more were in the womb of his mind, waiting to burst forth and be transplanted from the intangibility of the mental image into the reality of paint. He knew that much of his work, like much of any artist's work, was purely aesthetic; having justified its existence by pleasing the eye it would perish. These were the pictures he painted as technical exercises, the pictures he had to paint in striving for a mastery over oils, but beyond that they held no importance for him. The only pictures on which he placed a value were those that expressed his personal philosophy, affirming life as a great adventure in the spirit as well as in the flesh. It was the total impact that counted. 'I don't care a damn for technical imperfection in my work', he once told his sister Mary, 'as long as it has the power to convey a concept touching the profundities of human life'.

He had never worked with more zest than at Bridge Street, nor had he ever thought of leaving there, but Rose's insistence on going to America played havoc with his intentions. Somebody had to hold the fort at Springwood, and so, against his inclinations, Norman went back to live in the mountains. Jane went also. The two had never been particularly close—Norman thought her capable and self-assured but combative, and all his life preferred the placid and tolerant Honey, whom he once described as 'the best-balanced and sanest woman I've ever known'—but he and Jane rubbed along well enough at Springwood; they did not jar on one another because they had, in common, a partiality for being left alone and for leaving others alone.

Norman kept the tenancy of Bridge Street and still spent a good slice of his time there. He sometimes caught the train down to Sydney and stayed for two or three days together, and when he came to town, Douglas Stewart has written, 'the whole place seemed to catch fire'. The studio flat was invaluable to him when he needed to work from the model; his Springwood studio was adequate for all his other needs but he preferred his models to go to him at Bridge Street—it saved his time and theirs.

Like every kind of worker, good models became scarcer as the war went on and the demands of the armed services and industry mounted, yet that was when he found Rita Lee. An artist named Joe Holloway took her to meet him. She was eighteen years old; tall, and statuesque (if less so than Norman's fondness for painting buttocky women was apt to make her); the daughter of a Chinese father and a white mother. Norman counted Rose, in youth, and Rita, with her dark eyes and alabaster skin, the only two truly beautiful models he ever had. To him, Rita was the perfect model for oil painting, not only for her physical qualities but also, and no less, for her faculty of reticence, aloofness and repose.

They never talked much, but now and then, in a rest interval, she made some remark which told him that a questing mind was at work behind the quiet mask of her face.

'Art is a sort of religion, isn't it?' she said one day.

'That's about as good a definition as you'd ever find for it', he agreed.

She was the model for some of his best oils, *Mantilla*, *Rita of the Nineties*, and *The Black Hat* among them. She posed for him for six years until she married a naval photographer, George Young, and settled down to make a home and raise a family. Norman regretted one thing; he tried time and again to paint her breasts but never quite succeeded in capturing their tender loveliness. The defeat always galled him a little.

His wartime struggle with oils was immeasurably more important to him than any reputation the Americans might award him for the pictures which Rose had taken across the Pacific. Even the catastrophe which occurred soon after her arrival in the United States did not unsteady his painting hand. He told himself wryly that those blasted illustrations to the *Memoirs of Casanova* were at the bottom of it! He was tempted to agree with Hugh D. McIntosh that there was 'a jinx on those damn' things', and when Rose had packed them for America he had privately hoped never to see them again. He never did. A railroad freight car in which the collection was crossing America caught fire. The *Casanova* drawings and many other of Norman's best works were destroyed. It was a diabolical misfortune. The loss was not even covered by insurance— through some mischance the policy had lapsed when the pictures were landed in America.

Perhaps the episode persuaded Rose that the expedition was ill-starred. At any rate she and her party came home, bringing with them any pictures which had survived the fire. When Norman greeted her at Springwood he felt she was taking the blow too hard. He refused to think about it. By his reckoning the price a work would fetch in the market-place was nothing, the doing of it everything.

The war rumbled on. Many of his circle were caught up in it and carried overseas. He particularly missed Slessor, who was a newspaper correspondent with the Australian army in the field, and Blunden, who went off to report the fighting on the Russian front. Each of them sent a note now and then but they were too busy to write much.

Other of his friends fell away because they had lived their span. 'Banjo' Paterson died in Sydney, quietly lamenting that at seventy-six he was too old for soldiering. A little later Hugh D. McIntosh, who had gone back to England some years before determined to recover his lost affluence, died in London, flat broke but unvanquished in spirit. Norman did not sorrow for them—Paterson, the aristocrat, and McIntosh, the inspired plebeian, had each in his own way lived life to the full. He never doubted that he would meet them both on that other plane 'behind the curtain' when his time came to follow them.

Japan's entry into the war did not upset him. Indeed it helped his work as a cartoonist by broadening his field of attack. He still delighted in lampooning Hitler, Mussolini, Goering and the rest of the Nazi-Fascist gang, and now he was able to extend the gallery to include the Mikado, as an undersized monkeyish figure strutting and smirking in a sloppy military uniform. Neither on the outbreak of the Pacific war nor even after the Japanese swarmed southward and appeared to be unstoppable did he grant them the slightest chance of invading Australia.

When they were landing troops in New Guinea and the neighbouring islands in 1942, in preparation for a drive on Port Moresby, he chanced to meet Robert Menzies in Sydney. A Labour government—headed by John Curtin, one-time office boy of the weekly *Rambler*, which had failed to flourish in Melbourne in 1899—was in power, but Menzies still knew more about the ominous realities of the war situation than most Australians outside the War Cabinet. As a member of the Advisory War Council and a dominant figure of the Federal Parliamentary Opposition, he was privy to most of the secrets.

'At the moment there's nothing to stop the Japs', he told Norman. It was true. Australia was ill prepared and American reinforcements had only just begun to arrive. 'They could be in Sydney in a few months.'

'No', said Norman with supreme assurance. 'The gods won't allow it while there's a poet like Doug Stewart in Australia.'

This assessment of the prospects was evidence not only of Norman's faith in the power of the gods but also of his opinion of Douglas Stewart's poetic stature. That opinion was to strengthen in the years ahead as Stewart's talent revealed itself in such verse plays as *Ned Kelly*, *The Fire on the Snow*, and *Shipwreck*, but even his early poetry had persuaded Norman that he outshone McCrae or Slessor or any other of his Australian forerunners and contemporaries. That he had been born in New Zealand was immaterial. Of what importance was twelve hundred miles or so of ocean? Stewart had left his native land and adopted Australia as his own, and in Norman's eyes he was as Australian as Henry Lawson or Joseph Furphy.

Even as early as the day he startled Menzies with his affirmation of the gods' readiness to frustrate Japan's designs, Norman was beginning to think of Stewart as a genius. By the time the war ended he had thrown aside any remnant of doubt and ranked his friend as the supreme English language poet of the century. Whether or not others thought the finding tenable, Norman never changed it.

The events of the war all served to affirm Norman's faith in the gods: his gods. They were wise, powerful, benevolent, whereas the Christian God was a mischievous invention of latter-day myth-makers and responsible for endless human misery. Douglas Stewart once heard a Sydney printer and occasional publisher, Charles Shepherd, suggest to Norman that he illustrate the Bible.

'Oh, no, no, no, couldn't think of it, Charlie', Norman replied. 'It's a very dangerous book, had a very bad influence.'

He could be tolerant of Christian leanings in his friends, however. John and Mae Frith's only son, Jeff, was born in 1941. They wanted Norman and the other *Bulletin* cartoonist, Ted Scorfield, to be godfathers. Scorfield accepted, and then the Friths put it to Norman.

'But I'm an atheist', he objected.

They told him that it didn't matter, so Norman said, 'Well, if you're sure!', and was duly registered as one of Jeff Frith's godfathers. But he was not present at the christening ceremony at St Chad's Church of England, Cremorne. That would have been going too far.

And perhaps he was right about the gods, because the Japanese were stopped and turned. As the war stretched out he went on painting, drawing, etching, writing, modelling ships. He also went on looking for poets and writers. He could never resist the possibilities lurking in a manuscript. He supposed he was driven by the identical instinct which makes old prospectors go trudging out into harsh and trackless country in search of gold.

An unpromising package arrived at Springwood one day in 1943. It consisted of a weather-beaten army kitbag holding a jumbled mass of 300-odd typewritten sheets, crammed in anyhow. Only an incurable optimist would have wasted time on it but he sorted the sheets into their right order and started reading. He had a prickling sensation in the

region of the spine long before he reached the last page. It was an unfinished novel about the siege of Tobruk; comic and tragic, harsh and
tender, as authentic as the thud of gunfire. Norman wrote a glowing
letter to the author, a young citizen soldier—and peacetime newspaper-
man—named Lawson Glassop, who was back in Australia with his unit
after three years in the Middle East. The letter told him he must finish
his novel at once: it was a matter not of choice but of duty. Glassop did
so, and *We Were the Rats* was published in 1944 and scored a big
success.

It also achieved the distinction of becoming the subject of a prosecution
after it had been in the shops for eighteen months and had sold 15,000
copies. A Sydney magistrate deemed parts of it obscene and fined the
publisher ten pounds. The fine did not matter but, for all practical purposes, the decision constituted an Australia-wide ban, so shopkeepers took
fright and stopped selling the book.

'It's hard luck, Lawson', Norman sympathized, 'but what could you
expect? If I sponsored a cookery book some magistrate would smell
obscenity in it and order it to be publicly burned.'

Germany surrendered, but the Pacific war was still dragging on in the
second half of 1945. The Japanese were beaten but their fanaticism
seemed limitless—they seemed ready to fight to the last man and last
bullet. And then Hiroshima was rent by the first atomic bomb on 6
August, Nagasaki by the second on 9 August, and suddenly, it was all
over. Norman's cartoon on VJ day, 15 August, was among the best be
ever drew. A sombre Amazonian warrior, Nemesis, one hand resting on
the hilt of her sword and the other on an atomic bomb, stood with brooding eyes fixed on a pallid little man labelled Science who stared back
fingering his chin and stuttering in agonized indecision. The title was
'Little Man, What Now!', followed by the words, 'Take your choice! The
end of the war or the end of everybody and everything.'

Norman put a wealth of feeling into that drawing. He abominated the
nuclear physicists—'The most dangerous bastards', he said, 'who have
ever threatened the very insecure foothold man has on this planet'. They,
the wreckers, were in the ascendant and he wondered if his kind, the
creators, could stand against them or would presently, along with
everybody else, be blotted out in a carnival of man-made fire and fury.
He did not doubt the power of the gods to stop it if they chose. He was
only afraid they might be running out of patience.

33    John Hetherington with Norman and Armstrong Jones

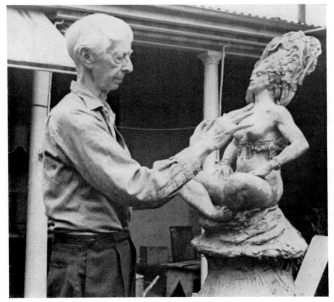

34    Norman working on the sculpture seen as Plate 31

35  Norman with Black Sammy

36  Norman in the gallery at Springwood with Harry McPhee

# II

# Twilight of an Olympian
# 1945-69

────ᴧᴧᴜᴜᴜ/◉/ᴧᴧᴧᴧᴧ────

The years immediately after the war flicked by like milestones seen from an express train. Norman hardly noticed how fast they were passing. He had never thought much of human devices for measuring time, and clocks and calendars bothered him even less as he grew older.

While nothing ever counted with him so much as his own work, Australia's progress in building a cultural identity of its own was still close to his heart, and whether he was at Springwood or Bridge Street, or travelling between the two places, he saw hopeful signs. Although writhing under the persistence of modernism in painting and sculpture, he believed that what he called 'the cult of infantile formlessness' would soon pass. Meanwhile he was convinced that Australian poets and prose writers had at last found a robust national voice. It did not surprise him; he held that war was the great energizer—it stirred men's minds to their depths, sweeping away stagnant and sick ideas and breeding a set of fresh and virile ones. He did not know if he would live to see the intellectual tide reach its flood, but at least he had seen it begin to rise. It expressed itself in the work of new poets like Kenneth Mackenzie and Francis Webb, of new prose writers like Mackenzie and the New South Wales school-master, John Tierney, who wrote under the name of Brian James. Tierney was, for Norman, the finest Australian writer of imaginative prose since Lawson, and one with 'a much larger view of humanity and a delightful power of ironic humour'. Above all, the upsurge expressed itself in the work of Douglas Stewart. As Stewart's talent flowered Norman's admiration turned to wonder, and soon after the war he was describing the New Zealander as 'the sort of avatar who arrives once in a century—the only creator of poetic drama comparable with Shakespeare'.

Q

'Large words, Norman', grunted one of his friends.

'I'm talking of a large man', said Norman.

He was overjoyed when Stewart and Margaret Coen married in 1946; he had no doubt that the marriage would be successful in itself and would also strengthen and enrich Stewart's poetry.

There were disappointments too. Lawson Glassop was one. Glassop, although industrious, lacked the essentials of a novelist—*We Were the Rats* was a happy literary accident which he could never repeat. Glassop kept at it, even when publishers rejected one novel after another and he had to take a journalist's job to earn a living. In 1949 he found a publisher for a novel about a gambler, *Lucky Palmer*, but it was a failure. After that his efforts to write fiction were desultory, and Norman could not pretend regret. He liked Glassop, but saw him as a writer who had spent himself in one freakish sprint and had no more to give.

He could not feel like that about Godfrey Blunden, who decided not to come home after the war. While understanding Blunden's reasons, which were deeply personal, Norman was sorrowful. He believed that, working in Australia on Australian themes, Blunden could have become a major novelist, but saw no hope for him as an expatriate, drifting from Europe to America, then back to Europe. He never abated his views on expatriates. 'The expatriate is only half a man', he told a magazine interviewer less than five years before he died. 'Half his identity is lost. A man must work at his desk in his own country.' Blunden published two widely admired novels, *A Room on the Route* and *The Time of the Assassins*, based on his wartime experiences in Russia. Norman acknowledged their technical excellence, but felt they were mere shadows of what might have been. He was only mildly consoled when, in 1968, Blunden, with whom he always kept in touch by letter, published *Charco Harbour*, a novel built around the character and Pacific explorations of Captain Cook.

Kenneth Slessor shed his war correspondent's uniform and became a civilian again as if he had never been away. He went back to journalism, writing leading articles for a Sydney newspaper—one of the hated 'news-rags'—but Norman did not hold it against him. Slessor was a paradox He had always lived in two distinct worlds. In one, he was the poet striving with his own spirit, as solitary as a deep-sea diver on the ocean floor; in the other, he was the hard-drinking and gregarious newspaper-man, romping and junketing with his own kind. Norman knew that Slessor could exist in no other way: the journalist and the poet were separate yet indivisible; and the combination was effective, for of the young group of the 1920s Slessor was the one whose work would live. To Norman, Slessor and Hugh McCrae were the great forerunners of the school of Australian poets which had now come into being, with Stewart towering above all the rest. It was a joy to know that Slessor was back and apt to walk in at any time, unleashing laughter and argument and a gust of memories.

The end of the war also brought Jack back into Norman's life. Jack, who had stayed on in England patiently building a reputation as a writer, had served in the British Army for most of the war, and he wrote his father a cheerful letter soon after the peace came. Norman was glad to respond. He had been grudgingly impressed by Jack's erudition and industry which had resulted in the publication of a stream of novels, biographies, historical studies, volumes of poetry, classical translations, and other books. Now he even succeeded in swallowing the knowledge that Jack, caught up in the anti-Fascist struggle of the 1930s, had become a communist. At first Norman had been aghast, as if Jack had embraced Roman Catholicism and entered the priesthood. 'Communism is not a political dogma but a state of mind', he often said. 'A man does not become a communist—he is one already.' Although he held to that conviction for the rest of his life, he did not let it chill the tone of his letters to Jack. It was enough that the long and sterile estrangement was over. He sent Jack photographs of a number of his big oil paintings. Jack showed these to Dylan Thomas who stared, swallowed hard and said, 'To think there are fairies in the world'. Jack thought it discreet not to report the remark to his father.

Norman dared to hope that five years of agony and peril had broadened Australia's mind. Then he had to admit himself wrong. The banning of *We Were the Rats* in 1946 was the first heavy jar. It was only the beginning. Presently the puritans were on the march, with the mob cheering them on. Sex was *prima facie* obscene, and a nude body an affront to man, if not to God. It was all horribly familiar. He wondered if he was back in the 1920s.

A deputation of journalists called at 12 Bridge Street one afternoon. They told him they were alarmed by the outbreak of censorship and the threat to free speech. They intended making a fight of it and wished to marshal public and political opinion on their side. Would he be their leader?

'No', said Norman. 'I won't have anything to do with attacking the Wowsers who are responsible for what's going on. But, I'll tell you what! I wouldn't mind leading an attack against those who are responsible for the Wowsers.'

They asked what he meant.

'I mean you fellows,' he answered. 'What I've stood for, the right to free expression in the arts, you have incessantly attacked. Your newsrags have given the Wowsers such a conviction of their power and their right to set standards that no judge or magistrate would have the moral courage to throw out a police prosecution of a book or a picture. It's a bit late to come asking me to help you remedy the bloody mess you've made of things.'

They filed out and went quietly down the stairs. Norman hoped his words had struck home.

His working hours were as full as ever and he still seemed tireless. His almost emaciated frame appeared to house limitless energy. He needed it. His Daemon never slept. Wanting more time for serious work, he persuaded the *Bulletin* to ease his load late in the 1940s. His salary went on unchanged and he continued turning out joke drawings and illustrations in a steady stream, but from early in 1948 Scorfield and another staff artist, Heth,* did nearly all the topical cartoons. Norman drew an occasional cartoon, but for the first time in more than fifteen years Cartoon Day no longer rose up every week like a minatory spectre.

The battle with oils still dominated his life and he did some experimental portrait painting. While doubting if it was worth doing for itself he kept at it because it forced him to concentrate and discouraged any temptation to slip into easy formulas. His aim was to define his sitter's personality while yet giving a literal delineation of the face. 'If a painter has to distort', he said, 'he isn't a portraitist but a caricaturist'. Poets were his favourite subjects. He worked hard over Robert D. Fitz-Gerald, but was not happy with the result. He was a little better pleased with Rosemary Dobson, but still felt he had missed some vital emanation of her personality. Hugh McCrae was hopeless. The wild and unruly current of life which coursed through him made him incapable of sitting for two minutes without bursting into talk or laughter—his face was like quicksilver.

'It's no good, Hugh', Norman said in the end, throwing down his brush. 'I'll have to hang on for a while and take your death-mask.'

McCrae howled with delight.

No portrait that Norman did ever satisfied him, but he felt that one of Douglas Stewart had some merit. It captured something of the man's controlled and sombre power.

The work never ceased and, like a river taking hold of fallen leaves, it caught up the weeks and months and years and carried them away. One day in 1949 Norman noticed the date on a newspaper which somebody had left lying on a side-table at Springwood. God almighty, he thought, I turned seventy nearly a week ago! He was old as men counted age, old enough to die, but he did not feel old and he was damned if he was going to die yet. They would keep his seat in Olympus until he arrived to claim it.

The death of a contemporary never made Norman brood on his own

* Norman F. Hetherington, who had joined the *Bulletin* in 1946.

mortality. He did not measure his expectation of life nor the length of his artistic reach against any other man's, so when those who were more or less of his age began falling around him he did not pause to wonder if time was running out for him too.

He was not at all surprised when Syd Ure Smith, a comparative stripling in his early sixties, died in October 1949. 'The belly god did for Syd', Norman said. 'All that good eating was too much. He's the perfect example of a man who stabbed himself to death with a pork chop.' Being indifferent to food, Norman could not understand the lure of the table to a gourmet. The strain of asceticism in his nature made him see eating for eating's sake, instead of to live, as rather shameful. He indulged his appetite for tobacco and, especially as he grew older, for tea, vowing that he could not work without them, but Savonarola would have approved his abstinence in all else. He deserved no credit for it—gluttony was a sin he had no mind to.

The hapless Katie's death, which followed soon after Ure Smith's, did not shake him at all. Remembering the young Katie, he marvelled that she should ever have so roused his senses as to make him throw caution aside and saddle himself with a wife and family he did not want. Yet he could not persuade himself that the essentials of his life would have been much different if he had not known her: he was a prisoner of his own character—if there had not been one Katie there would have been another. Trying to find the right key for a letter of sympathy to Ray, who had never flagged in caring for his mother, Norman finished by composing a lame note in which he said that Katie's death was 'a happy release'. He hoped Ray would forgive him that tired *cliché*.

Unless a death, birth or marriage had a direct impact on his life, Norman could never bring himself to rouse anything but cursory interest in it. He had done little more than shrug when Honey's marriage to Bruce Glad had broken down during the war and ended in divorce; however, he missed the gentle and equable Honey, who married an American doctor and went to live in South Carolina. Nor was he ruffled when Jane married her former brother-in-law, Bruce Glad, some years later. Norman thought them temperamentally well suited and capable of looking after their own affairs without his help.

Although Phil had a daughter, Norman had never seen the child and it did not occur to him that he was a grandparent until Jane and Honey began raising families. Then he was aghast. 'I never dreamed I'd figure in the ignominious low comedy character of a grandpa', he said. As his daughters' families grew he had to resign himself to the situation, but he was always vaguely astonished and slightly aggrieved that this should have happened to him.

He was living most of his time at Springwood now and finding it a secure refuge from the irritations of life, including grandchildren. He had liked his own small corner of Sydney when he was at Bridge Street, but he no longer felt drawn to the city for any but fleeting visits. He had been glad to sub-let the flat to the Stewarts at the end of 1947; it suited them, and Norman's need of it had diminished almost to vanishing point. He was doing most of his painting at Springwood by that time, and whenever he wished to spend a few days working in Sydney he could stay with the Stewarts. They did not think of him as old; nobody who knew him ever did, for even when the indefinable but unmistakable patina of old age settled on him his spirit did not change. He and the Stewarts did not see eye to eye on every question, but these were only the divergences of outlook inevitable between intelligent people; age had no bearing on them.

When Norman faced the bluster and turmoil of the Sydney streets he felt like a man in a strange and hostile land. He disliked the jostling rivers of people, all hurrying somewhere with set and anxious faces. He disliked even more the new buildings which rose all over Sydney as the war receded. To his eyes, the modern city building resembled nothing so much as a huge anthill, and he reasoned that people, having been reduced to the comparative proportion of ants, must in time come to think like ants and act like ants. He tried to tell himself that architectural ants' nests were only a passing fashion but did not really believe it; he supposed that the architect, demoralized by the challenge of creating cities capable of holding vast masses of people, had abdicated in favour of the engineer.

The buildings were only one symptom of the new world he did not understand. The spread and vigour of radical sociological doctrines made him tremble for the future. His innate political conservatism became more impenetrable, his distrust of reformers more profound. Given the power, he would have turned the clock back to his childhood world when class distinctions had been fixed and clearly defined. This was not conventional snobbery. He did not think that dukes were necessarily better than butlers, or bank managers than dustmen, but he maintained that there were immutable disparities, and that, left to himself, every man would find his natural level and be happy in it; or as happy as earthly men were ever intended to be. He had nothing but derision for the theory that administrative conjuring tricks would enable the world's underdogs to lift themselves up on to a plane with the world's top dogs; they would merely, he said, pull the topdogs down to their own level. He took the view that capitalism, with all its imperfections, was the one and only system capable of stimulating a great civilization. Nothing else, he insisted, could create an upper class which would build beautiful houses and fill them with objects produced by the finest artists and craftsmen, or generate the wealth which would provide great public galleries and museums.

His revulsion from the vision of a socialist world, which he saw as a grey and joyless place bossed by theorists, bigots and bureaucrats, accounted for much of his ardour in pursuing his dream of Atlantis. He had long accepted Plato's version of the Atlantean legend, and its appeal to his romanticism strengthened as he grew older. He read everything he could find bearing on it and, tumbling these facts and fancies over and over in his restless mind, moulded them into something superficially akin to historical truth. He believed in the dream because he needed to believe in it: a land like Atlantis should have existed, therefore it must have existed. For him, it was not only a lost world but the model of a perfect world, warm and lucent, as different from the world about him as his gay and resplendent Olympus was different from Grandpa Williams's Methodist heaven.

He could persuade even sceptics to swallow the idea while he was talking with them. Once out of range of his voice and his contagious enthusiasm they might reject it as nonsense, but anyone facing him in the long living room at Springwood had to listen and had to believe. It was all so intricately fashioned, and yet so simple. Atlantis, he said, bolstering the assertion with a wealth of spellbinding deduction, had been destroyed by a man-made nuclear cataclysm some 20,000 years ago, and the physical evidence of its existence lay buried hundreds of feet beneath the floor of the North Sea. He did not doubt that within a few years—perhaps twenty, more likely fifty, not more than a hundred—underwater archaeologists, having invented tools capable of delving down into the coverlet of ooze, would bring to light incontrovertible proof that Atlantis had been a highly developed civilization, with nothing to learn, technologically, from the twentieth century. Its extinction, according to Norman,

> was due to a communistic uprising of the lower orders who destroyed all the higher classes in whom are vested the powers of government, social order, cultural achievement in all its forms and an enlightened knowledge of man himself and the conditions which surround him. And in a final holocaust of civil war they destroyed the island of Atlantis itself.*

He wrote several letters pressing his theory on the English author, Leonard Cottrell, who achieved international recognition after the Second World war with a succession or books on archaeological exploration. Cottrell, unimpressed although courteous, sent a reply dismissing the Atlantis story as 'pure mystery-mongering' but Norman's faith remained unshaken.

The depressing thing was the prospect that what had happened to Atlantis might be about to happen again. Watching 'the nuclear bastards'

* Article in the *Bulletin*, 23 October 1957.

devising weapons which dwarfed the Hiroshima and Nagasaki bombs, Norman agonized over the possibility that men were about to obliterate themselves and their world. Even though a poor kind of world, drab and shoddy alongside his Atlantis, at least it was a foundation, something to build on. To think of it transformed into a charred wilderness populated by a handful of deformed cave-dwellers grubbing in the mud for roots to stay their hunger made him shudder.

Norman had never imagined Australia without the *Bulletin*. All his life it had been there, secure in its red cover, a counterweight to the 'damned newsrags'. Even in Archibald's day he had not agreed with everything it said and he agreed with a good deal less in its later years, but he had always counted it the one journal with an authentic national character whose voice could rouse Australians and rally public opinion on crucial issues. Then, early in the 1950s, he began to wonder if the *Bulletin* could survive. It was still widely read but seemed to have lost its galvanic power, like a man forceful in his prime whose personality softens with age. He traced the beginning of the decline to Webb's editorship when the *Bulletin* had begun to pursue a policy of, in Norman's phrase, 'Wowserism, humourlessness, and frenetic anti-communism'. This was an artless diagnosis and grossly unjust to Webb. The *Bulletin* was a casualty of far-reaching social and technological changes which had appeared on the heels of the first war. Although a poor organizer, Webb was in many ways a brilliant journalist, and only a fraction of the blame for the *Bulletin*'s failure to meet the challenge confronting it between the wars and later could be debited to him when he retired in 1948.

The process of dry rot had been under way for three decades before Norman became fully aware of it in the 1950s, but he believed it could still be arrested and cured. It was not his business to offer advice but if the men who were running the *Bulletin* had asked him he would have urged them, for one thing, to go all out to build a new school of black and white artists. That department had gone to hell. Archibald had understood the surpassing importance of forceful artists to the *Bulletin*; but Archibald was thirty years dead and nobody had inherited his genius.

'Look at it!' Norman grunted one day when Slessor was at Springwood. He threw Slessor an open copy of the *Bulletin*. 'Drivelling gags about missionaries being boiled by cannibals and Indians reclining on spikes! They've no relation to Australia, and all the time there's a wealth of material going begging here. The artists are too bat-eyed to see it.'

He hoped he was being too pessimistic. Ken Prior, and David Adams, who had succeeded Webb as editor, must be awake to the danger. And, after all, Norman told himself and others, they had something to work on. The *Bulletin* was as good as ever in some departments. Verse was one; Stewart selected the verse, and his influence was clearly stamped on it. His Red Page was even more potent. He had given it an authority and decisiveness which had been missing since A. G. Stephens's day; more, the articles, whether written by Stewart himself or by others, had a balance and impartiality sometimes missing when the talented but erratic Stephens had been in control. Norman, who was not alone in seeing Stewart's Red Page as an unequalled force in quickening and strengthening the post-war literary advance, often contributed an article. These writings naturally reflected some of his antipathies, although not the more intemperate ones—no organ of popular opinion could have given space to these without causing riots. 'My hates', he said, 'are among my most treasured possessions. I could not do without them.' The list—it included Christianity and all religions claiming divine inspiration, Jews with only a few exceptions and Negroes with none, all Messiahs of the people ('There is no distinction between a Jesus and a Hitler in their effect on the mass mind', he declared), and all corruptions of the Greek philosophy of life—lengthened as he grew older, but one item overshadowed all others; this was the modernist revolt in the creative arts, and above all in the field of painting.

He had been foretelling modernism's imminent collapse for some thirty years and his confidence that it was about to disintegrate and vanish remained unshaken. When the Art Gallery of New South Wales put on a show of French modernists in 1953 he made one of his rare trips to Sydney to see it, then flayed it in a full-page *Bulletin* article headlined 'An Emetic in Oil-Paint'. The pictures, he wrote, revealed that the painters' mental level 'was hardly up to that of a child of eight, and a backward child at that'. The exhibition rekindled all his long-standing detestation of Paris as the cradle of modernism—the place in which, he said, Picasso and Matisse, Gertrude Stein and Ezra Pound, Stravinsky and 'all the other noisy revolters' could be heard shouting 'I am the greatest ever'.

A Sydney Abstractionist once challenged him on the modernist issue. 'You've no right', the objector said, 'to criticize contemporary art since you don't practise it'.

'Indeed', said Norman. 'Then I suppose a doctor has no right to diagnose cancer in a patient unless he's infected by it himself.'

He believed most modernists had produced nothing of value, excepting only that one here and there had evolved pleasing colour patterns which had influenced commercial fabric designers and thereby helped to brighten a stodgy world. Otherwise he abhorred what they did and was dumbfounded by anyone's readiness to buy their works.

'But surely', an innocent friend asked him, 'you admit that a lot of these modernists are sincere?'

'Yes', he said. 'So is every murderer—he risks his own life to attain his end. All fanatics are sincere. That's the damnable thing about it.'

He laid much of the blame for modernism's longevity at the door of the 'newsrag' art critics, first in Europe and America, then in Australia. For most of his life he had fought a running battle with the critics—'literary frustrates who have failed to achieve any distinction as writers, so that they must seek to salvage their self-esteem by resorting to the assassin's knife'. He could pass off their jeers at his own work with some such quip as, 'Good Lord, I've had generations of them trying to brain me with their feeding bottles', but their professed approbation of modern art made him gag. To him, they were wreckers who would destroy his world if they could.

One day a friend reported to him a comment on critics attributed to Sir Thomas Beecham, the British orchestral conductor. 'Critics', said Beecham, 'are like eunuchs: they know what to do but they can't'. Norman loved it. He said it ought to be inscribed on the walls of every artist's studio, every concert hall, and every writer's study; and, pre-eminently, on every critic's tombstone.


Bushfires ran wild through the Blue Mountains in December 1956 and January 1957. A dark and acrid fog of smoke swirled overhead for weeks, and even at night the parched and reeking air was never cool. Great tracts of forest and scrubland were burnt black. Many of the mountain towns were threatened, and hundreds of outlying houses overrun and reduced to smoking ruins. This was nature in its most evil mood. Norman had faced many bushfires since he and Rose had first gone to the mountains, and at times the house and those in it had been in dire peril, but he had never before seen anything so rampant and awesome as this. It had been bad enough five years earlier—he'd been doing a series of illustrations for a *Bulletin* serial 'The Letters of Rachel Henning',* and the air had been so hot, he remembered, that he'd had the devil's own job to keep the ink from drying on his pen—but that outbreak had been no match for this ungovernable tempest of flame. Familiarity with bushfires had never lessened his hatred and fear of them. They had all the insensate fury of a blood-crazed mob bearing down on a victim.

He walked out of the house one afternoon and wandered around the grounds. He did not know where the nearest fire was burning, but judging by the smoke it was not far off, probably gnawing its way through heavy

* Serialized in the *Bulletin* in 1951 and early 1952, *The Letters of Rachel Henning* was later published as a book by the *Bulletin* in 1954.

timber within a mile or so. And a mile was nothing in this country; given a helping wind, a bushfire could travel faster than a man could gallop on a good horse. Norman had always kept a belt of the grounds cleared of scrub but he knew this could not arrest a major fire for long. If it came this way it was almost certain that the house and everything in it would go. He could not even telephone for help, because the lines were down. Anyway every able-bodied man within miles was already out helping to fight the fires in his own neighbourhood. There was one shred of comfort. He was alone at Springwood and had only his own skin to worry about. Rose had been seriously ill some months before and had gone into hospital in Sydney. That had been the only sensible course; times having changed, she and Norman could get no regular domestic help worth having, and she'd have died of creeping starvation if she had relied on him to feed her. Her recovery had been slow and she was still in Sydney, making her home with Bruce and Jane Glad at Hunters Hill while regaining her strength.

Norman was prowling between the house and the outside studio when it happened. He heard a noise like the roaring of a great wind and saw a wall of fire rolling towards him. It had a mad and terrifying beauty, like the bursting of a great dam filled with molten gold. Driven by a strong wind, it leapt all spaces and surged onward at racing speed. Wind-blown particles of glowing bark set shrubs and tinder-dry grass alight. These small fires, merging, swept down on the stables, garage and outhouses, all covered with a mass of honeysuckle which blazed up like a monstrous torch. An inflammable track of hedges, trees and grass led from the stables to the studio, and thence across a gap of thirty yards or so to the house. Norman, standing and watching, thought, 'This is it at last. The whole place must go.'

Fifty men might have checked and turned it, but what could one man do unaided? And yet he couldn't stand and do nothing. There was just one hope: if he could burn a break behind the studio there might be a fighting chance of steering the fire away. He set off at a run, fumbling in his pocket for matches. The flames were soaring forty or fifty feet above the stables and the heat was satanic. The miniature jungle of dry grass behind the studio flared like paper the moment he touched a match to it. When his fire threatened to get out of control he beat it out, then set the grass alight once more. He repeated the action of lighting and beating out again and again, while turning away every now and then to heave buckets of water into a mass of creepers alongside the studio which kept bursting into flame as sparks and other fiery particles fell among them. The fire from the stables flowed toward the studio. Well, he could do no more. If his break did not work, it was all up with the studio and the house; more than likely, with him too. The oncoming fire reached the edge of the break. And there, miraculously, it faltered. It tried to nibble a way forward but, finding nothing to feed on, lurched aside and veered off across the grounds away from the studio and the house. It wiped out years of growth in hedges, flowering shrubs and ornamental trees as it went, but the peril was over.

Half blind from smoke and heat Norman dragged himself back to the house, fell into his chair and closed his eyes. Every nerve was jangling, every muscle taut, and yet he had a sense of elation. He had not dreamed that, at seventy-seven, so much strength remained in his body.

Some time after that trial by fire one of his friends, making a joke of it, said, 'Good God, Norman, you might have been gobbled up and we'd never have known what had become of you. There isn't much of you to burn!'

'It'll take more than a bushfire to finish me', Norman said, sitting and rolling a cigarette. 'Anyway they'd have found enough of me for a coroner's inquest—the fellows who make a hobby of collecting any bit of old rubbish I've handled would have rushed up here and sifted the ashes until they came on a charred shinbone or my false teeth. What treasures those would have been!'

No collector himself, Norman could not comprehend the collector's instinct. He accepted it in the connoisseur of pictures or in the biblio-phile; there was something to be said for having a house decorated with fine pictures or a room lined with rare books. But he was baffled by the jackdaw spirit of grown men who devoted their time and energy to track-ing down the trivia he had scattered in his wake—a crude sketch done in childhood, a pen or brush he had discarded, an old hat, anything else which his touch had sanctified. He was patient even with those of the brotherhood who believed their devoted fribblings gave them a vested right in him, but his private comments were caustic; he labelled one 'a complacent Babbitt', another 'an aggravating barnacle'.

One of them went to Creswick at Mary's invitation and prowled about 'Lisnacrieve' in quest of unconsidered trifles. Mary happened to make mention of an old wooden privy seat bearing the carved initials of sundry Lindsay boys, including Norman.

'Where is it?' the collector cried.

'I'm afraid we used it for kindling', she confessed.

She vowed that he turned white to the lips.

For many years Norman had to contend with every kind of collector. Owners of what he called 'those damned autograph albums' were always at him and few of them were content with a simple signature; prac-tically every one asked him not only to sign the page but also to 'dash off' a sketch for good measure. Collectors of his books also continually pestered him to 'draw something' on the fly-leaf. He did thousands of such impromptu sketches, spitting curses under his breath but unable to refuse because, as he put it, 'any postures of intellectual exclusiveness' were obnoxious to him, and he would not send somebody away supposing that he put an academic value on a trifling pen or pencil drawing.

He was less amenable when portable tape-recorders came into fashion and enthusiasts began pursuing him. He supposed the tape-recorder had its uses, although the world seemed to have done well enough without it for some thousands of years, but he disliked few things more than having a microphone pushed under his nose and being commanded to talk. His vehemence persuaded most tape-recorder enthusiasts that they were wasting their time, but one woman appeared to imagine that pertinacity would triumph in the end. She kept telephoning and Norman kept saying no. The telephone conversations grew terser and his refusals gruffer, but she persisted. One morning he was in the town of Springwood on his weekly shopping visit. He went into the library to return a batch of books and borrow more.

'Ah, Mr Lindsay, I've caught you at last!' a voice trilled. Recognizing it as the tape-recorder woman's, he swung and faced her. She had followed him into the library and stood, bright and smiling, tape-recorder in hand.

He snapped out a few words and she recoiled, then a few more and she fled.

'I heard later that she complained I was very rude to her', Norman said. 'I probably was. I dislike rudeness and laxatives, but I've used each to good purpose in times of need.'

He never renounced his belief that life was inextinguishable. It enabled him to hear without a quiver the news of Phil's death in January 1958, and then of Hugh McCrae's death a few weeks later. He considered it a fatuous assumption that spirits so vital as Phil's and McCrae's could ever die. Phil, at fifty-one, and McCrae, at eighty-two, had each been in failing health, and as Norman saw it each had shed his used-up body and, reborn, gone off to new adventures.

Even some people who were familiar with Norman's belief that earthly death was merely a change of direction expected him to put on a show of mourning his youngest son. After all, the proprieties called for a tear or two! Norman had none to shed. A few years earlier he had refused to grieve when Ruff Tremearne, and then Bert and Percy, had died in quick succession, so why lament for Phil? Phil had made a name as a writer of historical novels and for the screen. He had also earned big money, although his financial irresponsibility had kept him at ceaseless war with duns, bailiffs and process-servers. His letters had continued to be indomitably cheerful when he had fallen chronically ill with heart disease, kidney trouble and dropsy, but they had not fooled Norman. To Phil, an invalid's life was torment and he was better out of it.

Shoals of letters came to Springwood, most of them filled with commiserating platitudes. Jack wrote from England in refreshingly unsentimental style. He gave an unvarnished account of the circumstances of Phil's death and sent on a letter which Phil had been writing to Norman when his last illness had made him put it down. It was a remarkable letter. It almost seemed that Phil, knowing his life was running out, had thrown the remnants of his energy into an effort to dispel any shadows still lingering over the relationship between his father and brother. He had worked specially hard to make the point that Jack, shocked by the Soviet Union's ruthless crushing of the Hungarian uprising in 1956, had turned his back on communism. This was an oversimplification but superficially true, and Norman was eager to take it at face value.

Letters were more important to Norman than they had ever been and the reading of the mail was usually a pleasant interlude; but not always. One day in the middle of 1958 he opened a letter from David Adams. The short typewritten note told Norman that his *Bulletin* salary would be discontinued at the end of the following week. To be dismissed by a letter dictated to a stenographer was a jarring blow to his self-esteem. It left him bitter and resentful.

'Damn it', he said, 'I'd expect an association lasting sixty years to count for something. You'd think I was an office boy they'd caught pinching the stamps.'

Ever since realizing that the *Bulletin* was losing ground he had watched it go downhill. Such efforts as had been made to arrest the slide—for example, a change from the old-style 'folded broadsheet' to *New Yorker* size—seemed to him hopelessly inadequate. The sickness was too deep-seated to be cured by surface treatment, and months before Adams's letter reached him Norman was saying 'The poor old *Bulletin* is dying of senile decay'. Yet it did not occur to him that he had become an expensive luxury. As cartoonist-in-chief he would have been well worth his £800-odd a year, but the drawings and articles he supplied after choosing semi-retirement did not justify such a salary when the *Bulletin* was fighting for its life and had not paid a dividend since 1955.

The break left his friendship with Douglas Stewart untouched. Nothing could disturb that. Norman said their association was 'an intellectual rather than an emotional intimacy because of the difference in our ages', but it was no less deep on that account. He valued it above his friendship with McCrae or Slessor, or even with Tremearne, and considered it the richest of his life. The Stewarts continued to be frequent weekend visitors at Springwood, and Norman found solace in their companionship.

Stewart still wanted him to write for the Red Page and, swallowing his anger with the *Bulletin*, he began turning out articles again. He enjoyed the mental exercise, and an article by him—opinionated, blunt, challenging, crusty—always gave the Red Page a special tang. Now that he was no longer on the salaried staff he was paid like any other outside contributor. He did not need the money, but it kept him in tobacco.

He hoped that some miracle would save the *Bulletin*, because he believed the Red Page was essential to Australia's intellectual health. The puritans were, however stubbornly and reluctantly, yielding a little ground at last, and he gave much of the credit to Stewart's calm perseverance. It was true that he still wondered if Australia would ever rout the moral cranks. A controversy which boiled up in 1959 around a print of his picture, *The Court*, nurtured his doubts. The manager of the Hotel Acton, Canberra, ordered one of the resident guests, an English-born geologist named Doctor H. T. P. Hyde, to remove the print from his bedroom wall because the housemaids had complained that they were embarrassed by having to look at the nudes in it. Doctor Hyde refused and the affair ballooned into a national controversy, then after a few tense days fizzled out.* Notwithstanding such outbreaks of pietism, there was a brighter side, notably the Australian government's easing of literary censorship late in the 1950s. Norman's two long-banned novels, *The Cautious Amorist* (which a British producer had some years earlier turned into a film, called *Our Girl Friday* in England and *Adventures of Sadie* in America, bearing only accidental resemblances to the original story) and *Redheap*, were among a large group of books declared unobjectionable. The first Australian edition of *Redheap* appeared in December 1959. The event interested Norman only as evidence of the censorship thaw. 'I'm afraid the vanity of the author is dead within me', he told a newspaper interviewer. 'All I can hope now is that the lifting of the ban will make the way a bit easier for other writers of the truth—not that I think things should ever be too easy for the artist, who always needs the stimulus of conflict.'

None of the echoes reaching him from the outside world made him hanker to leave the quiet of Springwood and he swore that nothing would ever again induce him to set foot in Sydney. With real or simulated reluctance, he let Rose and Jane persuade him to break this pledge and go down in July 1960 for an afternoon performance of the Elizabethan Theatre Trust's marionette version of *The Magic Pudding*,

---

* This was not Norman's last brush with holier-than-thou self-righteousness. In 1966 a Melbourne citizen complained to the police that a Lindsay painting *Bacchanalian Festival*, on show in a city commercial gallery, was obscene. The Vice Squad raided the gallery and questioned the proprietor, but took no other action. The daily newspapers printed the story under bold headlines, and a buyer quickly snapped up *Bacchanalian Festival* for $700.

which had just begun a successful Australia-wide tour. He went backstage afterwards to congratulate the puppeteers, and while there gave an extended television interview. Although he said later that he had been 'tricked' into it, some observers thought he had known exactly what was happening and had secretly revelled in it.

But his few hours in the city were enough and he was glad to get back to Springwood. It was the rowdy uglification of Sydney that repelled him. Having surrendered the Bridge Street tenancy in 1956, soon after the Stewarts vacated the flat and moved into a house at St Ives, he never suffered the smallest twinge of nostalgia, except in the recurrent dream which sent him back there at night to hammer vainly on the street door. He could perhaps have shut his eyes to any other of the changes in Sydney but not to what he called 'the rape of Circular Quay'. He had fallen in love with the Quay when he first saw it, in the days when sailing ships still crowded Sydney Cove; it was holy ground to him, if only because Joseph Conrad had served in ships which had berthed there, had eaten in the Chinese restaurants in Lower George Street, and had bought tobacco at a little neighbourhood shop kept by a Frenchman who had lost both hands and rolled cigaretes with his stumps (Conrad had borrowed the tobacco-seller's externals for one of his unforgettable characters, the handless French villain in the short story *Because of the Dollars*). Some of the Quay's old-time charm had lingered when Norman lived at Bridge Street, and late on warm Sunday afternoons he had now and then strolled down to watch the laden ferry-boats coming and going through the shimmering haze lying over the Harbour. Now, buried under an overhead railway track mounted on crude pillars, where trains continually thundered back and forth, the Quay was like a well-loved picture defaced by vandals. The ferry boats had dwindled to a handful. Norman saw them as sad and tired ghosts of a vanished yesterday.

His tendency to look back and see the past in roseate hues hardened as he moved into his eighties. But he yearned to forget one long-ago episode, and his anger overflowed when Jack innocently reminded him of it. While lustily damning the 'newsrags' Norman often dipped into them, and one day in 1960 his eye lighted on a Sydney review of Jack's second volume of autobiography, *The Roaring Twenties*. The reviewer noted that the book mentioned the Springwood ouija board experiments. Norman at once wrote an irate letter, accusing Jack of having chosen to 'stigmatise' him as a spiritualist and saying that no further amiable relations were possible between them. Jack replied that the passage (pp. 67-9) was a brief and factual report of what he had seen with his own eyes; if he had omitted it, he said, he would have been guilty of misrepresentation. Norman ignored Jack's letter, and the lately healed rift opened wide again.

A few months later Norman was again jolted into recalling his spiritualistic dabblings. Lionel died and the news woke poignant memories of the episode which had wrecked their friendship. Norman pretended to take his brother's death in an offhand way. 'Poor old Joe!' he said. 'A pity he took himself so seriously, with his ridiculous brewer's label of "Sir Lionel".' In Norman's view, Lionel's knighthood had diminished his essential distinction instead of adding to it. 'He was really a very likeable chap.' The seemingly careless words masked a sense of loss. The consciousness of their shattered comradeship had been a weight on Norman's heart for nearly forty years.

He was much alone at Springwood now—more alone than he had ever been in his life. Rose was often away for many weeks at a time, staying with the Glads in Sydney. She was better and happier there. Her health was still troublesome, and the rigours of the mountain climate, not to mention the trials of keeping Springwood going with incompetent or casual domestic help, were a strain. And Rose did not share Norman's liking for isolation. She hated being cut off from people and having to rely on newspapers, television, the radio and the telephone for contact with the world at large. Life with the Glads was never dull. Their friends came and went all the time, and Rose, who had lost none of her social ease, enjoyed meeting them. The children also gave her endless pleasure. Unlike Norman, she found nothing ignominious in being a grandparent. Jane drove up to Springwood every week or two to see if her father needed anything, and to gather up any pictures he had done and take them to Sydney for sale. Rose often accompanied her. Norman liked seeing them but did not miss them when they left.

He found his deepest refreshment in Douglas and Margaret Stewart's visits. They and he talked the same language and when they were at Springwood he had a sense of completeness and relaxed contentment. He was not much surprised when Stewart broke the news that he was leaving the *Bulletin* and going into book publishing. The Packer newspaper group, Australian Consolidated Press, took over the ailing *Bulletin* in November 1960, and a few months later Stewart joined Angus and Robertson. While sorry that Stewart would no longer be guiding the Red Page, Norman thought the change no bad thing. He had never altered his view that book publishers were cynical, overbearing and rapacious, and he believed Stewart would lose no chance to improve the author's lot.

Living alone, Norman managed well enough. He had recruited a Springwood man named Jack Ramsdale, who drove out once a week and spent the day washing out the kitchen, cleaning the workroom and the living room, putting underclothing and sheets through the washing

R

machine, and doing other chores, then drove Norman into the town to do his shopping; Ramsdale lent a skilled hand also at refurbishing the garden statues, and mounting and framing pictures, as well as at the delicate operation of cleaning the ship models. An Englishman long settled in Australia, he lived in the town with his wife and was glad to supplement his military pension by working for Norman, but there was nothing of master-and-man about the arrangement; Norman called him 'my henchman' and admired his character and integrity, and they were on easy-going first-name terms. Ramsdale and another local man, Harry McPhee, who went every weekend to trim the lawns and keep the grounds in order, did all the tedious jobs between them. Norman was grateful for that; he had no energy to spare for the drudgeries that Jack and Harry took off his hands.

Meals were a nuisance when first Norman was alone. Being convinced that Australian professional cooks were all 'food murderers', he elected to look after himself and subsisted for a while on grills and Irish stew. This represented the limit of his culinary skill until, fossicking in a kitchen cupboard, he came on some of Rose's cookery books and started experimenting. He was surprised to find that he not only liked eating what he cooked but took pleasure in cooking it. After some early failures he learned to produce such items as thick soups, suet dumplings, rich gravies, steak-and-kidney pudding, casseroled meat and vegetables, pickled steak and walnuts, curry and rice, and steak, ham and egg pie; he even became proficient at biscuits and lemon cheese tartlets.

A Katoomba doctor who sometimes dropped in for an unprofessional visit called one day. As they sat yarning, Norman began boasting of his kitchen prowess and described the kind of meals he was cooking and eating. The doctor was horrified.

'Look here, Norman', he said, 'you'll kill yourself if you go on eating such stuff. I'm not going to leave this house until you let me prescribe a balanced diet and you promise to abide by it.'

'No you don't', Norman replied. 'I've had a few balanced diets prescribed in my time and they damn' nearly finished me. I've now arrived at the satisfactory understanding with my belly that what I like to eat suits it also. My gastric juices are the best diagnosticians. I leave it to them.'

Apart from its practical usefulness, cooking—which Norman, once converted, called 'an art like any other'—was an entertaining way of using up time, and he had lately made the unsettling discovery that although the years were short the days were long. Where there had never been enough time, there was now occasionally too much, for a man who was usually awake for eighteen or nineteen hours a day. It did not often happen that he could find nothing to do but when he was idle for even ten minutes he grew bored; and, to Norman, boredom was worse than an aching tooth. An early riser by long habit, he usually woke about six o'clock. He would pull on slippers and dressing-gown and make a large pot of strong tea, then go back to bed and stay there until nine o'clock or later, reading, smoking and thinking while nerving himself to get up and shower and shave. He had never before cared to lie in bed, but getting up had now become a daily trial. He was always more weary at the beginning of the day than at the end, when work, or the mental concentration which work forced on him, had invigorated him. Otherwise, his body gave him little bother, except for a cold now and then, or a periodic attack of lumbago which he calleed 'one of the comic ills of the flesh, but a damn' painful one'.

Once on his feet, with a bowl of oatmeal porridge and more strong tea in his stomach, the habits of a lifetime bore him along. He often started his working day by giving two hours to a pen drawing while the light was at its best, then spent the next two hours on a water-colour. In the afternoon he worked at oil painting until the daylight faded, loving and hating the struggle, groaning under his breath and sometimes aloud, striving for mastery and never admitting defeat. He once said that he had acquired some competence in oils at 'the unseasonable age of eighty', but he knew the battle was endless and that neither he nor any other man would ever win it. One of his few later oils which gave him some satisfaction was a large canvas, *The Black Rider*. Painted when the nuclear arms race was at its height, *The Black Rider* portrayed a man on a black horse galloping at top speed, whooped on by jeering devils, against a sullen and thunderous sky and a flaming horizon. It defined Norman's outlook at a time when he believed the earth was doomed to man-made annihilation, and he liked it well enough to keep it hanging on his own wall; he still valued it as a workmanlike expression of his former state of mind when his despair turned to hope some years later as events allayed the world's terror that one or another of the nuclear powers would inevitably destroy mankind.

He liked going out in the late afternoon and fiddling away in the grounds with a rake or mattock. Harry McPhee left little to be done, so Norman dug up a patch of earth and started a kitchen garden. He planted turnips, carrots, tomatoes and sweet corn, and soon had them flourishing, but drew the line at green vegetables. He insisted that green vegetables were evil, and that vegetarians were either a product of that evil or were drawn to green vegetables by a species of morbid attraction. 'I never knew a vegetarian who wasn't either mentally enfeebled or a sociological fanatic', he said. 'Look at Hitler and Bernard Shaw.' Ever since his first visit to Europe he had abominated Shaw as an 'arrogant and outrageously conceited tub-thumping Utopian'.

Evening dinner was his one substantial meal of the day, and after it he would settle into his battered old armchair in the livingroom, a cup of coffee beside him and a supply of the cigarettes which he rolled for himself at hand. He loved that chair, with its extension for his feet and legs; over the years it had moulded itself to his body and, reclining in it, he was completely relaxed. When the Stewarts or somebody else came to stay, he would lie back talking and listening, his Roman senator's head, with the fringe of silver hair falling over the forehead, poised on the lean and corded neck. He was a compelling talker and his voice, which never became an old man's unsteady pipe but kept its vibrant male quality to the last, gave a stamp of decision to everything he said, even when the logic was shaky. Yet he never wanted to hold the floor and talk other talkers down; he had the gift of being able to listen and of wanting to listen. He took in what anybody else said, tested and dissected it, seized on any novel idea and, crowing over it, embroidered it with fancies of his own.

When alone, as he usually was, he wrote thousands of words nearly every night while stretched out in his chair. Sometimes it was a chapter of a novel, sometimes a study of Pepys, Browning, Cervantes, Conrad, Burns, or another of his literary gods, sometimes a short story, sometimes an essay on the evils of nuclear fission or on the mystery-detection novel as a twentieth-century phenomenon. And sometimes a letter. Whether typed or handwritten his letters, to Mary or to any of the two or three friends he wrote to regularly, were as provocative, vivacious, combative and headstrong as ever, pieces of rich and glowing verbal tapestry running in length from seven or eight to twenty-odd pages. The syntax was often carefree and the spelling unique, but the meaning was always crystal clear.

Books had been of first importance to him all his life and now they were indispensable. Weakening eyesight had made him abandon etching in his seventies but he could still read all night without discomfort. He was a fast reader, so his problem was to find enough books. Friends often sent him books, and he picked up seven or eight every Friday from the Springwood library. Many books of the moment disappointed him but he was driven to them by the discovery that he knew his favourite prose writers too well. When he was in a browsing mood he could still open Dickens, Scott, Cervantes, Boswell, Hazlitt, Pepys, Balzac, Conrad, de Maupassant or any one of a few others at random and ramble through two or three pages which he knew almost by heart, but they did not meet his need for prolonged reading; and although he kept Beerbohm, Mencken and Norman Douglas at his bedside he called on them not for stimulus but only to soothe his mind with old remembered fragrances when sleep eluded him. Among modern books he turned first to reminiscences by men of action such as soldiers and seamen; he also revelled in good travel narratives, particularly anything by Peter Fleming, 'who couldn't write a dull page'. Biography came next. Lytton Strachey's 'flawless technique' bewitched him, and he was hardly less taken with S. N. Behrman, William Manchester and some of the other American biographers. He saw merit in few modern novelists. James Gould Cozzens—'the greatest novelist America has produced'—was a soaring exception. Hemingway was 'a fraudulent tough guy', Faulkner 'unreadable', and Steinbeck 'a mountebank'. None of the 'serious' European novelists of the time pleased him at all, but he could not get enough of the French writer Gabriel Chevallier, whose anti-clerical ironies in *Clochemerle* made him writhe with joy, nor of the Englishman Robert Harling's elegant and sophisticated psychological thrillers.

Australia's tardiness in breeding a larger group of high-grade novelists saddened him. So did Australia's reluctance to recognize Brian James. Norman raged to see James passed over while Patrick White was read and honoured both at home and overseas. He would admit no virtue in White, 'one of those abysmal fellows who think life is a terrible penalty and that a realistic presentation of it must concentrate on all that is neurotic, suffering, gloomy, and hopeless'. He sometimes delivered such judgements on the basis of slender knowledge. He was incensed that 'a lousy play like *The Seventeenth Doll*, I think it's called' (he meant *The Summer of the Seventeenth Doll* by Ray Lawler) should win popular acclaim in Australia, Europe and America while Douglas Stewart's verse dramas were comparatively neglected.

'You've seen it?' a friend asked when he was blasting it.

'No.'

'Read it then?'

'No. I tried to read the damn' thing and couldn't get through the first act.'

Like the great authors, the great music composers also failed him. Beethoven and Wagner remained on the very summit of his Olympus but he could no longer clamber up to their heights and find them emotionally and mentally exhilarating. Hungry for some kind of music, he thought of military bands. He sent to Sydney for two or three records of famous marches and, liking them, ordered more. Night after night he put in an hour listening to *The Thin Red Line*, *The Stars and Stripes Forever*, *Liberty Bell*, *Voice of the Guns*, *By Sword and Lance*, the evergreen *Colonel Bogey*, and others of the kind. John Philip Sousa had toured Australia with his band before the First World War and given more than fifty concerts in Sydney, but Norman had not bothered to go. Fifty years later he cursed himself for having missed that feast.

His cats either shared his liking for band music or endured it for the sake of his company. He had a succession of cats, among them such notables as Pangur Ban, Black Sammy and Burly Bill, and each liked to sit with him after dinner, stretching at ease on his extended legs or curled on his lap. Only one of his latter-day cats—Armstrong Jones by name—was truly domesticated; all the others started life as members of a large feline colony infesting the heavy bush. Descendants of domestic cats gone wild, these animals lived by their wits, courage, strength and speed of claw. Norman held that 'a cat is always entertaining which human beings rarely are', and was inexhaustibly patient in taming one whenever the office of Springwood cat fell vacant. He spent three months winning Black Sammy's trust, feeding meat to him at the same time every day and steadily narrowing the distance between them. Once Sammy stood to have his ears scratched and his tail stroked the rest was easy. Norman had a large number of wild or half-wild friends, ranging from the kookaburras, magpies, currawongs and other birds, who came and fed round his kitchen door every evening, to a school of red ants who shared his dining table, a family of marsupial mice who presented themselves nightly for a meal of biscuit crumbs, and a rather forbidding spider who throve on finely shredded raw meat.

So the years went by in an outwardly uneventful procession. Norman gave little thought to them—he knew when it was spring or summer, autumn or winter, and that was enough. He might have been living on an island which he left only for his weekly shopping excursion to the town of Springwood. The few friends who counted with him—a shrinking handful, because death had taken so many and others had drifted away—were always welcome but he detested intruders. At one time strangers came knocking on his door every few days, wanting to look at his pictures. He sent them packing but others came, and in the end he had to paint a sign and nail it to his front gate: *This Is a Private Residence. It Is Not Open to the Public. There Are No Pictures on View Here.*

Although finding it increasingly hard to pump up excitement about anything, his nerves tingled one day in 1965 when his eldest son broke the silence which had lasted between them for five years. Jack published a biography of Turner, the English painter, and in a forgiving mood posted his father a copy. Norman sent back a friendly letter which did not mention their conflict over *The Roaring Twenties*; he possibly grasped the olive branch so readily because Jack was his only surviving son, Ray having died five years before. Jack could never again be Norman's disciple, but harmony was restored and after that they wrote to each other more or less regularly. Their letters ranged over a wide field but shunned one topic. By tacit agreement spiritualism was taboo.

Norman always chuckled when he quoted a scrap of ribald verse which Mary sent him in one of her letters.

> The years come in and the years go out
>   As I totter towards my doom,
> Still caring less and less about
>   Who goes to bed with whom.

That quatrain expressed his outlook to perfection. He had not lost interest in women and never did, but he saw them now with an old man's detachment. 'The failure of desire, by which that old goat who wrote *Ecclesiastes* means copulation, is the best reward of age', he wrote in his autobiography,* and possibly meant it.

The knowledge that his life must end soon did not seem to weigh on him. He talked about his death as casually as a man might about an impending journey. He often told the story of the American comedian, W. C. Fields, lying in a coma with friends gathered about his bed, waiting for the end. A woman sat holding his hand. Suddenly Fields opened his eyes and, touching his lips with a finger, winked at her, then died. 'In short', said Norman, 'he imparted to her the final secret—that death was the last great joke of all. I hope I'll do half as well when my turn comes.' He said that any of his half-wild cats could give most men points in how to die. Each of them disappeared into the bush at the approach of death and, with impeccable good taste and enviable tact, died alone.

His one dread was that, suddenly struck helpless, he would be kept going as a bedridden hulk, condemned by medical sorcery to continue breathing against his will. The manner of Mary's death strengthened his resolve that he would never die lingeringly while he had the use of his hands. Mary had trimmed off all the loose ends of her life before subsiding into a Ballarat old people's home. She had presented furnishings, pictures and other items from 'Lisnacrieve' to the Ballarat Art Gallery, to enable a replica of the drawing room to be put together as the focus of a display of works by Percy, Lionel, Norman, Ruby and Daryl, and made a Will leaving the Gallery the bulk of her estate; she had also arranged for the sale of 'Lisnacrieve', which was demolished later to make way for a modern house. As time passed and her body failed she had little use for life but her strong heart went on beating. Toward the end she lay for many months, unable to read or write and hating every burdensome day, until death came in January 1968.

Although Norman was what he called 'damnably slowed down', his output still far exceeded that of most artists in their prime. In one sustained burst, beginning in 1965 and running into 1966, he turned out oil paintings at the rate of three a month. He did it while leaving nothing else undone, even continuing to play the literary steersman to several poets and writers who seemed to have something of value to give.

---

* *My Mask* (Sydney, 1970), p. 242.

He faltered briefly when Jack Ramsdale collapsed with a heart attack early in 1967 and had to leave him. After an anxious week or two he found a local woman, Molly Fisher, who agreed to come and do Jack's domestic work; Mrs Fisher had been with the Lindsays in her single days many years before and knew the run of the place. Harry McPhee, who was still keeping the grounds in order, took over the mounting and framing of the pictures and, having proved himself, succeeded to the ill-defined but demanding post of Norman's 'henchman'. Harry, slight but strong, dark, lean-faced and quiet, turned out to be the best handcraftsman Norman had ever known, equally adept at framing a picture, enlarging a room, cleaning a statue, laying down a path, or doing any other practical job.

Norman quickly accustomed himself to the slightly changed system of daily existence and went striding on. His productive velocity—'that incessant, that appalling, that driven and magnificent industry!', in Douglas Stewart's words—could be explained in no known terms; it came flooding up out of some well deep inside him. When a de luxe edition of his pen work was being made ready in 1968—de luxe editions devoted to his water-colours, pencil drawings, and ship models also appeared in the late 1960s—he was not satisfied with some of the drawings and did a number of new ones. It was years since he had worked with the pen, and he admitted that getting back to it was 'a sweat'. He also complained that he could keep at it for only about three hours a day. In his prime some of his pen sessions had lasted from nine o'clock in the morning until midnight.

He was less concerned than ever by what any 'newsrag' critic said of his pictures when they went on exhibition. He thought the critics kinder on the whole but doubted that this denoted any change of heart. 'It's simply', he said, 'that there isn't much satisfaction to be got out of heaving a brick at a man who has one foot in his coffin'. He kept thinking more and more, however, about the survival of his work and his name. He believed that the greatest artists produced something good, something that deserved to outlast them, only now and again, and did not see himself as an exception. 'If only two per cent survives I'll be happy', he told John Frith. 'That's the most that any man dare expect.' His dream had an element of personal vanity but his spirit of evangelism was the stronger motive force. He hoped to leave behind him something that men yet unborn would see and, having seen, make the keynote of their own philosophy. For the blood of Grandpa Williams ran strong in Norman to the last. As early as June 1947 he had written to the Board of Trustees of the Art Gallery of New South Wales offering a large and representative collection of his works as a gift. He had imposed one condition: the collection must be shown in perpetuity. The Trustees had consulted the Crown Solicitor, who advised that the Gallery could not accept the gift on this condition. The discussions had dragged on for a long time but the legal obstacle had proved to be insurmountable. At last, in May 1950, the Trustees had received a letter from Norman and Rose withdrawing the offer.

He had no patience with the opinion that *The Magic Pudding*, probably *Saturdee* and *Redheap*, and perhaps one or two other of his books would be cherished and read when his pictures were forgotten and rotting in dark cellars. To him, the idea was unutterably silly. He did not class his writings with his paintings, drawings and etchings, or think of them as anything but marginal expressions of himself. 'My individual concept of the enigma of life is defined in a form imagery', he said, 'and if that has potency, as I believe it has, it might take centuries to percolate into man's consciousness'. He was determined not to leave that process to chance, and, his approach to the Art Gallery of New South Wales having been rejected, he searched for other ways to ensure that an adequate collection, or collections, of his best works should be preserved and kept on permanent show. This was the motive of a plan he evolved in his middle eighties which ultimately led to the acquisition of the Springwood house and grounds by the National Trust of Australia (New South Wales), as a Norman Lindsay gallery and museum.* To stock it, Norman left the Trust a group of oil paintings, water-colours, pen drawings and pencil sketches, as well as ship models and other items. A year before his death he gave a smaller collection—six large oils, eight water-colours, and three pen drawings, with two wooden ship models, and a plaster model for a fountain—to the Norman Lindsay Gallery in the University of Melbourne School of Architecture. He told a *Sydney Morning Herald* reporter:

> The national galleries of Australia don't want me. I don't want to make money. It's no damn use to me. Australia has been good to me despite the fact that they wanted to hang me at one stage . . . I want to leave behind a definite statement of my work and this is the only way to do it. People who are interested in Australian galleries don't know that we have any art. The rubbish they have in the galleries is this European stuff and it's dead . . .

He knew that he could not hope for widespread recognition and understanding in his lifetime. That realization was implicit in a curious book, *The Scribblings of an Idle Mind*, which he had put out in 1966. This collection of loosely linked essays on art and life, in which he assailed most of the fashionable liberal tenets. angered his enemies and dismayed many of his friends. His enemies greeted his strictures on Jews, Negroes, homosexuals and humanism with cries of 'Racist! Fascist! Reactionary!' Those of his friends who took the book at face value, as

* For an extended account see Appendix I.

most of them did, pardoned it as an old man's indiscretion, but others, more perceptive, read it as Norman's retort to the intelligentsia—a class he despised for what he saw as their subjection to aesthetic fashion, their enslavement by Picasso, James Joyce and the whole modernist movement, and their sheeplike conformism under a guise of philosophical emancipation. The intelligentsia had rejected him and his art, so in *The Scribblings of an Idle Mind* he took vengeance by rejecting them and their creed, and as a gesture of scorn defiled their altars and spat on their gods.

Time alone will settle Norman's place in the pantheon of art. Opinion among his contemporaries ranged from the mocking to the idolatrous. It could not be otherwise. He was too controversial, this man with fire in his brain and fire in his heart, to be objectively assessed while he lived, or perhaps until fifty years after his death. What he did with his brush, pen or etching needle was so often blurred or distorted by the storms of controversy he let loose, or coloured by the impact of his dynamic and overflowing personality. It was blurred also by his propensity for overdoing sex themes. Lionel said that Norman 'fell for anything about sex like a woman for fashion', but it was not so simple as that. To him, sex was not only the dominant motive of the human animal, and therefore the element essential above all others to the work of any artist intent on exploring the human ego, but also the most powerful weapon to his hand in his campaign against the narrow-minded provincialism of the Australia into which he was born. If it is true that he seemed unable to stop fighting that war after it was won, it is incontestable that nobody else of his or any other time did nearly so much to free the Australian creative artist from moral shackles.

Whatever his shortcomings, men as cultured in mind and as far apart in outlook as Godfrey Blunden, Kenneth Slessor, Leon Gellert, Douglas Stewart, and Jack Lindsay ('With all his limitations he was built on the grand scale', Jack said some months after his father's death), ranked him as a genius. Each reached that conclusion on the basis not of any single branch of his work but of all of it: the paintings and black and whites, the novels and short stories, the philosophical writings and literary essays, the topical cartoons, the ship models—so exquisite that they transcend craftsmanship and take their place as works of art; even his role as a literary inspirer and guide had to come into the balance, for it had its roots in the same soil as the work of his own hands. 'Add it all together, the brilliance and the mass', Stewart has written, 'and surely genius is the only word for it'.

It is too soon for that or any other definitive judgement on Norman Lindsay to command acceptance. For good or ill—and the pejorative opinions are no less numerous than the ecstatic—his own time cannot say the last word about him. Only the years can condemn him to oblivion or award him immortality. He knew it. 'If there are genuine values, those will endure and be affirmed—all that is valueless will perish', he said as his life moved toward its close. He was content to accept the verdict of time. He never seemed to doubt what it would be.

Norman's ninetieth birthday generated a burst of television, radio and newspaper publicity. 'I'm damned if I understand it', he growled. 'Anyone would think I'd arrived at the age of ninety by a unique exercise of agility and sagacity.' His privacy was shattered for weeks. Letters and telegrams flooded in, his telephone rang and rang. Strangers hammered at his door bringing gifts of iced birthday cakes, roast chickens, boxes of biscuits and sweets, baskets of fruit—he supposed that after seeing him on their television screens, as sere and wrinkled as an old dry branch, they imagined him to be on the brink of starvation. In the end he took his telephone off the hook and, refusing to answer the door, stayed in hiding, brooding on human perversity. This was the same old mob, only now they loved him instead of hating him. Once they had wanted his blood, now they clamoured to kiss his hands. Liking them no better for that, he kept his door barred.

The excitement subsided but not until it had cost him precious time. He wanted Springwood—the grounds as well as the big old house, shabby and echoing—to be shipshape when it passed to the National Trust. Months of work were necessary and he could only guess how long he had left. Harry McPhee went out every afternoon, when he finished his regular job as an electrical linesman in Springwood, as well as every Saturday and sometimes on a Sunday, and he and Norman never let up. The preparation of the pictures Norman was leaving to the Trust, the re-rigging of the ship models, structural alterations inside the house, the cleaning of the garden statues, and other tasks absorbed all their energies. Norman saw no reason why the museum should not be a going concern within a few weeks of his death, and under his direction Harry reconstructed one room to provide a public entrance and exit, even fitting it up with a counter. Norman nodded approvingly when it was finished. 'Now', he said, 'the Trust can start making money as soon as I've gone out'.

He never went into the town now; he did not want to go. The place had become a small metropolis, with new buildings shouldering up everywhere and cars fouling the air with vile fumes. He had liked the sleepy calm of the old Springwood, but he found the new one bustling, brisk, efficient, and as bloodless as an adding machine. Harry fetched most of his supplies, and the butcher delivered meat which Norman ordered by telephone—while detesting the tyranny of the telephone he had to grant its usefulness for some purposes. His interest had waned. Ready-cooked deep-frozen food was nutritious enough and saved work. To be sure, it had less flavour, but his palate was tired so he rarely knew what he was eating anyway.

A worry which he had not known for nearly seventy years began haunting his mind: money. His bank balance was running low. The cost of getting the National Trust project under way was proving heavier than he had foreseen, and he'd soon be broke if he went on spending at this rate. He regretted now that he had always left business affairs to Rose and never bothered to build up substantial savings of his own. Rose was ready to provide whatever he needed for living expenses and ordinary working materials, but, doubting her enthusiasm for the large gestures he was making to perpetuate his name, he balked at pressing her for extra money. He watched his reserves dwindle until a time came when he knew he'd have to earn some money or go into debt. He sent a message to Anne von Bertouch, who ran a commercial gallery in Newcastle, asking her to come and see him. He had never met Mrs von Bertouch but had heard well of her. She came and he told her the story. For many years, he explained, he'd devoted himself to producing pictures and letting Rose sell them; now, for a change, he intended to do some selling on his own account. Would she look after it? Mrs von Bertouch jumped at the invitation and they settled everything in a few minutes. Then he led her out into the great kitchen and served her tea and English biscuits.

He was torn between elation and misgiving when she left.

'Fancy me holding an exhibition at my age!' he said to Harry McPhee. 'I'm too tired to hold an exhibition.'

'You could do worse', said Harry.

'Do you think so? . . . Well, we've got to get some money somewhere.'

He wanted to talk about it and Harry listened while he ran on, chewing over the pros and cons.

'I don't know', he said. It was early April and, having told Mrs von Bertouch he could be ready inside five months, he knew he'd have no time to spare. 'I wonder how I'll get enough pictures?'

'You'll manage', Harry assured him. 'I'll look after the framing and do everything I can to help.'

'All right then', Norman said. 'All right, it's on!'

Although he had some pictures in hand he needed more, but he had never failed to meet a deadline and he'd damn' well meet this one. He slogged away, fussed over by Harry and watched with mild surprise by the reigning Springwood cat, Burly Bill. It was a race against time but he won it. The exhibition opened on 22 August and closed on 15 September. Three of the four oils, four of the twelve water-colours, both pen and inks, and all six pencil drawings had sold. Norman was mildly disappointed that buyers had left anything, but at least his money worries were over. The exhibition netted him $5,606.69. He could once again write cheques without a qualm.

The September winds were keen and, do what he would, he could not keep warm. Life was damnably uncomfortable, but he tried to believe he'd be better when summer came. He could not quite convince himself, and in the end he had to admit that his body was letting him down. Although he still disliked medical mumbo-jumbo, he had made friends with a young Springwood doctor, Ian Florance, and set some store by his advice. Florance overhauled him and prescribed a course of treatment to eliminate the body fluid which had caused his legs to swell and his breathing to become troublesome. Norman was sceptical but to his astonishment the treatment worked. His legs began to shrink and his breathing was easier. It seemed a miracle. Perhaps he'd been too hard on the doctors and their nostrums.

But he knew it was only a respite, and when he finished a large water-colour, *For King and Parliament*, he inscribed it in the lower right-hand corner, 'September 1969. This is the last painting of Norman Lindsay'. He, who had been so quick in all his actions, moved like a tired old man. His strength went on ebbing even in the softer winds and milder airs of October. Some weeks earlier he had taken to sleeping in his living room chair, with a blanket for covering. Harry wanted to make up a bed for him in the living room but Norman vetoed the proposal.

'I'm more comfortable in the chair', he said.

He had no appetite or energy for work. He told Harry he was too tired and felt he had earned a rest. He scribbled an occasional letter but could never manage to write more than a few sentences at a time; it took too much out of him. He could not even read for long; after a few pages he would shut the book on his finger and lean back with closed eyes, letting his mind roam off down long-ago paths. In a letter to Jack, he said that, like all mad hatters, he found himself talking to unseen enemies, but drew comfort from saying aloud, 'Oh, well, it can't last much longer'.

He was accustomed to living in silence and even a year or so earlier it had not mattered; now each day was interminable and his thoughts were stale and leaden. The greatest bore, he decided, was himself. He was always eager for a yarn when Harry arrived to go to work. Harry was a steward of the Springwood Methodist Church, and Norman liked to hear even about that. He was taken with Harry's account of the minister, the Reverend Harold J. Gorrell, a simple man of unwavering faith.

'He sounds a good fellow', Norman said. 'Could you get him to come out here and see me?'

Harry said yes and meant to pass the message but it kept slipping his mind. Mr Gorrell would have gone at once. Even unprompted, he thought of calling but decided against it; he had heard of Norman's antagonism to Christianity and was fearful of appearing to push in.

'I'm going to die soon, Harry', Norman said one day. It was about the middle of October. 'And when I do I don't want to be burned.'

'Burned?'

'Cremated, as they call it. I don't want that. I want to be buried out there in the bush.'

'All right', Harry promised. 'Who do you want to bury you? Roman Catholic, Presbyterian, Methodist, Church of England?'

'You're a Methodist, aren't you, Harry? That will do me.'

The conversation cut itself into Harry's memory because Norman was rarely serious about his own death. He liked to make light of it, tossing off remarks such as 'Don't make any mistake, Harry. After I die I'll be coming back to keep an eye on you!'

On Saturday 25 October he was so feeble that he could hardly walk but he groped his way across from the house to the outside studio and sat down in front of an unfinished and untitled oil painting.

'I'll do a bit of this painting and leave it on the easel', he said. 'Give me a hand, Harry.'

Harry supported the thin old body on the chair and Norman picked up a brush. He added a few strokes to the picture, then fell back, spent, and let Harry help him back to the house. That was the last time he touched a brush.

Four days later Harry's telephone rang at 5.45 in the morning.

'I'm sick. I haven't slept all night', Norman's voice said. There was a metallic clatter as he dropped the handset.

Harry called into the telephone but no answer came. He flung on his clothing and, after leaving a message for Doctor Florance, got into his station wagon and made fast time to Norman.

Norman was sitting hunched in his chair, pitifully small.

'I'm freezing cold', he said. 'This is death.'

'There's only one place for you', Harry told him. 'That's hospital.'

He made a pot of strong tea and Norman drank some. Florance arrived and gave Norman an injection, then telephoned the Springwood Convalescent Hospital. With Harry half-carrying him, Norman stumbled out to the station wagon and got in. He looked back at the house and raised a hand in a shaky salute.

'Goodbye, bloody old house', he said. 'I hope I never see you again.'

Burly Bill, glowering and muscular, sat on the veranda, his lambent eyes following every movement as they drove off. Norman had left precise instructions for Burly Bill's care and feeding pasted to the kitchen wall, but the cat was unco-operative. He remembered Harry as the man who had taken Norman away and declared war on him. Lurking in the shrubbery until a chance came, he would charge out like a small black and white thunderbolt, and bury teeth and claws in Harry's leg. Some time after Norman's death Burly Bill went back to the bush and was not seen again.

Norman had two days in the Springwood hospital. Then he was moved to the Royal North Shore Hospital, in Sydney. They talked of operating and that put him in a rage. He told the surgeons to go to the devil—he wanted no knives prodding into his worn-out carcase. While yearning all the time to be back in the mountains, he stood the Sydney hospital as long as he could. Then it became intolerable. Two young nurses found him walking about his room and, having steered him back to bed, tied him to it. He was in a scorching fury that evening when the Stewarts called to see him. 'I'm going to get up and walk out of here and cut my wrists', he told them. They calmed him and had him freed, and next day, 12 November, Jane Glad and Margaret Stewart drove him back to the Springwood hospital.

Harry went in to see him there every afternoon and took anything he needed. One day it was a pencil and white paper because some of the hospital girls wanted him to draw koalas for them; the koalas he drew had all the inimitable Lindsay touch. Another time it was the cheque book; he wanted to get his bills paid and wrote cheques for everything. Next day, Friday 21 November, he was talkative and cheerful. When Florance called Norman said he wanted to go back to the old house—he seemed to be hankering to feel a brush in his hand. 'All right', Florance promised. 'I'll take you out this afternoon, but you have to sleep first.' That satisfied him. He went to sleep, and at about three o'clock in the afternoon his heart stopped beating.

They buried him three days later in the Methodist section of the Springwood cemetery—a clearing surrounded on three sides by bush and sweet with bush scents. There was a service first in the crowded little Methodist Church; Rose was too ill to make the journey from Sydney but Jane and two of her children were there. Mr Gorrell conducted the service in words which Grandpa Williams would have approved, and Douglas Stewart gave an address.* From the church everybody drove out to the cemetery. The morning was warm and sunny, with white clouds sailing across the sky like great icebergs, and cicadas shrilling in a vibrant chorus. After the ceremony at the graveside some of Norman's friends went back to a Springwood hotel and, at a kind of wake, gave three cheers for him. Then they went their separate ways, leaving him to the whispering of the gaunt eucalypts and the high, clear bugling of the magpies.

* For the full text of Douglas Stewart's address see Appendix II.

# *Appendix I*

## Norman Lindsay Gallery and
## Museum, Springwood

The Norman Lindsay Gallery and Museum was opened to the public on 24 February 1973. It is owned and controlled by the National Trust of Australia (New South Wales). Thus the home in which Norman lived and worked for most of his life from 1912 until his death in 1969 stands as a permanent memorial to him. The exhibit includes oil paintings, water-colours, pen drawings, etchings and pencil sketches, as well as personal relics, such as facsimiles of Roman swords and helmets which Norman made, pieces of his pottery and sculpture, and letters and manuscripts.

Norman began to develop the idea some years before his death. Several delegations from the National Trust visited him at Springwood in 1967 and 1968 to assess the possibilities. They were generally enthusiastic over the concept of preserving the old sandstone house as a gallery and museum but less hopeful than Norman that it would pay its way as a popular showplace. There was one formidable obstacle: the house and its forty-two acres of grounds belonged not to Norman but to Rose, and would have to be purchased.

In a Will signed on 7 March 1969 Norman made a bequest to the Trust; the detailed list (later expanded by acquisitions) named sixteen oil paintings, sixteen water-colours, and nine pen drawings, and items including ship models and sculptures, paints and painting table, bookcases and other furniture, and books comprising 'works of the writers who have meant most to me in prose and poetry'. It was conditional on the acquisition of the Springwood property by the Trust, 'so that the various items and works of art the subject of this my bequest may be preserved in the said premises . . .'

In February 1970 the Trust opened a public appeal for $250,000. It estimated that this amount would be required to buy the property for the agreed price of $50,000, to restore and modify the buildings and grounds, and to establish an endowment fund of $150,000 to meet anticipated maintenance costs. The response fell far short of the target—by October 1972 the total raised was still below $90,000—but the Trust, having concluded that the place would probably attract 20,000 visitors a year at $1.00 each and be self-supporting, decided to go ahead. Renovations, repairs and alterations included repainting and rewiring the house, retiling the kitchen and courtyard, and cutting archways through the walls so that visitors could flow from room to room. Stone paths were laid in the grounds, and Arthur Murch, a Sydney painter and sculptor, overhauled and waterproofed the garden statues, patching cracks and replacing missing bits. A caretaker's flat was built on to the outside studio, and, as stipulated in Norman's Will, the caretaker's post was offered to Harry McPhee. He accepted it.

The Trust has a future plan to broaden the scope of the Springwood place. This envisages the building of a gallery in the grounds, and the conversion of the house into a museum of the Lindsay family. Material for this purpose is already being acquired.

# Appendix II

This is the full text of the funeral address spoken by Douglas Stewart at the Methodist Church, Springwood, on 24 November 1969.

The best thing I ever saw done at a funeral was when Percy Lindsay died. Percy was Norman Lindsay's eldest brother, and a landscape painter of rare and delicate quality. There were mostly artists and writers and bohemians of various sorts at his obsequies, and we were all hanging round some dreadful funeral parlour in Sydney, for hours it seemed, when suddenly somebody got utterly fed up with the whole thing and called out 'Three cheers for Percy!' And everybody did cheer, and those cheers rang out in that dismal place, defying death, denying that a Lindsay could die.

I am not going to call for three cheers here, but I should like to; for if ever a man defied extinction in his work and in his spirit, it was Norman Lindsay.

His own view of death, as his friends have so often heard him say, was that it is no more than a walk into the next room; and all he ever said when his brothers Percy and Lionel died—and he was really very fond of Lionel, underneath their conspicuous differences—was, 'I'm glad poor old Perce got out of it', 'I'm damned glad Lionel got out of it'.

I could not go so far as that myself and say I am glad Norman Lindsay has got out of it. He was the king of good fellows, he shone up here like a light in the sky, and we are all going to miss him very much.

But in a sense, if I am not glad, I cannot be altogether sorry; for he would never have wanted to outlive his capacity for work, and it has been obvious for the last six months, particularly in the last three weeks, that to do any more work was really getting beyond him. He stuck it out right to the end. In the last few years of his life he filled his house with pictures for a bequest he wanted to make; and, to keep himself while he did it, he painted enough additional pictures for two exhibitions, one in Sydney and one in Newcastle. And if he did not quite manage to die, as he would have liked to, with a brush in his hand, he very nearly did; for on the very morning of his death he was making arrangements with Doctor Florance, his medical man, and Harry McPhee his henchman, to go out from the Springwood hospital to his studio and see what was next to be done.

Work, of course, was his gospel, his whole reason for existence. He was like some whirling solar force, incessantly pouring out work of art, and inspiring and invigorating everyone who came into contact with him.

It is astonishing in fact how much of his work is in active movement at this moment. His book of pen drawings has just been published in America. His book of pencil drawings has just been published in Sydney, and will shortly be published in London. There is a reprint of his book of water-colours. The film of his novel *Age of Consent* is still showing to packed houses in Sydney, and I don't know in what other countries of the world. His book for children, *The Magic Pudding*, transformed into a marionette show, is going to Japan next year for what is called the Expo, and negotiations are now under way to take it also to Korea, Singapore, Kuala Lumpur and Indonesia. All round the world this man's work is sparkling and flashing and alive.

But that is just what happens to be going on at this moment. What we have to think about today is the work he did that will live as long as our civilization lasts, and longer than that too. I can't enumerate now everything he did. He did too much. But when you think about his novels and his children's books, his beautiful pencil drawings, his pen drawings which many connoisseurs rate equal to the world's best, his etchings which personally I consider the finest ever done anywhere, his sparkling water-colours, his rich and sumptuous oils, surely all this amounts to nothing less than genius. This has been said before; it is almost a cliché. But it must be said again. And what a resounding cliché it is. There are very few people in the whole history of art to whom you could seriously apply a term so majestic. Australia has had many artists of talent, and fine talent too; but only one genius, capable of this heroic mass of work, always first-class at its best; only one Norman Lindsay.

Let us give him, at least, three silent cheers.

# Bibliography

## BOOKS BY NORMAN LINDSAY

### FICTION

*A Curate in Bohemia*. New South Wales Bookstall Company, Sydney, 1913.
*The Magic Pudding*. Being the Adventures of Bunyip Bluegum and his Friends Bill Barnacle and Sam Sawnoff. Angus & Robertson, Sydney, 1918.
*Redheap*. Faber and Faber, London, 1930. (Published in America as *Every Mother's Son*)
*Miracles by Arrangement*. Faber and Faber, London, 1932. (Published in America as *Mr Gresham and Olympus*)
*Saturdee*. Endeavour Press, Sydney, 1933.
*The Cautious Amorist*. T. Werner Laurie, London, 1934.
*Pan in the Parlour*. T. Werner Laurie, London, 1934.
*The Flyaway Highway*. Angus & Robertson, Sydney, 1936.
*Age of Consent*. T. Werner Laurie, London, 1938.
*The Cousin from Fiji*. Angus & Robertson, Sydney, 1945.
*Halfway to Anywhere*. Angus & Robertson, Sydney, 1947.
*Dust or Polish?* Angus & Robertson, Sydney, 1950.
*Rooms and Houses*. Ure Smith, Sydney, 1968.

### NON-FICTION

*Creative Effort*. Cecil Palmer, London, 1924. (The first edition was published by Art in Australia, Sydney, in 1920, but the London edition, an extensively revised version, is the one quoted in this biography. Norman considered it to be the more precise statement of his ideas.)
*Hyperborea*. Two fantastic travel essays. Fanfrolico Press, London, 1928.
*Madam Life's Lovers*. A human narrative embodying a philosophy of the artist in dialogue form. Fanfrolico Press, London, 1929. (Not being a true novel *Madam Life's Lovers* is listed here as non-fiction.)
*Bohemians of the Bulletin*. Angus & Robertson, Sydney, 1965.
*Norman Lindsay Ship Models*. Preface and Commentary by Norman Lindsay. Foreword by Douglas Stewart. Photographed by Quinton F. Davis. Angus & Robertson, Sydney, 1966.
*The Scribblings of an Idle Mind*. Lansdowne Press, Melbourne, 1966.
*My Mask*. An Autobiography. Angus & Robertson, Sydney, 1970.
(Many of the above books of fiction and non-fiction were illustrated by Norman Lindsay.)

### PICTORIAL WORKS

*The Pen Drawings of Norman Lindsay*. Special number of *Art in Australia*, edited by Sydney Ure Smith and Bertram Stevens. Angus & Robertson, Sydney, 1918.
*Pen Drawings: Norman Lindsay*. Arthur McQuitty, Sydney, 1924.
*The Etchings of Norman Lindsay*. Constable, London, 1927.

*Art in Australia: Norman Lindsay Number.* Art in Australia, Sydney, 1930.

*Norman Lindsay's Pen Drawings.* Art in Australia, Sydney, 1931.

*Norman Lindsay: Water Colour Book.* Eighteen reproductions in colour from original watercolours with an appreciation of the medium by Norman Lindsay and a biographical survey of the artist's life and work by Godfrey Blunden. Springwood Press, Sydney, 1939.

*Paintings in Oil.* Fourteen reproductions in colour from original oil paintings, and sixteen half-tone plates reproduced in black and white. Essays by Douglas Stewart and Norman Lindsay. The Shepherd Press, Sydney, 1945.

*Norman Lindsay: Selected Pen Drawings.* Introduction by Douglas Stewart, and preface by the artist describing his technique for pen work. Angus & Robertson, Sydney, 1968.

*Norman Lindsay Watercolours.* Nineteen reproductions in colour from original watercolours, with an appreciation of the medium by Norman Lindsay and a survey of the artist's life and work by Godfrey Blunden. Ure Smith, Sydney, 1969. (This is an extensively modified and revised version of the 1939 watercolour book.)

*Norman Lindsay Pencil Drawings.* With a foreword by A. D. Hope. Angus & Robertson, Sydney, 1969.

## ILLUSTRATIONS IN BOOKS

This chronological list is not intended to be exhaustive but it embraces all books by authors other than Norman Lindsay considered to be significant examples of his work as an illustrator.

*Oblation* (A. G. Stephens). Printed for the authors and publishers, A. G. Stephens and Norman Lindsay, by Websdale, Shoosmith, Sydney, 1902.

*Satyrs and Sunlight* (Hugh McCrae). Published for the author by John Lane Mullins, Sydney, 1909. (London edition, revised and enlarged, by the Fanfrolico Press, 1928)

*Satyricon* (Petronius).. Privately printed by Ralph Straus, London, 1910. (A translation by Jack Lindsay, with the 1910 illustrations, was published by the Fanfrolico Press, London, undated, but about 1927.)

*Songs of a Campaign* (Leon Gellert). Angus & Robertson, Sydney, 1917.

*Isle of San* (Leon Gellert). Art in Australia, Sydney, 1919.

*Colombine* (Hugh McCrae). Angus & Robertson, Sydney, 1920.

*The Man from Snowy River* (A. B. Paterson). Angus & Robertson, Sydney, 1920.

*Idyllia* (Hugh McCrae). N.L. Press, Sydney, 1922.

*Fauns and Ladies* (Jack Lindsay). J. T. Kirtley, Sydney, 1923.

*Thief of the Moon* (Kenneth Slessor). J. T. Kirtley, Sydney, 1924. (A London edition of Slessor's early poems was published by the Fanfrolico Press in 1927 (but dated 1926), under the title *Earth-Visitors.* It carried the same illustrations as *Thief of the Moon.*)

*Lysistrata* (Aristophanes). Translated by Jack Lindsay. Fanfrolico Press, Sydney, 1925. (London edition by the Fanfrolico Press, 1926)

*The Passionate Neatherd* (Jack Lindsay). J. T. Kirtley, Sydney, 1926. (London edition by the Fanfrolico Press, 1926)

*The Works* (Petronius). The complete works translated into English by Jack Lindsay. Fanfrolico Press, London, 1927.

*Loving Mad Tom* (edited by Jack Lindsay). Fanfrolico Press, London, 1927.

*Propertius in Love.* Translated by Jack Lindsay. Fanfrolico Press, London, 1927.

*The Antichrist of Nietzsche*. A new version in English by P. R. Stephensen. Fanfrolico Press, London, 1928.
*Women in Parliament* (Aristophanes). Translated by Jack Lindsay. Fanfrolico Press, London, 1929.
*As It Was in the Beginning* (Dulcie Deamer). Frank Wilmot, Melbourne, 1929.
*Cuckooz Contrey* (Kenneth Slessor). Frank Johnson, Sydney, 1932.
*The Animals Noah Forgot* (A. B. Paterson). Endeavour Press, Sydney, 1933.
*Our Earth* (Kenneth Mackenzie). Angus & Robertson, Sydney, 1937.
*Five Bells* (Kenneth Slessor). Frank Johnson, Sydney, 1939.
*Elegy for an Airman* (Douglas Stewart). Frank Johnson, Sydney, 1940.
*Sonnets to an Unknown Soldier* (Douglas Stewart). Angus & Robertson, Sydney, 1941.
*Ned Kelly* (Douglas Stewart). The Shepherd Press, Sydney, 1946. (First published in book form by Angus & Robertson, Sydney, 1943, unillustrated)
*Great Expectations* (Charles Dickens). The Shepherd Press, Sydney, 1947.
*Shipwreck* (Douglas Stewart). The Shepherd Press, Sydney, 1947.
*Sun Orchids* (Douglas Stewart). Angus & Robertson, Sydney, 1952.
*The Letters of Rachel Henning* (edited by David Adams). The *Bulletin*, Sydney, 1954.
*Fisher's Ghost* (Douglas Stewart). The Wentworth Press, Sydney, 1960.

## OTHER AUTHORS' WORKS USED IN REFERENCE

Ashton, Julian. *Now Came Still Evening On*. Angus & Robertson, Sydney, 1941.
Blainey, Geoffrey. *The Rush That Never Ended*. Melbourne University Press, Melbourne, 1963.
Chaplin, Harry F. *Norman Lindsay: His books, manuscripts and autograph letters in the library of and annotated by the author*. Foreword by Norman Lindsay. The Wentworth Press, Sydney, 1969.
Glassop, Lawson. *We Were the Rats*. Angus & Robertson, Sydney, 1944.
Graham, John A. *The Creswick Grammar School History*. Brown Prior Anderson, Melbourne, 1940.
Henderson, G. C. (ed.) *The Journal of Thomas Williams*, 2 vols. Angus & Robertson, Sydney, 1931.
Hetherington, John. *Australians: Nine Profiles*. Preface by Norman Lindsay. F. W. Cheshire, Melbourne, 1960.
———— *Forty-two Faces*. F. W. Cheshire, Melbourne, 1962.
———— *Australian Painters*. F. W. Cheshire, Melbourne, 1963.
———— *Melba*. Faber and Faber, London, 1967.
Lindesay, Vane. *The Inked-In Image*. Heinemann, Melbourne, 1970.
Lindsay, Daryl. *The Leafy Tree: My Family*. F. W. Cheshire, Melbourne, 1965.
Lindsay, Jack. *Life Rarely Tells*. The Bodley Head, London 1958.
———— *The Roaring Twenties*. The Bodley Head, London, 1960.
———— *Fanfrolico and After*. The Bodley Head, London, 1962.
———— 'Norman Lindsay: Problems of his Life and Work', *Meanjin Quarterly*, xxix (1970), pp. 39-48.
Lindsay, Jane. *Kurrajong*. Angus & Robertson, Sydney, 1945.
Lindsay, Lionel. *Addled Art*. Angus & Robertson, Sydney, 1942.
———— *Comedy of Life*. Foreword by Peter Lindsay. Angus & Robertson, 1967.
Lindsay, Philip. *I'd Live the Same Life Over*. Hutchinson, London, 1941.
Lindsay, Rose. *Model Wife*. Ure Smith, Sydney, 1967.
Low, David. *Low's Autobiography*. Michael Joseph, London, 1956.

Mackaness, George & Stone, Walter. *The Books of the Bulletin*, Angus & Robertson, Sydney, 1955.

McCrae, Hugh. *Story-Book Only*, Angus & Robertson, Sydney, 1948.

Meudell, George. *The Pleasant Career of a Spendthrift*. Routledge, London, undated, but about 1929.

Nichols, Beverley. *Twenty-five*. Jonathan Cape, London, 1926.

Slessor, Kenneth (ed.) *Southerly; Norman Lindsay Number*. No. 1 of 1959. Articles by Douglas Stewart, Kenneth Slessor, Brian James, George Mackaness, Norman Lindsay. Angus & Robertson, Sydney, 1959.

Stewart Douglas. *The Fire on the Snow*. Angus & Robertson, Sydney, 1944.

———— *The Flesh and the Spirit*. Angus & Robertson, Sydney, 1948.

Stone, Louis. *Jonah*. Methuen, London, 1911.

Williams, Thomas. *Fiji and the Fijians, the islands and inhabitants*, Vol. 1, Alexander Heylin, London, 1858.

# Index

# Index